THE POLLOCK - HOLMES LETTERS

MR. JUSTICE HOLMES
In old age

The Pollock-Holmes Letters

Correspondence of Sir Frederick Pollock and Mr Justice Holmes 1874-1932

EDITED BY

MARK DeWOLFE HOWE

Professor of Law, University of Buffalo School of Law

WITH AN INTRODUCTION BY

SIR JOHN POLLOCK, Bart.

VOLUME II

CAMBRIDGE

AT THE UNIVERSITY PRESS

1942

CAMBRIDGE
UNIVERSITY PRESS

University Printing House, Cambridge CB2 8BS, United Kingdom

Cambridge University Press is part of the University of Cambridge.

It furthers the University's mission by disseminating knowledge in the pursuit of education, learning and research at the highest international levels of excellence.

www.cambridge.org
Information on this title: www.cambridge.org/9781107512092

First published 1942
First paperback edition 2015

A catalogue record for this publication is available from the British Library

ISBN 978-1-107-51209-2 Paperback

CONTENTS

Volume II

ILLUSTRATIONS

Volume II

THE POLLOCK-HOLMES LETTERS

VOLUME II

VI

1919-1921

WASHINGTON, January 24, 1919

Dear F. P.:

Your studies in Natural Law are not forthcoming on a rapid look around. I remember your writing on the subject but I couldn't recite on what you said, although of course I read whatever I know of yours. But I didn't expect you to agree with me altogether. As to Ethics I have called them a body of imperfect social generalizations expressed in terms of emotion. Of course I agree that there is such a body on which to a certain extent civilized men would agree — but how much less than would have been taken for granted fifty years ago, witness the Bolsheviki. John M. Zane walks into me in the *Mich. Law Rev.*[1] and later in the *Ill. Law Rev.*[2] and thinks I am hopelessly precluded from the place that otherwise I should occupy by accepting the old notion of a sovereign being superior to the law that he or it makes and by believing that judges make law. I suspect he means a different thing from what I do by law and that the fight is more about words than he thinks. But there is a real difference expressed by him in a tone of dogmatism upon which I should not venture, although I think I could smash him if he would say what he thought and not only what he didn't believe. He does believe that Hobbes, Bentham, Austin, and every German jurist that ever was were asses. So he has taken rather a large contract. My brother Brandeis, Okakura [3] a Japanese writer on art, and a dame who showed me early Chinese paintings that she thought showed spiritual heights never

[1] "German Legal Philosophy," 16 *Mich. L. Rev.* 287 (March 1918).

[2] "A Legal Heresy," 13 *Ill. L. Rev.* 431 (June 1918).

[3] Kakuzo Okakura; author of *The Ideals of the East* (1903), which Holmes had recently read.

reached by us, have happened to concur in assuring me in their several ways of the superiority of the oriental mind to ours. I said to Brandeis produce the documents; I can show you any number of books that I believe touch life and the world more profoundly, more exquisitely, and at more points than anything I know of or believe exists in the East. As to the Jap writer I content myself with the contempt of the dame for the whole Jap lot as an inferior offshoot from the Chinese (not that I believe that an adequate statement by any means), and as to the dame I think she has wrought herself into a hyperaesthesia on her theme. I have bought an etching of Ostade — a peasant family saying grace over their bowl of porridge that is as tender as Millet's *Angelus* and without any touch of melodrama. I saw the reproduction in Hind's *Short History* [4] and have kept a dealer on the lookout for a good while. It makes me want to cry — κ. τ. λ. You remember what Lord Coke says of Littleton's "etc." [5] There is much general discourse remaining. My love and thanks to Lady Pollock for a charming short letter which I hope soon to answer — but work is humming just now.

Yours ever,
O. W. H.

LONDON, January 30, 1919

My dear Holmes:

As soon as I could get free of the Attorney-General's Committee on Breaches of Law (problem thereof shortly stated being: Expand "Hang the Kaiser" in rational terms), my wife and I went to Bath, not for the waters but as a pleasant place where we knew of a really good hotel, and so continued for a week. . . .

We know now from a Russian engineer who has come to London via Norway that he saw Jack in Moscow on Sept. 8, well and unmolested — my wife has seen him and I am going to see him on Sunday.

[4] Arthur Mayger Hind, *A Short History of Engraving and Etching* (1908).

[5] Describing the virtues of Littleton's treatise on Tenures, Lord Coke said: "Certain it is, that there is never a period, nor (for the most part) a word, nor an *etc.* but affordeth excellent matter of learning." (Preface to *Coke on Littleton* (15th ed.), p. XXXVII.)

The *Law Reports* have changed their printers and I am striving to teach the new people divers things they ought to know — such as not meddling with punctuation out of their own heads. General difficulties of printing are no way abated so far.

The League of Nations appears to be making itself at Paris under pressure of events, so fast as to supersede all private discussion and speculation. I am glad it is settled that the Germans are to have none of their colonies back.

Three weeks ago, I installed my successor in the Royal Colonial Institute Lodge, so masonic duties will be less pressing. During the war masonry did work in consolidating relations between G. B. and the Dominions which will probably never be known to the general public. Also, to a certain extent, with the U. S.; but I suppose that for some reason masonry is more active in the central and western states than on the Atlantic Coast, so I feel that the time given to it has been well spent. . . .

Yours ever,
F. Pollock

London, February 17, 1919

My dear Holmes:

On Saturday we had a further telegram from Jack notifying his arrival at Helsingfors.[1] I have ascertained that the Foreign Office is instructing our consul there, and we may hope to see Jack in his proper person within a month or so. Details are wanting until we have a letter.

I share your feelings under talk about the superiority of "the Oriental mind," or art or most things to ours. There are many schools of Eastern thought and Eastern art agreeing together in very little except that their several assumptions and conventions are different from ours, and there is no common standard to enable one to talk of superior or inferior. (To talk of Japanese art as an inferior offshot from Chinese is even worse than it would be to talk of the French landscapist as an inferior offshot from Constable). On our part we have to remem-

[1] In a Cablegram to Holmes, dated Feb. 6, 1919, Pollock said: "Jack safe Finland escaped Bolshevists."

ber that the Bible is Oriental before we talk of *our* superiority. There is one thing common to the thoughts of the farther East, a certain contempt for transitory matters of fact — strongest in India, where I believe the whole of Sanskrit literature has not a single historical work to show, perhaps weakest in Japan.

Zane's belated storm in a teacup is almost comic. Any medieval man would have said that of course the king's judges can't sit in judgment on the king — not to mention that the Court of K. B. was formally *coram ipso rege* — and would have thought it odd if not perverse to ask for any more reason. At the same time he would have admitted that there are some things neither the King's Courts nor Parliament can change, such as the law of Holy Church — not however meaning thereby anything any Pope chooses to say. The Pope can't repeal the Decalogue, as Cardinal Merry del Val remarked to me when I saw him at the Vatican to get some information about the canon law of marriage and divorce, being about to give evidence before our Royal Commission. [2] (Gorell Barnes was an excellent modern reformer but weak in knowledge of ecclesiastical jurisdiction).

On looking up the report of *Kawananakoa* v. *Polyblank* [3] . . . I find Harlan seems not to have wholly approved your reasons. I wonder why.

I have just finished Boethius (*De Consolatione Philosophiae*) in the Loeb Classics edition — not only a curious and historically rather important book but of greater intrinsic merit than I expected to find it. The other contents — theological tracts, *De Trinitate*, etc., which the best recent critics accept as genuine Boethius — I have left alone.

[2] In 1912 Pollock had testified before the Royal Commission on Divorce and Matrimonial Causes, the Chairman of which was John Gorell Barnes, First Baron, (1848–1913), Judge of the Probate, Divorce and Admiralty Division of the High Court of Justice, 1892–1905; President, 1905–08.

[3] 205 U. S. 349 (1907). It was Holmes's opinion in this case which John M. Zane had criticized in his article, "A Legal Heresy," 13 *Ill. L. Rev.* 431 (1918). In the course of his opinion, holding that the territory of Hawaii was not a necessary party to the suit, Holmes had said: "Some doubts have been expressed as to the source of the immunity of a sovereign power from suit without its own permission, but the answer has been public property since before the days of Hobbes. . . . A sovereign is exempt from suit, not because of any formal conception or obsolete theory, but on the logical and practical ground that there can be no legal right as against the authority that makes the law on which the right depends." 205 U. S. at 353. Harlan, J., concurred in the result.

The 17th century translation which was found good enough to use for this edition with no great amendment, is quite remarkable, especially the versified parts.

Yours ever,
F. P.

WASHINGTON, April 5, 1919[1]

Dear Pollock:

. . . I am glad that the hitches in Jack's coming over are coming to an end. You know that I have sympathized with you both, but I didn't dare to write while you were in doubt. I am beginning to get stupid letters of protest against a decision that Debs, a noted agitator, was rightly convicted of obstructing the recruiting service so far as the law was concerned.[2] I wondered that the Government should press the case to a hearing before us, as the inevitable result was that fools, knaves, and ignorant persons were bound to say he was convicted because he was a dangerous agitator and that obstructing the draft was a pretence. How it was with the Jury of course I don't know, but of course the talk is silly as to us. There was a lot of jaw about free speech, which I dealt with somewhat summarily in an ealier case — *Schenck* v. *U.S.*[3] . . . also *Frohwerk* v. *U.S.*[4] . . . As it happens I should go farther probably than the majority in favor of it, and I daresay it was partly on that account that the C. J. assigned the case to me.

Your mention of Boethius made me want to get it but our book sellers in this one horse place no longer keep the Loeb series. I believe I have mentioned before what a shame I think it that such a good plan should be so spoiled by not giving critically accurate translations. As to Harlan's qualified concurrence[5] in *Kawananakoa* v. *Polyblank*, that sage, although a man of real power, did not shine either in analysis or generalization and I never troubled myself much when he shied. I used to say that

[1] A short note from Pollock, dated March 18, 1919, is omitted.
[2] Debs v. United States, 249 U. S. 211 (1919).
[3] 249 U. S. 47 (1919).
[4] 249 U. S. 204 (1919).

he had a powerful vise the jaws of which couldn't be got nearer than two inches to each other.

For the moment my work is done and I hope for a little leisure during the next week. I propose to devote it first to Laski's new book *Authority in the Modern State*, which he dedicates to me and Frankfurter. Do you know anything about him in Oxford? People in Boston [5] seem to have got the idea that he is a dangerous man (they used to think me one). I don't know whether because he is inspired by Figgis [6] more or less in his discourse on sovereignty or because (as I am told) his wife has written some come-out or subversive articles — I know not what. I have had the greatest pleasure in his conversation as he is a portent of knowledge though still very young. There is also a prejudice against Frankfurter; I think partly because he (as well as Laski) is a Jew. I believe him to have been very valuable as a stimulus in the Law School,[7] but Boston is nothing if not critical. It never occurs to me until after the event that a man I like is a Jew, nor do I care, when I realize it. If I had to choose I think I would rather see power in the hands of the Jews than in the Catholics', — not that I wish to be run by either. I have let the League go its way without much study. I have my hands full and am too old and too busy to take a part, and futile worry is waste.

I got a rattling good French book on Rembrandt's etchings the other day—*Coppier*, the author.[8] Just now I am looking a gift horse in the mouth and trying to ascertain whether an Ostade is first, second, or third state: also I read with great interest Rhodes's *History of the Civil War* — a real work of art I think — although I hate to read about those times and read this only because his sister sent it to me. My love to Lady Pollock.

Yours ever,
O. W. H.

[5] Laski was a lecturer and instructor in History at Harvard University, 1916–20.

[6] Rev. John Neville Figgis (1866–1919). Figgis, a distinguished churchman and political philosopher, was largely concerned with the conflicts between church and state, and was insistent upon the value and significance of the independence of church from state.

[7] Felix Frankfurter had been appointed Professor of Law at the Harvard Law School in 1914.

[8] André Charles Coppier, *Les Eaux-Fortes Authentiques de Rembrandt* (1917).

LONDON, April 7, 1919

My dear Holmes:

Our young poet John Drinkwater has produced a chronicle play on Abraham Lincoln — acted by a Birmingham company at Hammersmith with considerable success: we saw it on Saturday afternoon, my wife for the second time. It is curious to see how many different worlds there are in London: the audience was not the least like the audience at a west-end theatre — likewise the acting, which was conscientious, rather heavy and sometimes amateurish. For the play, it is in good dignified English frankly renouncing any attempt at local colour, except the disastrous one of making F. Douglas[s] (the negro) a grotesque figure talking a sort of pidgin English. There was then a real negro dialect it seems (*ex relat.* E. Robins), but Douglas[s] would not have talked it. Lincoln made too solemn and preacher-like I think, but it is honest work. Two things really interest me: the proof that the revival of the chronicle play is possible at all, and the desire of the intelligent middle class Briton to know about Lincoln and the Civil War. They go to learn American history from Drinkwater as their ancestors did to learn English history from Shakespeare (and his half forgotten predecessors) at the Globe, and the necessary defects of a chronicle play from the point of view of dramatic art trouble them as little.

. . . The uniforms were presumably after authentic models, but I did not know that U. S. general officers had a frock-coat undress of a slaty gray tint — this must have been a passing fashion. Lee appeared in Appomattox Courthouse (an effective scene this) in a much smarter uniform of bright blue, verging on green to my eye, but my wife saw it as sky-blue. Can that be right? I don't know where authority for the Confederate uniforms is to be found in Europe — possibly in the great military museum of the *Invalides* in Paris. . . . Of course Drinkwater's play would not do in America unless it were revised from top to bottom in concert with a competent American: I have not heard that any such thing is thought of. His worst mistake is making Lincoln deliver the Gettysburg speech in Ford's theatre: not that great novelists and dramatists have not taken as great liberties with history, but because transposing that speech to the end from the middle of the war robs it of its moral and historical greatness.

Another and very different American function last Friday — a memorial service for those fallen in the war, at the Abbey — massive, simple, impressive, ending with the *Battle Hymn of the Republic* and the *Last Post.*

I have got Lord Charnwood's *Life of Lincoln* — more instructive to the English reader but less human than Norman Hapgood's which seems not to be generally known.

Did I tell you I am starting on a new book — on the League of Nations, bespoken by my law publishers, rather a new venture for them. It will not be a large book, and I shall cut the historical inducement short. "Precursors" have been overdone I think. They are a fatal temptation to doctoral theses which magnify them as prophets, whereas when you turn up the original you find oftener than not that the precursor was grinding some other axe (Alberico Gentili [1] always excepted to the honour of Italy and Oxford.) On which there will be just a hint for the judicious. . . .

Yours ever,
F. Pollock

Washington, April 27, 1919

Dear Pollock:

A good one from you, April 7, came a few days ago. As to the play A. Lincoln and F. Douglas[s], I believe Douglas[s] was a man of considerable education and rather a handsome old boy. I don't imagine that he talked negro any more than you or I. I hate to recur to Civil War times — yet a while ago I read Lord Charnwood's *Life of Lincoln* with pleasure and recently Rhodes's *History of the Civil War* with much ditto. Both books seem to me extremely well done. As to Appomatox, Lee met Grant in full uniform, but of course it was Confederate gray. As to the other uniform you mention I can't speak by the book but I am sceptical. . . . I await the appearance of your book on

[1] 1552–1608; Italian jurist; Regius Professor of Civil Law, Oxford.

the League of Nations with interest — but the subject hitherto has left me a little cold. What you say about Precursors has been illustrated in connection with our Constitution, *e.g.*, Hannis Taylor made a great pother about Pelatiah Webster [1] which seemed to me more inspired by the desire to show H. T. as a discoverer than by importance — and others have blown the horn of others. I received last night from Laski a copy of a handsome reprint of the *Political Works of James I*, with an introduction by McIlwain. . . . It sounds as if it might be useful. Of course at present I have little or no time for reading and even for writing (letters). At this moment however I am awaiting the assignment for this week and am free until it comes, except that I ought to be looking at one or two cases that went over yesterday for further examination. I have run across your Chief Justice once or twice; went there to luncheon a week ago, etc., but haven't seen much of him.[2] I really don't know how considerable a lawyer he is. I tell the men I meet nowadays that I think them promising young fellows but that I sat on the bench (or whatever it may be in Chancery) with Lord Cranworth (in '66 — when they were unborn or children). I now look forward to what impressed my childhood as most wonderful — to being carried in a civic procession as a survivor. It doesn't matter very much of what. Meantime things have gone pretty smoothly. Of course there were people who pitched into the Court for sending Debs to prison under the espionage act, but there was no doubt that the Jury was warranted in finding him guilty or that the act was Constitutional. Now I hope the President will pardon him and some other poor devils with whom I have more sympathy. Those whose cases have come before us have seemed to me poor fools whom I should have been inclined to pass over if I could. The greatest bores in the world are the come-outers who are cock-sure of a dozen nostrums. The dogmatism of a little education is hopeless. Be sure to give my love to Lady Pollock — that kindest of hostesses and friends. In memory I look out of your back windows

[1] In *A Memorial in Behalf of the Architect of Our Federal Constitution* (1907) and *The Real Authorship of the Constitution of the United States Explained* (1912).

[2] The Earl of Reading, Lord Chief Justice of England, in January 1918 had come to Washington as High Commissioner and Special Envoy to the United States.

and sigh to doubt if I ever shall again. However you and I have had our whack and can't complain.

Yours ever,
O. W. Holmes

London, May 8, 1919

My dear Holmes:

Guess, if you like, what book inspired the enclosed aphoristic reflections:[1] if you guess right note for caution that I don't commit myself to my reading of the book being correct. Some people are born with an invincible distrust of the world and themselves which they can't help, and that may be a better explanation for anything I know.

We are struggling here with a laggard and niggard spring — as it were reflecting the state of Europe. But the peace terms as they have now emerged are not bad.[2] On this side most of us think (except the partisan journalists who think any stick good to beat Lloyd George with) that it is no way to peace and harmony to address an allied Great Power, even if it is too greedy, in the manner appropriate to a college class of freshmen.[3] It is said to please your public, but I doubt, for in the long run the American Public is no fool. . . .

I am giving up the editorship of the *L. Q. R.* after this year and looking out for a successor: it is not easy to find a man who is competent and also willing to do it practically for love, but I do not despair of finding him.

Yours ever,
F. P.

[1] [Enclosure]: A common Prig does not know he is a Prig.

An advanced Prig knows it and is proud of it.

But a consummate Prig humbles himself before his own lofty conception of priggery, and writes a large book to demonstrate to himself that he is only a Flat.

Dicit stultus superbus: Omnia vanitas quia homo vanus.

Dicit stultus abiectus: Homo vanus quia omnia vanitas.

Dicit vir prudens: Homo minimus sed non vanus, quia nulla in Deo vanitas.

[2] On May 7 the terms of the Treaty of Versailles were printed, and on the 9th a Plenary Session of the Peace Conference accepted those terms.

[3] Probably Pollock here refers to President Wilson's public declaration on April 23 that he was opposed to the Italian claim for Fiume, and to his threat to withdraw from the Peace Conference if the claim should be allowed. Lloyd George supported the Italian claims under the Treaty of London.

WASHINGTON, May 26, 1919

My dear F. P.:

What an aggravising (a good child's word) cuss you are! To give me your admirable aphorisms and leave me — me who have so little time here to read anything but records — to guess what inspired them. I haven't the slightest idea. I *have* just read Marvin, *The Century of Hope*, an interesting conspectus of the modern period inspired by a rather deeper belief in the spiritual significance of man than I am able to entertain and a consequently greater faith in the upward and onward destiny of the race. But the note of hope is the best for achievement and so the book seemed to me worth writing and reading. Laski suggested it to me and then sent to me Graham Wallas's *Life of Francis Place* which I have begun. Until I read the first mentioned volume I am afraid I never heard of Place. . . . To recur to your aphorisms and to avoid a possible misinterpretation of my criticism of Marvin: I fully agree to the *nulla in Deo Vanitas* — in the sense of the little article that I sent to you some time ago.[1] I only don't believe, *i. e.* have no affirmative belief, that man was necessary to God in order to find out that he existed (if the cosmos wears a beard, as to which I have no opinion). It seems to me probable that the only cosmic significance of man is that he is part of the cosmos, but that seems to me enough.

Brandeis the other day drove a harpoon into my midriff with reference to my summer occupations. He said you talk about improving your mind, you only exercise it on the subjects with which you are familiar. Why don't you try something new, study some domain of fact. Take up the textile industries in Massachusetts and after reading the reports sufficiently you can go to Lawrence and get a human notion of how it really is. I hate facts. I always say the chief end of man is to form general propositions — adding that no general proposition is worth a damn. Of course a general proposition is simply a string for the facts and I have little doubt that it would be good for my immortal soul to plunge into them, good also for the perform-

[1] Presumably his "Natural Law," 32 *Harv. L. Rev.* 40 (1918); *C.L.P.* 310. See *supra*, Vol. I, pp. 270–71.

ance of my duties, but I shrink from the bore — or rather I hate to give up the chance to read this and that, that a gentleman should have read before he dies. I don't remember that I ever read Machiavelli's *Prince* — and I think of the Day of Judgment. There are a good many worse ignorances than that, that ought to be closed up. I don't know how it will come out. The spring here is enchanting. Since the last sentence I have been over in Georgetown with my wife and had a glimpse of the park — noble oaks — the air full of the smell of box and roses and what Bob Barlow [2] once called the yelling of birds. Really if a glance at the *New Republic* had not thrown the customary gloom over life it would seem fair once more. With which I close my potato-trap — for speech — to open it again to take in luncheon. . . . My work is done for the moment and there can't be much more of any sort before vacation.

Yours ever,
O. W. Holmes

Beverly Farms, June 17, 1919 [1]

Dear Pollock:

. . . We are just settling down here — where we arrived Saturday evening, and gradually recovering from the almost collapse from work, Washington's heat — so different from that further north — and the tiresome journey through, from Washington to Boston. I don't know what it is about the Washington weather but I have a brown plush mouth there all the time as if I had been on a spree but without having had the fun. Coming on I reread most of *Present Philosophical Tendencies* by Perry (professor I believe at Harvard College), a clever book made somewhat obscure at moments by professorially technical language. It strikes me that these philosophers have gone round the globe to get to the spot close to which they stood before they began to philosophise — also that they still show their theological inheritance by assuming the special cosmic importance of man. I see no reason to believe that God needs

[2] Robert Shaw Barlow, Boston lawyer and personal friend of Holmes.

[1] The letter from Pollock to which this is apparently responsive is missing.

him otherwise than as he may need all that is. But I am not quite sure how far we agree in our fundamentals — I can't believe that we differ greatly. I agree with you as to war crimes, and have said whenever it was proper that I thought the President should pardon a lot of poor devils that it was my misfortune to have to write opinions condemning. I suppose it was those opinions that led them to want to blow me up — but it showed that they were fools and didn't understand the situation. The country people here show a little additional *empressement* in their greetings which I take to mean satisfaction that the experiment did not succeed.

I hear that there are orders to keep a special eye on this house, which I believe to be quite unnecessary. In Washington after a second attempt to blow up the Attorney General [2] I found a policeman stationed near my front door — which was my first news of the business. My last opinion was in favor of the constitutionality of a state law throwing all the risks of damage to employees on the employers in hazardous businesses.[3] To my wonder four were the other way, and my opinion was thought too strong by some of the majority, so that Pitney spoke for the Court and I concurred, with what I had to say — Brandeis and Clarke only with me. I pointed out that even in what was supposed to be the Constitutional principle of basing liability on fault it meant that a man had to take the risk of deciding the way the jury would decide — in doubtful cases. But already law grows remote and as soon as I feel a little brisker I expect to forget it altogether. My love to Lady Pollock.

Yours ever,
O. W. H.

LONDON, July 7, 1919

My dear Holmes:

So now you know what high officials in Ireland felt like in the '80's, and I hope you will have no more trouble than the

[2] Alexander Mitchell Palmer (1872–1936); Attorney General of the United States, 1919–21.

[3] Arizona Employers' Liability Cases, 250 U. S. 400, 431 (1919). Justices McKenna and McReynolds wrote dissenting opinions in each of which Chief Justice White and Justice VanDevanter concurred

sight of a discreet policeman. Your authorities seem to have the ramifications of Bolshevism pretty well in hand. . . .

It is long since I have looked at any general history of philosophy. Talk about man's cosmic importance has very little meaning for me. From the exterior or natural history point of view — the sensible universe as a continuous orderly whole — one phenomenon is as important as another. From the interior point of view of man as a living soul we know nothing of his importance among the infinite possible orders of intelligence in the spiritual world, assuming them to be commensurable — which may be a large assumption.

Provided that captains of U boats and such like are brought to justice, which now seems assured, I feel about William of Hohenzollern rather like the Cornish juryman: "Hang en or no, 'tis n't a halfpenny odds."[1] But his counsel should have some sport unless he takes Charles I's line of merely denying the jurisdiction. Will he have the sense to retain a good English criminal lawyer? *sed qu.* whether professional etiquette requires counsel to accept such a cause, or any cause, outside regular courts known to the law of England.

I should like to see the opinions in that constitutional case of employer's liability in hazardous business. The supposed principle of no liability without fault is certainly not to be found in the medieval Common Law, nor do I see how it can be arguable in any jurisdiction where *Rylands* v. *Fletcher*[2] is received. Not but what there is some kind of presumption of fault at the back of most rules of absolute liability. And how about libel? It is settled by *Hulton* v. *Jones*,[3] right or wrong, that talk of an imaginary J. S. may bring upon me an action at the suit of a real J. S. whom I knew not to be *in rerum natura*. And if I remember right it is immaterial whether by any diligence I could have known.

[1] In article 227 of the Treaty of Versailles, which had been signed on June 28, 1919, it was stated that the Allies "publicly arraign William II of Hohenzollern, formerly German Emperor, for a supreme offence against international morality and the sanctity of treaties." It was then contemplated that he, like others charged with the commission of war crimes, should be tried before a military tribunal which, in its decision, should "be guided by the highest motives of international policy, with a view of vindicating the solemn obligations of international undertakings and the validity of international morality."

[2] L. R. 3 H. L. 330.

[3] Hulton & Co. v. Jones, [1910] A. C. 20. See *supra*, Vol. I, p. 156.

Laski seems to be a rather important rising author. His publishers have never sent anything of his to the *L. Q. R.* So I am not acquainted with his work.

Your Ambassador [4] is exercised about the plague of inordinate reporting: the only remedy I can think of is action by the Bar Association somewhat on the lines of the Uniformity of Laws Committee.

The other day at a masonic dinner I sat next a brother from Arizona: he told me there is a large Mormon community in that State, gave them an excellent character as citizens and said they furnished some of the best U. S. troops in the war. If and when I cross the Atlantic once more I hope — now having a fairly considerable standing in the Grand Lodge of England — to find masonry a key to some new aspects of American life.

My wife sends her love.

Yours ever,
F. P.

Beverly Farms, June 27, 1919

Dear Pollock:

Your letter of June 9? came last night and gave me additional pleasure by reporting Jack well.[1] Success to the book and relief from his dentist to him! As I read in my youth that the embalmers in Egypt were pursued with stones when they had finished their job so would I fain pursue this other accursed tribe. However, to be just my man treats me well but I have it on my conscience that I didn't go to him for inspection before coming north. My wife hasn't been well but she is getting better and everything is going most satisfactorily. I am glad that you don't treat my proposed excursion into facts as of the essence of salvation. I have sent for books but ten days have gone by without answer. I think of a Catholic lady who on a fast day called for bass, then terrapin — not forthcoming —

[4] John W. Davis.

[1] The letter referred to is missing. John Pollock had just returned from Russia and had completed his volume *The Bolshevik Adventure* (1919).

and then said, "Bring me a mutton chop. God knows I have tried for fish." If I am destined to lapse from facts back into ideas, God knows I have tried for the facts.[2]

I knew Henry Adams quite well.[3] He had two sides. He had distinction, great ability, and great kindness. When I happened to fall in with him on the street he could be delightful, but when I called at his house and he was posing to himself as the old cardinal he would turn everything to dust and ashes. After a tiresome day's work one didn't care to have one's powers of resistance taxed by discourse of that sort, so I called rarely. I think his dabbling with branches of knowledge and then finding that they were not it — and in short his philosophizing didn't amount to much. But he did first class work — wrote the best piece of American history there is, etc., etc. When he gave up his professorship he sent me all his German books on law and the sources — a noble present — and always was most kind even when he professed to grumble, as when I first went to England.

Apropos of Education I have been rereading the *Education Sentimentale* which you praised for its account of the revolution of '48. I admire the solidity — and virtues of style that take more than my knowledge of French to appreciate — but when a producer goes into the market the consumer has the first word and I don't care for overt presentations of the ignoble. I followed it up with Scott: *Talisman* and felt as if I had got into the air and Paul Veronese. What do I care for impossibilities if the author can fire off my emotions?

Yours ever,
O. W. H.

My love to Lady Pollock.

[2] It appears from Holmes's Journal that during the summer he read the *Report on the Strike of Textile Workers in Lawrence*, 1912, (Sen. Dec. 870, 62nd Cong. 2nd sess.) and *Summary of the Report on Condition of Women and Child Wage Earners in the United States*.

[3] Apparently the missing letter from Pollock contained an explanation of the allusion in his letter of May 26. *The Education of Henry Adams* was published in September 1918. Holmes, according to his Journal, read the book in 1907 when it was privately circulated among Adams's friends.

BEVERLY FARMS, July 22, 1919

My dear Pollock:

Yours of July 7 comes this morning.[1] There are implied references to things I had said that I don't remember now. You, I infer from things that you have written from time to time, take more stock in idealism than I do. I think when you give up solipsism (odious word) and admit the existence of other people you admit the *ding an sich*. Of course, however, I agree that the cosmic importance of man we know nothing about. . . . I don't know your libel case, *Hulton* v. *Jones*, but it coincides with a dissent of mine in Mass.,[2] and also with a decision of the Supreme Court of U. S. that I wrote in *Peck* v. *Tribune Co.*, 214 U.S. 185,— in principle at least. As I said in the last:—"If the publication was libelous the defendant took the risk." But that hardly reaches the necessary height as the publisher knows that his act will be detrimental if it hits and the plaintiff has no share in bringing about the situation. Laski certainly is a man of importance and gives me great pleasure in the way of intellectual companionship and also of putting me on to and lending me books. The last I haven't cared so very much for — Brown, *The French Revolution & English History* — an honest bit of work, but with details that don't interest me as much as they do an Englishman.

The Journal of a Disappointed Man — Barbellion — with introduction by Wells.[3] Some things look as if Wells wrote it, but I don't see why he should have thought it worth while — and Benn — *The Greek Philosophers*. I had just read his *History of English Rationalism in the Nineteenth Century*. He seems to be an enthusiastic atheist. I got but moderate pleasure from *The Greek Philosophers*, though it led me to send for the *Memorabilia* of Xenophon. Like most literary histories when he gets into causes of movements he names a lot of impalpables that I can't remember and that for all I see might be replaced by another lot with equal plausibility. It reminds me that I don't retain an impression that the cross examinations of

[1] See *supra*, p. 15.

[2] Hanson v. Globe Newspaper Co., 159 Mass. 293, 299 (1893). See *supra*, Vol. I, p. 46.

[3] Bruce Frederick Cummings (pseud. W. N. P. Barbellion), *The Journal of a Disappointed Man* (1919).

Socrates were so ineluctable as convention avers. My impression — mostly from youth — is of postulates that oughtn't to have been granted and of consequences that do not follow. As to the multiplication of reports I don't bother much — I always say the last twenty years takes up most of the law into itself.[4] I hope indeed that you will cross the Atlantic again for I grow more doubtful whether I ever shall. As to the Mormons I know not. I imagine from what I have heard that it is a disadvantage not to be of them if you live at Salt Lake. Give my love to Lady Pollock — I think of her often — and am not sure that I ought to let my letters to you take the place of writing also to her direct.

Yours ever,
O. W. HOLMES

P.S. All that I mean by the *ding an sich* is a somewhat, independent of my thought, presumably amounting to more than I know.

O. W. H.

RYE, SUSSEX, August 6, 1919[1]

My dear Holmes:

. . . I answer your last by return, for I shall have no patience with you till you have read *Hulton* v. *Jones*: for it is a mighty amusing case.[2] The plaintiff there did contribute to bring about the situation, for he had changed his original name of baptism to Artemus at confirmation: the only historical case of such change I know since Gawdy, J. noted in Coke on Littleton.[3] But no point was made of that. What makes it quite odd is that when the defendants, Hulton & Co., the owners of the newspaper, said they did not know of any real Artemus Jones's existence the plaintiff magnanimously accepted the denial and went on the pure point of law — but the damages look uncommonly as if nevertheless the jury did not believe the defendants,

[4] See "The Path of the Law," 10 *Harv. L. Rev.* 457, 458 (1897); *C. L. P.*, p. 167, at 169.

[1] A letter from Pollock, dated July 24, 1919, is omitted.
[2] The facts of the case are stated *supra*, Vol. I, p. 156.
[3] Book I, Chap. 1, Sec. 1, p. 3a.

and why the plaintiff took that line I don't know. Moulton's dissenting judgment ought to have prevailed,[4] I thought at the time — the reasons given in the House of Lords are very slight. I can't give you the reference here, but it must be in every book on or including defamation published within the last ten years.

Thanks for the opinions in the Arizona cases also to hand. It is amazing to my English mind that four judges of your Court should be found to assert a constitutional right not to be held liable *in a civil action* without actual fault. What do they make of the common *respondeat superior* rule? For it really won't do to say a man is in fault for not providing himself with infallible servants. I like your short opinion better than the larger one.[5]

I have been an idealist about thirty years in the sense of holding unknowable reality not only a chimerical but a contradictory term. Not that J. S. can expect to know everything — or that John Doe can have any direct knowledge of Richard Roe. Whether there is such a thing as knowing everything is an open question on which idealists of different schools hold widely different opinions.

Some want a universal mind to hold the world together, others do not. For myself I find it difficult to believe that the universe is reasonable, but impossible to believe that it is not.

I know Benn's *English Rationalism*, and met him once in London: he lived in Florence — a kind of Greek pagan I think— not a vulgar half-educated atheist at any rate, such as Bradlaugh, who was merely a ranting Calvinist preacher turned inside out.

I have looked through Laski's new book[6] before turning it over to a reviewer, and collect that he was brought up a Catholic or in Catholic surroundings — Polish? It is good for Protestants to be reminded that the Roman Church is a great political organism behaving very much like a State. . . .

Yours ever,
F. P.

[4] In the Court of Appeal, Sir J. Fletcher Moulton, Lord Justice of the Court of Appeal, wrote a dissenting opinion in which he maintained that the defendants were not liable. See [1909] 2 K. B. 444, 458.

[5] See *supra*, p. 15, esp. note 3.

[6] *Authority and the Modern State* (1919). The book was reviewed by H. J. R. (presumably H. J. Randall) in 36 *L. Q. Rev.* 93 (1920).

BEVERLY FARMS, August 21, 1919

Dear Pollock:

This morning brings a letter from you. . . . I shall keep your letter where I shall see it on my return in order to read the case you speak of. . . . As to the Arizona case I agree with you on all points. I thought the dissent amazing and that the opinion, which I agreed to make the opinion of the Court in order to get something that could be called that, was but a flabby performance. As to the universe my formula as a bettabilitarian (one who thinks you can bet about it but not know), is a spontaneity taking an irrational pleasure in a moment of rational sequence. . . . Laski was an Oxford man and I believe took honors there. The queer ecclesiastical interest in an unbelieving Jew is due I think to his having studied under Figgis whose propensities no doubt you know. . . . My latest reading has been Gooch, *History of English Democratic Ideas*, an excellent little book, which makes me wish I had Laski's gift of swiftly swallowing and assimilating the dull books of the past, such as Harrington's *Oceana* or Sydney.[1] I blush to say I never read Locke's treatise on Government. Now I am in rather a deliberate French work, Chauviré on Bodin. The old cuss reminds me somewhat of Coke. On the whole I am getting my money's worth for the trouble. I borrowed the book from Laski, who has a flair for picking up curiosa. A platitude has come home to me with *quasi* religious force. I was repining at the thought of my slow progress — how few new ideas I had or picked up — when it occurred to me to think of the total of life and how the greater part was wholly absorbed in living and continuing life — victuals — procreation — rest and eternal terror. And I bid myself accept the common lot; an adequate vitality would say daily: "God—what a good sleep I've had." "My eye, that was dinner." "Now for a rattling walk —" in short realize life as an end in itself. Functioning is all there is — only our keenest pleasure is in what we call the higher sort. I wonder if cosmically an idea is any more important than the bowels.

Yours ever,
O. W. H.

[1] James Harrington, *The Commonwealth of Oceana* (1656); Algernon Sydney, *Discourses Concerning Government* (1698).

RYE, SUSSEX, September 3, 1919

My dear Holmes:

Now I have two letters of yours on hand.[1] The learned Frenchman's book on Bodin is not known to me: I rather think there was no monograph on the said J. B. when I skimmed the cream, or what I thought so, of his political doctrine to dish up in my little book on the *History of the Science of Politics*. Rousseau's *Contrat Social* is awfully clever (I dished that up too): brilliant development of consequences from assumptions which unfortunately are contrary to the governing facts. Having read Rousseau you must certainly read Locke's *Essay on Civil Government* to observe the contrast of method. It is not long — of course nobody need at this day read the first part which pulverizes poor Sir. R. Filmer's patriarchal system of divine right[2] (Locke however, I have little doubt, was aiming at Hobbes through Filmer, who was really a Hobbist in temporal matters and all but said so). And on the whole it is quite readable though sometimes the arrangement is rather confused, and a few points I think there is a wilful smoke-screen (politer term than fog). Consider the *Essay* as a political pamphlet on the Revolution side, and the fact that it was the Whig gospel for a century, and you will see its working merit. If I have a spare copy of a bicentenary paper I wrote about Locke for the British Academy[3] — unless I have sent it to you already — I will send it from London towards the end of the month. We are here till the 24th.

You seem to agree with my ingenious friend G. E. Moore of Cambridge (whose *Principia Ethica* I recommend if not already known), that all good things are absolutely and so to speak incommunicably good in their several kinds — in which I think he is right, though that leaves the problem of the scale of values outstanding.

As for the small proportion of life that can be given to the *vivendi causae*, the things that make it as a whole worth living, that is all of a piece with the ways of nature. Most invertebrate

[1] Only the letter of August 21 has been found.

[2] *Patriarcha* (1680).

[3] "Locke's Theory of the State," *Proceedings of the British Academy*, 1903–1904, p. 237; reprinted, *Essays in the Law* (1922), p. 80.

and even cold-blooded vertebrate life is the residue of enormous potential fecundity gone (as we say) to waste — I forget how many thousand eggs go wrong for one codfish that gets hatched. But, as Berkeley said long ago, it is idle to censure the creation as wasteful if you believe in a creator who has unlimited stuff to play with. And anyway, why be sorry for the things we don't miss? Anyhow there will be new ideas in the future that can't come into our knowledge in this world: and what does it matter that there have been lots of old ones to you and me unknown, unless ignorance of them is a hindrance to knowledge of something we have a definite reason for wanting to know? People who are insensitive in certain directions (as Leslie Stephen was completely music-deaf) do miss a lot, but after all they never know it.

Yours ever,
F. POLLOCK

BEVERLY FARMS, September 19, 1919

Dear Pollock:

Your logical demand in your letter of Sept. 3 that after Rousseau I should read Locke I already had complied with — not merely the second part but the first. In these days one thinks of the C. J. (I can't remember his name on the moment) to Saunders: "Why do you labor so, for the Court is clearly with you?" [1] Rousseau got his ideas from Locke I suppose, and Locke, I rather infer from what Laski said some time ago, from his predecessors in England. But I can't recite, alas, on Sydney, Harrington *et al.* I hope it will carry only *levis nota infamiae* at the Day of Judgment. Just now I am rereading Heine's *Life* told in his own words, translated by Arthur Dexter formerly of these parts from the German of Gustav Karpeles with omissions and additions. Heine is the stingingest cuss ever. Did I ever repeat to you my division of "able lawyers" into kitchen knives, razors and stings?

[1] Presumably Holmes refers to the remark of Twysden, J. in Birks v. Trippet, 1 Saund. 32, 33: "What makes you labour so? The court is of your opinion, and the matter clear."

The other day Laski sent me E. S. P. Haynes, *The Decline of Liberty in England*, which seemed to me to succeed in being obscure in matters that had no obscurity in them. But I partly sympathized with his *animus*. The whole collectivist tendency seems to be toward underrating or forgetting the safeguards in bills of rights that had to be fought for in their day and that still are worth fighting for. I have had to deal with cases that made my blood boil and yet seemed to create no feeling in the public or even in most of my brethren. We have been comfortable so long that we are apt to take it for granted that everything will be all right without our taking any trouble. All of which is but a paraphrase of eternal vigilance is the price of freedom — and I would fain add, to the labor men, eternal hard work is the price of a living. . . .

Yours ever,
O. W. Holmes.

Rye, September 20, 1919

My dear Holmes:

Now I have got Laski's *Problems of Sovereignty* from the London Library, and think it was an ill day for him when he fell into the hands of Figgis. (There was a distinct cranky element in F. which became crankier in his later work. Once I caught him misunderstanding Maitland.) He is not too old to shake off the obsession of church history. If he does not his work will be permanently lop-sided. Certainly resistance to the temporal power for conscience sake has usually been the work of men acting in groups — even the late Conscientious Objectors were a group, though hardly a considerable one. I should have thought the fact too notorious to need enforcing by a minute study of the Scottish Free Church secession. Nor is it any discovery that in extreme cases disobedience to lawful authority may be a moral duty if conscience clearly forbids obedience (at the risk indeed that conscience may be wrongly informed, in which case wholly right action is impossible). This is explicitly allowed in Roman moral theology, see Newman's *Letter to the Duke of Norfolk*. On sovereignty in general Laski seems to me confused, and likely to be confusing to novices. In spite of Bryce's clear exposition, published sixteen or seventeen years ago, he fails to distinguish legal sovereignty — the formal authority to make rules not formally controllable by any other defined power — from political supremacy — the power of directing the action of legal sovereignty by lawful means: of which the first is matter of law, the second matter of fact. L.'s mind seems to me quite un-legal.

Then, what sane man ever maintained that it is a necessary attribute of a sovereign to be *always* obeyed? Not John Austin, to do him bare justice, though I love him not. Laski's Austinianism is a figment. Even less Jeremy Bentham: and when Hobbes says that the subject's duty is correlative to the sovereign's power to protect him he certainly does not mean that the sovereign is dethroned by every riot or rebellion. (Even habitual disobedience in some things is consistent with the rule of law: it is certain that only a minority of motorists observe the statutory speed limit on a clear road, but England is not therefore in a state of anarchy.) Hobbes's worst mistake was his dogmatic assumption that sovereignty is illimitable and indivisible: which Bentham distinctly refuses to accept in the *Fragment on Government*. Laski's talk about "Erastianism" (another figment, I think) is often loose and sometimes erroneous. More of the Figgis twist, I suppose. I don't think he realizes how much the temporal power interfered before the Reformation — not in matters of doctrine indeed, but very firmly on questions of property, including ecclesiastical patronage. Nor does he see the difference between a cosmopolitan and a merely intra-national church — the former can make a real treaty with the State, the latter can't. If he thinks the King in Council acquired any new ecclesiastical jurisdiction by the substitution of the Judicial Committee for the old "Delegates" I am pretty sure he is wrong, but cannot now verify.[1] A church by law established has to pay for its privileges, that's the broad fact.

[1] In his first chapter, "The Sovereignty of the State," Laski said: "An omnipotence that Cardinal Wiseman can overthrow in 1851, that J. H. Newman can smilingly dissolve in 1875, that constitutes in the Judicial Committee of the Privy Council a tribunal for ecclesiastical causes which clergymen of repute will regard as of no authority, and, therefore, neglect, seems to represent an abstraction of the facts." *Studies in the Problem of Sovereignty*, p. 13; see also pp. 101–108.

Doesn't it all come round to this? Conscientious resistance is a matter of conscience not of law: for that very reason, the servants of the law can take notice of it only *de gratia* or as an element in guiding judicial discretion. But administrators and law-makers remember, if they are wise, that bad trouble may come of provoking it. (Locke pointed out, against Hobbism, that formulas won't ensure obedience in fact.)

However, Laski is clever enough to put older men on re-examining and re-stating their own beliefs, and to be sure that is much. I would concede to him that in a state of society — if it ever comes about — where the risk of war is negligible and violent crime practically extinct, central government, apart from administrative public services like the post office, may perhaps be regarded as a kind of Supreme Court, political as much as legal, for adjusting the relative claims of semi-independent groups. You and I won't live to see that and I don't much think he will.

Yours ever,
F. P.

WASHINGTON, October 26, 1919

Dear Pollock:

Your criticism of Laski is very like those that I have made to him, and like you I have regretted the influence of Figgis. It is an odd thing to see an unbelieving Jew interested in a schism in the Scotch Church. In a Philippine case, *Cariño* v. *Insular Government*, 212 U. S. 449, 458, that I may have mentioned heretofore,[1] the question was of a native title to land. The Government urged that it was bad for want of registration under the Spanish law, while admitting that Spain could not have enforced its law and wouldn't have let the owner register if he ever had dreamed of trying to. I said that while in theory sovereignty was absolute and Spain asserted, as the U. S. would assert, absolute power, it did not follow that the U. S. asserted that Spain had absolute power, that apart from theory sovereignty was a question of strength, and might vary in

[1] See *supra*, vol. 1, pp. 147, 148, 152.

degree, etc. . . . By a side wind what I was saying reminds me of how people in the law as elsewhere hate to recognize that most questions — I think I might say all legal questions — are questions of degree. I have just sent back an opinion of one of our JJ. with a criticism of an argument in it of the "where are you going to draw the line" type — as if all decisions were not a series of points tending to fix a point in a line. The admission of an antithesis between extremes necessitates it. North and South Poles import an equator. To come back to your theme, of course the territorial club (*i. e.* the nation), while it lasts, must have the army. While it has the army the extent to which it will allow other clubs depends upon its will — subject to the chance that if it goes too far it will use its fighting power. I regret in view of present threats of strikes here, that having generally been on the labor side, I didn't publish a dissent on the labor side two years ago [2] in which, however, I said: "I have no doubt that when the power of either capital or labor is exerted in such a way as to attack the life of the community, those who seek their private interest at such cost are public enemies and should be dealt with as such," etc.. I referred to John Mitchell using words that imported "the preference of the welfare of his private club to that of the country at large." Well, I believe that this country like yours, if the issue is pressed too far, will crush those who set themselves against it, but I regret the persistence of the head of the Steel Co. in refusing to deal with the unions,[3] and should be sorry to see the issue take that form.

The work has got well under way — so well that we adjourn tomorrow for a fortnight. I see various conflicts of opinion ahead, and even have prepared dissenting statements in one or two cases, subject to what may happen. I hope that we have heard the last, or nearly the last, of the Espionage Act cases. Some of our subordinate Judges seem to me to have been

[2] Hitchman Coal and Coke Co. v. Mitchell, 245 U. S. 229 (1917). Mr. Justice Brandeis wrote a dissenting opinion in which Holmes concurred. Two drafts of Holmes's unpublished dissent in this case are bound with his copies of his Supreme Court opinions now in the possession of the Harvard Law School.

[3] On September 22 a strike had been called in the steel industry. From the outset Elbert Henry Gary, of the United States Steel Corporation, refused to confer with representatives of the Union, and eventually the strike was broken.

hysterical during the war. It is one of the ironies that I, who probably take the extremest view in favor of free speech, (in which, in the abstract, I have no very enthusiastic belief, though I hope I would die for it), that I should have been selected for blowing up. I don't understand the Government pressing those cases and trust cases against corporations for doing what it still is doing and what is likely to be sanctioned by legislation — but that is not my business. . . .

Yours ever,
O. W. H.

WASHINGTON, November 6, 1919

Dear F. P.:

At last your injunction has been followed and I have read *Hulton* v. *Jones* [1] with much inward satisfaction as it is bang on the point of a dissent of mine in *Hanson* v. *Globe Newspaper Co.*, 159 Mass. 293,299,[2] and I even venture to think that the earlier discussion, though rather too long, does not suffer by comparison. You will think I have begun to blow my own horn as the other day I ventured to concur in your preference of my opinion in the Arizona case (liability without fault) to that of my colleague. But my head has not swelled, the coincidence is an accident — no more. Today I am stirred about a case that I can't mention yet to which I have sent round a dissent that was prepared to be ready as soon as the opinion was circulated.[3] I feel sure that the majority will very highly disapprove of my saying what I think, but as yet it seems to me my duty. No doubt I shall hear about it on Saturday at our conference and perhaps be persuaded to shut up, but I don't expect it.[4]

[1] See *supra*, vol. I, p. 156; vol. II, pp. 16, 20–21.

[2] See *supra*, vol. I, p. 46; vol. II, p. 19.

[3] Presumably, Abrams v. United States, 250 U. S. 616, 624 (argued Oct. 21, 22; decided Nov. 10, '19).

[4] Only the first sheet of this letter, ending at this point, has been found.

LONDON, November 24, 1919

My dear Holmes:

Thanks for telling me of your old Mass. case of *Hanson* v. *Globe Newspaper Co.* I should have liked to know of it earlier, but it is noted for a new edition of *Torts* on which I am now at work. It is in Wigmore's *Select Cases,*[1] I now see, but I have never had time to go through that profitable and sometimes amusing book in order. I think the decision may be wrong without *Hulton* v. *Jones* being therefore right, see note enclosed.[2]

You seem to be much more scrupulous about giving dissenting opinions than noble and learned persons in the House of Lords here, whose dissents do not always look as if they had taken much trouble to appreciate the other point of view.

In the Senate on the other hand the peace of the world and the pacification of the still unsettled parts of Europe appear to be considered of less importance than a party score. I should not deny that the Republicans had substantial provocation in some ways. I am wondering what will be the final addendum to my little book on the League of Nations when the last proofs are passed two or three weeks hence. . . .

Keeping bad English out of the *Law Reports* does not become easier. The last vermin I slew was *intervenent* (the reporter spelt it — *ant*, moreover), for which I can find no warrant but an obscure writer on admiralty law *ad init. saec. xix.* And in the judgment (Phillimore in the Judicial Committee) it was intervener as it should be. In the lump, between ourselves, we are an illiterate profession.

Yours ever,

F. P.

[1] John H. Wigmore, *Select Cases on Torts* (2 vols., 1st ed., 1911).

[2] [*Enclosure*]: *Hanson* v. *Globe Newspaper Co.* is an interesting case. I am not sure that the minority judgment goes far enough to support *Hulton* v. *Jones*: the facts are not on all fours.

Here the defendant's statement was meant to apply & in fact did apply to a real person whose name in its usual written form differed from plaintiff's by only one initial, and the description as given was also applicable to the plaintiff. These are material differences.

It does not appear what the evidence was.

In *Hulton* v. *Jones* one may suspect that the jury, notwithstanding the plaintiff's acceptance of the defendant's explanation, did not believe it and acted on their disbelief.

LONDON, December 1, 1919

My dear Holmes:

Abrams v. *U. S.*[1]

Thanks for the opinions herein.[2] I am rather puzzled.

The monstrously excessive sentence — twenty years for an offense on which the sentence would have been about six months in England, or twelve at most — is enough to make one astute in favour of the defence.

But the extracts from the defendants' publication, which was issued in time of active war, seem to come to this:

Hostilities against the Bolsheviks are a crime against all workers, therefore if the U. S. includes any such hostilities in its military operations it is the duty of all workers to resist by (1) stopping or curtailing the production of munitions, (2) active rebellion, so as to cripple the military power of the U. S. altogether.

I don't see why there was not evidence to go to a jury on the fourth count.[3] So far as I can perceive from the judgments I should think the first three were bad.

It puzzles me also, I confess, that a special Act of Congress should be necessary to make seditious denunciation of the Government and incitements to rebellion, in time of war, offences of some kind. But, as matter of policy, I believe there were many leaflets of much the same kind distributed in this

[1] 250 U. S. 616, 624 (1919). The majority of the Court in this case, in an opinion by Clarke, J., held that the defendants' conviction under the Espionage Act should be sustained. The nature of the charge against the defendants is described in the majority opinion: "Each of the first three counts charged the defendants with conspiracy, when the United States was at war with . . . Germany, to unlawfully utter, print, write and publish: 'disloyal, scurrilous, and abusive language about the form of Government of the United States;' in the second count, language 'intended to incite, provoke, and encourage resistance to the United States in said war.' The charge of the fourth count was that the defendants conspired 'when the United States was at war with the Imperial German Government, . . . unlawfully and wilfully, by utterance, writing, printing and publication, to urge, incite and advocate curtailment of production of things and products, to wit, ordnance and ammunition, necessary and essential to the prosecution of the war.'" (250 U. S. at p. 617). Holmes, in his dissent, contended that there was no evidence to go to the jury on any count.

[2] If Holmes wrote to Pollock when he sent him the opinions in the Abrams case, the letter is missing.

[3] See note 1, *supra*.

country on which it was not thought useful to prosecute any one.

Yours ever,
F. POLLOCK

WASHINGTON, December 14, 1919

Dear Pollock:

As to the *Abrams case* your puzzle as to a special act of Congress being necessary is answered by the consideration that there are no crimes against the U. S. except by statute. I think it possible that I was wrong in thinking that there was no evidence on the Fourth Count in consequence of my attention being absorbed by the two leaflets that were set forth. But I still am of opinion that I was right, if I am right in what I devoutly believe, that an actual intent to hinder the U. S. in its war *with* Germany must be proved. As the *Debs case* and two others were assigned to me, in which the convictions were upheld,[1] I thought it proper to state what I thought the limits of the doctrine. The general principles laid down by me I think correct, and the particular conclusion I adhere to, because even if there were evidence of a conspiracy to obstruct, etc., the overt act laid must be an act done to effect the object of the conspiracy and it seems to me plain that the only object of the leaflets was to hinder our interference with Russia. I ought to have developed this in the opinion. But that is ancient history now.

You say in a letter received a few days before this one that we are an illiterate profession. My dear boy, if you can say that in England, what could I say that was adequate about us here! I see and hear things daily that would make me shudder if I had not grown hardened.

I have suffered a loss here through the closing of the print shop that I was wont to frequent — it didn't pay and the man has gone off. It takes away a weekly pleasure. Curiously, he told my pal, Admiral Davis,[2] with whom on Saturdays I would turn over a portfolio and jaw, that during the war he did a

[1] See *supra*, p. 7.

[2] Charles Henry Davis (1845–1921); brother of Mrs. Brooks Adams and Mrs. Henry Cabot Lodge.

good business but after the armistice it stopped. Perhaps it was the custom of foreigners that he got then, as I remember his telling me of having sold a lot of Zorns to one — and Zorns come high in these parts. I should like his Renan, but most of his etchings emphasizing facts about the naked female that generally are omitted in singing I don't care very much for. How I wish that you could look in here. I think you would like my library especially now that it is lightened up a bit by a few prints in the rare places where I can put one. Are you familiar with Nanteuil — individually, not taken in the lump with Masson, Drevet *et al.*? I think when he drew *ad vivum* and then engraved he was a king. One of his things with a fine bit of fur has been put up to a great price, I suspect largely by the conventional admiration of Charles Sumner — but it was from a painting, and I would rather have almost any one that he drew from the life. It is interesting to see how the big fellows, Rembrandt, *longo intervallo* Whistler, and with a further space Seymour Haden separate themselves from the second rate men more and more as you grow familiar with them. . . . I have bought a few of the second raters however that give me pleasure: Gravesande, a good deal of a master; Lalanne; — the more poetic Appian. Meryon I should think a first rater — and have stretched my purse for one of his. But this is cataloguing. Give my love to Lady Pollock, please.

Yours ever,
O. W. Holmes

London, December 11, 1919

My dear Holmes:

On Saturday week I am to be made a *docteur en Sorbonne* at Paris, the Faculty of Law there having been pleased to confer an honorary degree on me. This, with the Harvard degree, will be the honour I most prize, and moreover it is good to have an unexceptionable reason for going to Paris after being within the four seas these five years. It will be a short visit, Thursday to Monday, but well worth having. . . .

Yours ever,
F. P.

WASHINGTON, December 29, 1919

Dear F. P.:

Your note telling me that you are to have an honorary degree at Paris delighted me. You have deserved your honors and I am glad you are getting them.

I have just finished reading (with a dictionary) Ehrlich, *Die Juristische Logik* — which I might call an elaborate proof of my old thesis that the life of the law has not been logic; it has been experience. It is good though you and I hardly need it. I thought his *Grundelung der Soziologie des Rechts* the best book on legal subjects by any living continental jurist that I knew of. He has a keen sense of actualities.

I wish you and yours a happy New Year — happier than the last — and send you all my love.

Yours ever,
O. W. H.

LONDON, December 29, 1919

My dear Holmes:

It is a week since I came back from Paris a *docteur en Sorbonne* — passing by a narrow margin the strange medieval revival of a fiscal inquisition whereby one is forbidden to carry more than 10 francs out of France in coin — and bringing a parchment diploma, an artistic bronze medal, and the badge of my new degree, which is an ornament called *épitoge*. It is clearly described in Littré's *Dictionary*, and under the Latin form in DuCange one learns that though equivalent to our hoods in significance it has a different origin, from a small cape worn over the gown by medieval clerks. It is fastened on the left shoulder by buttons fixed for that purpose on the robe: but doctors who are not professors have nothing to fasten it to, for the robes are the badge not of the university degree but of the Faculty and are worn only by professors. It hangs like a stole, and broad end behind. Asking how it was worn made me a good opening with Madame Lucien Poincaré the Vice-Rector's wife (the titular Rector being the President of the Republic *ex officio*) when I sat next her at an exquisitely appointed dinner in the evening.

The ceremony was most impressive — do you know the amphitheatre of the Sorbonne and the great Puvis de Chavannes decoration filling the back wall? — the platform filled with doctors in divers colours, notably the canary yellow of Letters, and the central figure of the audience Marshal Foch, from whom I was no farther than the width of an ordinary-sized sitting room. The discourses very good: L. Poincaré spoke of the university's work in the war, Larnaude, Dean of of my Faculty, on the need to remember that what we fought for was right and justice, a professor from Strasburg, added it seems at the eleventh hour, and acclaimed of course, and the Deans of Faculties presenting the honorary graduates whom they had recommended to the University Board. Larnaude's praise would have made me blush all colours if I had been less old and hardened. I hope I maintained an air of decent and not over-elated acquiescence. I don't know yet whether there will be any official report. The press was naturally meagre: in London only a snippet or two though two of the five honorary graduates were English (the other one in Medicine, Greenish, a specialist in the chemistry of drugs, I had never heard of him before, nor probably he of me). Brachet, Belgian publicist; Volterra, Italian mathematician, in a dark cassock, broad green girdle, and black round cap with red tuft; and Nyrop, Danish philologist — *in absentia*, being old and blind, the Danish Minister receiving his insignia — made up the tale. It was good to see Paris and one's Paris friends again, in spite of the foulest weather I ever knew there.

Yours ever,
F. P.

I appeared, according to instructions, as a D. C. L. of Oxford — that gown takes careful packing.

Best wishes though somewhat belated to you and yours for the New Year. *Omnia bene* with us except the hopelessly moist elements.

WASHINGTON, February 1, 1920

Dear Pollock:

You and Jack are rivals for once before this modest tribunal. I have been having no time for reading and consequently have not finished Jack's very interesting book [1] as I shall very soon now, and your *League of Nations* has just come to interrupt that and my duties. I have only read the first 30 pages or so but I want to go on at once to the end. I must admit, however, that I am afraid that I am in a class that you rather despise pp. 25, 26.[2] I am not an admiral or a general. I loathe war — which I described when at home with a wound in our Civil War as an organized bore — to the scandal of the young women of the day who thought that Captain Holmes was wanting in patriotism. But I do think that man at present is a predatory animal. I think that the sacredness of human life is a purely municipal ideal of no validity outside the jurisdiction. I believe that force, mitigated so far as may be by good manners, is the *ultima ratio*, and between two groups that want to make inconsistent kinds of world I see no remedy except force. I may add what I no doubt have said often enough, that it seems to me that every society rests on the death of men — as does also the romantic interest of long inhabited lands. I should be glad, to speak Hibernianly, if it could be arranged that the death should precede life by provisions for a selected race, but we shall not live to see that. However, I dare say that all this is in the air and that you may say that on these or any other principles it is a good thing if we can unite forces to put down avoidable displays of force. I find it somewhat hard to believe that we can come to such intimate understanding with the East that future slaughters can be avoided. But I am very nearly an old man and must content myself with my job and

[1] John Pollock, *The Bolshevik Adventure* (1919).

[2] Describing one class of critics of the League of Nations, Pollock said: "One sees a little group of elders who stand aside and shake their wise heads. This new-fangled coercion, they say, will never do. Voluntary submission to an award and voluntary compensation according to the award are doubtless to be encouraged with discretion; but beware of laying profane experimental hands on the ultimate right of resort to the blood-feud. It is a venerable and sacred institution handed down by our valiant ancestors, bound up with the very life of the clan and the family."

leave this business to you young chaps. Now I return to your book. . . . Laski is getting up a collection of my scattered essays, etc., for a volume which I hope some day will be published in N. Y.. I signed a contract yesterday authorizing it.[3]

Yours ever,
O. W. H.

LONDON, Feb. 12, 1920

My dear Holmes:

Ouf! as Flaubert used to say: I am sending out the copy for a new edition of my book on *Torts*.[1] The part to which I had to do most was Chapter XII dealing with the duty of occupiers to "invitees." There are recent *dicta* here tending to multiply useless diversities, though I think no positively wrong decision. So far as I know American authority is rather scanty on this topic.

Another kind of invitation: the Chancellor[2] has just offered me silk — a thing seldom done, the usage being for men who want to become practicing K. C.'s, and think the time is ripe to execute a moult from junior to leader, to apply for it. His idea as explained to me by Claud Schuster (his private secretary and a fellow-Bencher of mine) is that speculative lawyers should now and then be recognized in this kind.

I have thought it right to accept, as there is a principle in it, though it means a heavy fee and the purchase of some useless and ugly raiment which I shall in all likelihood put on only once: the silk gown, however, will be a better dining garment for Lincoln's Inn Hall than my very ancient junior barrister's gown. The list of new K. C.'s will, I suppose, be public by the time you get this.

Last night in the House of Commons Lloyd George flattened out (the expression of a learned friend who was there) the spokesmen of the extremist miners' unionists who clamour for

[3] Published in 1920 under the title *Collected Legal Papers*.

[1] Eleventh edition.

[2] Lord Birkenhead.

something they call nationalization — which you may be rather pleased to hear.[3]

The so-called simplicity of truth seems to me an illegitimate converse of a much more guarded proposition, that a doctrine capable of being stated only in obscure and involved terms is open to reasonable suspicion of being either crude or erroneous.

Yours ever,
F. POLLOCK

March 14, 1920

My dear Holmes:

We have gone to Constantinople and don't know when we shall get out:[1] we may have to go to Berlin: stable government in Russia is still far off: prices are still at war level and all money values uncertain: the war may have made us a little better and rather more capable in emergencies but has not made us any wiser that I can see: and the business of making a new world is longer, tougher, and less pleasant than even the more prudent of us foresaw. The one abated plague of London is the scarcity of taxicabs: but they too are dearer.

Meanwhile one has one's own work to carry on. I am revising the old book on Contract, rather drastically in parts — some of it seems to me but callow stuff now. I have in my mind somewhat large rearrangement, such as a new head of Conditional Contracts with "frustration of adventure" prominent, but have not made up my mind whether it is worth the pains. After all, is not the implied condition in those cases something of a fiction to screen rules of policy imposed on the parties and becoming,

[3] Mr. W. Brace in the House of Commons moved for an expression of regret that the King in his recent speech on the opening of Parliament had not proposed the nationalization of the coal mines in accordance with the recommendation of the Royal Commission. Mr. Lloyd George promptly retorted, emphasizing the benefits of private ownership and competition in the industry. Mr. Brace's motion was rejected by a majority of 265.

[1] The Treaty of Sèvres, establishing the new rights of Turkish sovereignty was not signed until May 11. During the winter months, and until that time, there had been constant participation by the Allies in the effort of the Turkish government to suppress the Nationalist forces. On March 16 a French-Italian army occupied Constantinople.

like equity of redemption, a real part of the contract only after that pressure has been applied?

In the *Law Reports* I fight with wild beasts in the shape of grossly incompetent printers' readers. I wonder what has become of the old ones: they can't all have been killed or made fortunes.

The new list of K. C.'s is not out yet.

Yours ever,
F. P.

April 11, 1920

My dear Holmes:

This is written in the Angel at Guildford. . . . My wife and I are rusticating for a long weekend which she will prolong to a whole week. . . . The object of the excursion is her convalescence from influenza mixed with bronchitis: of which the best one can say is that it saves time to take them mixed rather than have the bronchitis as a sequel.

As to the sanctity of human life I quite agree with you that there is too much fuss about it.[1] My complaint against war is not that it kills men but that it kills the wrong ones, taking an undue proportion of the strong and adventurous and leaving too many weaklings and shirkers, thus working a perverse artificial selection of those who are least fitted to adorn or improve the commonwealth.

Exceptionally no doubt a physical weakling is a man of genius or great ability and a fine animal is a stupid lout: but taken all round the men fit for military service and willing to take risks are of better type than the unfit and unwilling.

Even worse is the enormous damage and destruction not only of fungible wealth but of what one may call the capital of the humanities, the possessions that make civilized life really worth living. Apart from the detestable Prussian *Kriegsräson* which openly disregards all this, and which one hopes may be finally suppressed by a solemn condemnation (though at present

[1] If in any letter subsequent to that dated February 1, 1920, Holmes had mentioned this subject, the letter is missing.

there are hitches), it seems to me that modern conditions of warfare increase this danger. Then the blow to the fellowship of humane letters is almost as great as at the Reformation. We have some compensation in the increased intimacy of English-speaking with French scholars, but the total balance is to the bad. No other remedy being in sight than the League of Nations — I don't say it is infallible — it appears to me the thing to do here and now is to put one's back into making it effective. *N. B.*: Its labour department, about which the public seems to know very little, is already getting to work: a solid peace-time activity wholly independent of the prevention of war machinery.

We are reading Henry James's *Letters*. If one thing strikes me more than another it is his swift and almost invariably correct appreciation of personal qualities, *e.g.* picking out Flaubert and Turgenev at sight from the smaller people about them. Apparently men of action interested him very little even if they were also scholars. Alfred Lyall, who would have been a grand study for a latter day Balzac, flits across as a mere name. Pampering an artistic conscience is among the most perilous of the higher temptations. The great British novelists — to Thomas Hardy inclusive — have escaped it.

Yours ever,
F. P.

WASHINGTON, April 25, 1920

Dear Pollock:

Your letter of the 11th has just this moment been received and read. My wife also has been down, not, the Doctor said, with influenza, but with a cold that has left her weak, so that she has kept the house for over a fortnight. She was ill last summer and is easily pulled down. She is better but is missing the double flowering cherry trees from Japan along the river front which is a world sight. Three of us Judges hooked off after conference yesterday and motored along a mile of wonder. They were just in perfection. I hope when you receive this Lady Pollock will be all right — please give her my love.

I agree of course with what you say about war. The C. J.

says, when I suggest that the replacing of the population is not a disagreeable task that the best part of the South simply was wiped out and cannot be replaced. Your remark that the men fit for military service on the whole are the better type, *non obstant* the possibility that a weakling may have genius, is precisely the reflection that makes me believe that it would be possible to breed a race. I agree also with what you say of H. James. As probably I have remarked before, to understand him or W. J. one must remember their Irish blood. I agree too that he narrowed his interests to a narrow circle of tastes, and I long have thought that there was a touch of underbreeding in his recurrence to the problem of the social relations of Americans to the old world. *Solvitur ambulando* — it seems to me a thing not to be dwelt on.

My latest interest was a case I gave the judgment in last Monday, affirming the constitutionality of a law in pursuance of a treaty with you for the protection of migatory birds.[1] Missouri said it invaded her rights, reserved in the instrument.

I also had a case in which Illinois tried to dodge the Constitutional requirement of due faith and aids to judgments in other states by denying jurisdiction to Courts otherwise competent.[2] They laid hold of a statement of mine in an earlier case that the Constitution did not oblige States to furnish a Court,[3] but we said the dodge wouldn't do.

This week ends our sittings for argument, though we don't finally adjourn until sometime into June. There are some important cases that I hope will be decided before we separate, including the validity of the 18th Amendment[4] and the right to tax Judicial salaries[5] — whether it is excluded by a provision that their compensation shall not be diminished during their continuance in office.

Laski is going to leave us for London to be a professor in — I forget the name, an economic thing — where I believe he will

[1] Missouri v. Holland, 252 U. S. 416 (1920).

[2] Kenney v. Supreme Lodge, 252 U. S. 411 (1920).

[3] Anglo-American Provision Co. v. Davis Provision Co., 191 U. S. 373 (1903).

[4] National Prohibition Cases, 253 U. S. 350 (1920). Holmes concurred in the prevailing opinion of VanDevanter, J., sustaining the validity of the Amendment.

[5] Evans v. Gore, 253 U. S. 245 (1920). The majority of the Court held that the tax was invalid. Holmes wrote a dissenting opinion in which Brandeis, J., concurred.

have a class from the Civil Service.[6] His knowledge is wonderful and he has put me up to many books that I should have missed. When he goes into a shop he spots a book as my wife would a flower. Incidentally, being here the other day he mentioned that in a place close by was a copy of the 1803 edition of Malthus — which was just what I wanted and I nailed it the next morning. I shall miss him badly. Wigmore in the *Ill. Law Rev.* goes for me *ex cathedra* as to my dissent in the *Abrams case.*[7] You didn't agree with it, but Wigmore's explosion struck me, (I only glanced at it), as sentiment rather than reasoning — and in short I thought it bosh. He has grown rather dogmatic in tone, with success, though he doesn't equal another Chicago man, Zane, who patronized and condemned me on other matters, and also with one sweep wiped all German jurists off the slate, and with another Hobbes, Bentham, Austin, etc., so that nothing seemed to remain but Zane, and what he stood for he didn't tell. Goodbye till next time.

Yours ever,
O. W. Holmes

April 14, 1920

My dear Holmes:

P.S. 1 (irrelevant). I am still at Guildford till Friday. As the wet Christmastide laid me by the heels with lumbago, this wet Eastertide has done the like — and literally by the *foot* — with something I will call *ejusdem generis* at large, for it would be absurd for a man of spare and active habits — and what many men would call abstemious — to confess to starting gout in his old age. However, it's subdued by a little care and dieting, only it is not worth while to go home for one day and come out again: and I am using the enforced leisure to set down without book some notes of my new ideas for recasting a chapter or so in *Contracts*, not a bad plan I think. Next week I will look up

[6] In 1920 Laski was called to the London School of Economics.

[7] "Abrams v. United States: Freedom of Speech and Freedom of Thuggery in War-Time and Peace-Time," 14 *Ill. L. Rev.* 539 (1920).

the Massachusetts judgment referred to in your letter to my wife.[1]

P. S. 2. Which reminds me how I might have reinforced my doctrine as to the contra-natural selection of war by the example of a certain stray bullet whose deviation by a fraction of an inch would have deprived the learned world of *The Common Law*, the law itself of the judgment aforesaid and many other profitable ones (the dissenting ones not the least so), and the present writer of a friendship nearing its jubilee, one of some three or four that have counted most in his life.

Confute that example if you can — it is stronger than speculation as to what the ingenious Mr. X who *was* killed would have done.

P. S. 3. Did you ever see or hear of a thin book called *A Reporter's Lincoln* by Walter B. Stevens — Missouri Historical Society, St. Louis 1916 — *penes me* as one of a batch of publications that Society sent me on making me an honorary member the other day. Presumably in the Library of Congress. The collection appears to be genuine, many of the anecdotes not generally known, (I had never read that A. L. was once on the point of fighting a duel with cavalry sabres), and much humanity in it. How it came to be gathered up in Missouri rather than Illinois does not appear. It pleases me to know that Lincoln abhorred starched collars.

Yours ever,
F. P.

WASHINGTON, April 28, 1920

Dear Pollock:

Anti P. S. (i.e. antistrophe to your P. S.):

1. A suggestion of gout strikes me as a mark of a good lawyer. My grandfather[1] had it and many of his descendants, though I have been free. An occasional transitory twinge in a toe has made me wonder once in a while but it vanished with the suggestion.

[1] The letter referred to has not been found, or the judgment identified.

[1] Charles Jackson.

2. As to war selection I have already told you of my agreement but I can't tell you what pleasure the expression of your friendship gives me from your reserved lips. Not, of course, that I didn't believe it before. It has counted enormously to me — in the earlier days when it was hard to keep up one's courage and in the later happiness of what is getting pretty near to old age. As Judge Lowell[2] once said in a case that I defended before him, when a man libelled a boat for salvage in which he had sailed 3000 miles from a sinking ship: "that account is *in equilibrio.*"
3. I do not know the book *A Reporter's Lincoln*. I will try to remember to ask about it when I get a chance to go to the Congressional Library as I hope to before long. The duel story sounds as if I had heard it and I rejoice with you that L. didn't like starched collars. I discovered soft shirts a year or two ago and when propriety permits a soft collar I get one on ὡς τάχιστα.

I made a little jest yesterday that pleased me. My brother Clarke was saying that knocking off wine and spirits had made it necessary for the clubs to raise their annual charges. I said they used to raise the Devil and now they raise the dues. . . .

My love to Lady Pollock.

Yours ever,
O. W. H.

London, June 3, 1920

My dear Holmes:

Having now before me a fuller account of *U. S.* v. *Abrams* in the April number of the *Harvard Law Review* in an article by one Zechariah Chafee,[1] (who were his ancestors? the name is puzzling), which backs up your opinion, I think the intent required by the language of the Act, and to be proved in order to support a verdict of guilty on the 4th count, is a specific intent in fact, and not an intent imputed to the defendant by way of

[2] Price v. Sears, Fed. Cas. No. 11,416 (1877).

[1] "A Contemporary State Trial — The United States versus Jacob Abrams et al.," 33 *Harv. L. Rev.* 747 (1920).

inference from what ought to have been his knowledge of probable consequences.

I can see no evidence of such an intent, and therefore humbly conceive that all the counts were unsupported and there was nothing that could properly go to the jury. (I thought 1, 2 & 3 bad from the first.) . . .

With the help of Mr. Z. Chafee's information I am making a note on the case for the July number of the *L. Q. R.*[2] (doing very well under my successor,[3] I think).

Last week I enjoyed a morning's cruise in a submarine under pretence of an International Law Congress at Portsmouth: and I have had a mighty pleasant weekend at Cambridge on the occasion of the College asking the new Hon. Fellows to dinner. Seniority cast on me the duty of returning thanks for them: I took some little pains about it and had reason to think my speech gave satisfaction.

Twopenny postage is a displeasing innovation, but I wish we had nothing worse to trouble us in public affairs.

Yours ever,
F. POLLOCK

If the printers of the *Law Reports* go on as they are still doing there will be manslaughter.

BEVERLY FARMS, June 21, 1920

Dear Pollock:

Your letter and postal card p.s.[1] greet me here, where we arrived Saturday evening rather seedy after Washington but reviving in the Beverly air. Chafee is a professor at the Harvard Law School and is said to be a very good man. In the few minutes talk I had with him a year ago he seemed unusually pleasant and intelligent. . . .

[2] See 36 *L. Q. Rev.* 210 (1920).

[3] A. E. Randall (1862–1925).

[1] The postal card is omitted. It stated only that Pollock would postpone publishing his comment on the Abrams case until he had seen a full report of the case.

I shall miss Laski sadly. He put me up to all sorts of new books and lent me many. . . . I am much attached to him, and now almost all my old friends and acquaintances in these parts are dead. Even in this village I shall see no more the most familiar faces. I will enclose in this a recent constitutional opinion of mine [2] — for no better reason than that it came to me here through the mail. It may give you a notion of the steady resistance of the States to new manifestations of national power. The later one to the 18th Amendment [3] I regarded as merely an illustration of what I said years ago in the *Northern Securities* case; that in what are called great cases (especially if there is a lot of money behind), a kind of hydraulic pressure is brought to bear that makes or tries to make just principles seem doubtful. I could not regard the attempt from many quarters to upset the 18th Amendment (teetotalism) as anything but taking a sporting chance for possible profit. I am hardly settled in my life yet, and am more or less distracted by the usual bothers of a change — including the non-arrival of two trunks, one containing my check books, etc.. So I will not expatiate. My love to Lady Pollock. I hope to begin to civilize up a bit, now that I am away from the job.

Yours ever,
O. W. H.

BEVERLY FARMS, July 31, 1920

Dear Pollock:

A month of vacation has gone and I have adjusted myself to the usual vacation life. The only events are books — and yet I don't read as much as it would seem that I ought to. Walks and solitaire take a good deal of time and one is liable, if one sits up late as I do, to drop into a nap over really improving studies. I read one little book of metaphysics by Hoernlé of

[2] Probably the dissenting opinion in Knickerbocker Ice Co. v. Stewart, 253 U. S. 149, 166 (1920). The majority of the Court held in this case that Congress could not constitutionally authorize the application of the workmen's compensation acts of the several states to injuries suffered in maritime employment.

[3] National Prohibition Cases; see *supra*, p. 41.

Harvard College[1]—going, I hear, to Oxford—clever but spending energy on some matters that seem to me futile, *e.g.* the suggestion that consciousness is an epiphenomenon. It seems to me that all we can say is that when the universe comes out in a certain knot of nerve tissues &c it also comes out in consciousness and that we have no more right to think away one part than another. I suspect that the suggestion is based on the humbug of degrees of reality. Also I have received some social theory books, (one of that name by Cole that seemed to me to take a good deal for granted that I shouldn't grant), the last the Webbs' *History of Trade Unionism* — alas not in the latest edition — an interesting and mighty solid piece of work; but it seems to me inspired by sentimental and dramatic economics so far as I can guess. I should think that they, like our Croly, thought that the universal standard of living could be raised if only they could lay hold of "the sums now withdrawn by capital," as if these sums did not now support labor. I wish the controversy could be reduced to the plain issue of fact: What do the luxuries of the few amount to? I believe them to be a drop in the bucket. The luxuries that really impinge upon the necessaries are the luxuries of the many, *e.g.* the Churches. And if you abolished them, do you doubt that the addition would be expended at once in more population? I don't.

I found Gooch's *Germany and the French Revolution* interesting and very instructive to my ignorance. And just now I am taking a brief turn at Aeschylus. I had Blackie's translation (in Everymans Library) and got the Greek. Poor old Blackie, obsessed by the mania of being poetical, he has blunted every sharp point of the magnificent original with the cotton wool of rhetoric. Just as Raphael Morghen did for Leonardo's *Last Supper*. Please give my love to Lady Pollock. I hope all goes well with you. I can make a good report for us.

Yours ever,
O. W. Holmes

[1] Reinhold Friedrich Alfred Hoernlé, *Studies in Contemporary Metaphysics* (1920).

THE OLD FLUSHING INN, SUSSEX
August 10, 1920

My dear Holmes:

We are settled here for a month, with a spell of fair weather after the wettest and coldest July these forty years or more. The first week of my vacation was spent at a Summer School of the League of Nations' Union near Worcester, and very pleasantly, as I was quartered on a hospitable house, whose old lady had known the Darwin family quite well. My special job was to give an elementary lecture on international law. Audience about half teachers as might be expected. Quality better than ordinary London lecture audiences, nearly up to the mark of University Extension or American university hearers (I don't mean the critical standard of the Harvard law school, still less the super-critical of the Lowell Institute, where at first I thought the people were bored to stiffness till I found out they were listening hard and reserving judgment[1] — but the average of a mixed lot in an epicene university, say Ann Arbor). Gilbert Murray of Oxford came for one night only and distinguished himself: he expounds very well and with an ingratiating manner.

Before leaving Lincoln's Inn I finished a new chapter for my old book of *Contract* — entitled "Conditions and herein of Frustration."[2] It will supersede "Impossible Agreements" which I now think was never a rational category and posed as such only by putting disproportionate emphasis on limiting hypothetical cases which don't occur in practice.

It is rather amusing to see your new lights trumpeting reasonable expectation as the real fundamental conception in contract: I agree of course, having put it in my 3d edition, *ad init.*, nearly forty years ago, only without a trumpet obligato. By the way I was sorry to see Wigmore carried away by the panic mongers.[3] His reasons amounted to saying that it is wrong to criticize an indictment for murder because homicide is a very dangerous offence and many murderers are very wicked men.

[1] In 1903 Pollock had delivered four lectures at the Lowell Institute in Boston. Their title was *The Theory of the State in English Publicists.*

[2] See 9th edition, Chapter VII.

[3] See *supra*, p. 42.

I had a glimpse of Brandeis in London: he was taken up with Zionist meetings.

Did you ever read Cowley's *Essays*? I am not sure that I ever did before, tho' my little reprint is dated in the '80's and has been long with me. He is reputed the father of modern English polite prose: not unjustly, but tho' fluent and lucid he is on the whole a learned *flat* with nothing that matters much to say, and in verse never achieves more than half a dozen good lines together, and often pretty bad ones.

Yours ever,
F. P.

I go on pegging away at Turgenev: a difficult author for a foreigner, but what an artist! If Tolstoy outweighs him on the whole as a bigger man, it is by weight alone. In form there is no comparison.

Have you seen that one of Scott's best "anonymous" mottos, "Sound, sound the clarion, fill the fife . . ." is run to earth as the one miraculous stanza in a long, otherwise wholly insignificant poem by one Major Mordaunt? [4]

BEVERLY FARMS, August 25, 1920

My dear Pollock:

Such a pleasant letter from you this week. I am afraid I don't know what you refer to when you speak of the trumpeting of reasonable expectations in contract. If I understand what substantive doctrine is meant I should think it was embodied in the *Kronprinzessin Cecilie*, 244 U. S. 12, which I think I mentioned to you when I wrote it (1917). I never read Cowley's *Essays*; as you imply, he wrote a good line or two of verse occasionally, but I have been in the habit of using him as an example of the power of fashion in art, once everybody read him — now no one. But as the object of art is to pull the trigger of an emotion, if it does, there is nothing more to be said — but

[4] Major Thomas Osbert Mordaunt (died, 1809) in *A Poem, Written during the last German War* (1791). See *Times Literary Supplement*, July 29, 1920, p. 487; Aug. 5, 1920, p. 504.

one thing does at one time and another at another. I have had and am having two great pleasures:

1. The book on *Political Thought in England from Locke to Bentham* in the Home University Library by my friend Laski whom I hope you will meet now that he is settled in London. The introductory Chapter seemed to me masterly. There are a few typographical errors in the book, and perhaps a little of the fault, natural to the young, of referring easily to books and people not generally known, without sufficient explanation. But Laski really is learned and reads the books he talks about — and I feel as if I knew nothing when I read him.

2. I now am in the middle of Pierre de Tourtoulon — *Les Principes Philosophiques de l'Histoire du Droit* — which is the bread of life. Perhaps occasionally he flats a little. Continental writers sometimes have trouble over what seems pretty plain to us, but on the whole I haven't for a long time read a book that embodies so many things that I believe, but that are not generally accepted, and so much that is new and instructive. I have not finished it yet but I am having a good time with it.

I read the other day two volumes that together make volume 1 (of 4!): *A la recherche du temps perdu* — Marcel Proust — closely printed — no intermissions. He is all there on the nuances of feeling and has a little talk about music that makes me wish I could hear him expound a sonata, but on the whole takes more time about things and people that he doesn't make me care much for than seems to me permissible *ici bas*. But I thought the same of H. James. Please give my love to your dear wife. We are well here and I hope you are.

Yours ever,
O. W. Holmes

Rye, Sussex, August 15, 1920

My dear Holmes:

Our last two letters (yours of July 31) have crossed. I have no use for materialists who talk of epiphenomenon. Experience in consciousness is the only kind of thing we know at first hand and (so far as its immediate contents go) are absolutely sure of. The rest is reflection, abstraction and reconstruction. To regard thought or consciousness as a by-product of something abstracted out of its own content is a ludicrous muddle. It also postulates the absolutely real space and time which Einstein seems to have demolished without recourse to metaphysic. The object of natural science is the world common to you and me, disregarding your and my individual points of view (but Einstein seems to suggest doubt whether, in the last resort, there is not a necessary fiction there): and that world is itself an ideal construction. Just now I am about to tackle a book by Whitehead of Cambridge and now of the Imperial College of Science — *The Concept of Nature* — one of the few men who really know all the mathematics there are, and co-author with Bertrand Russell of a work which perhaps a dozen other men in the world are competent to estimate. I don't know whether I shall be satisfied with its philosophical conclusions, if there be any, but it is bound to be solid stuff without any nonsense.

Aeschylus: I suppose that signifies the *Agamemnon* in particular: you should see Headlam's recent edition with translation if you can: he was one of our most brilliant scholars though now and then erratic in judgment and his early death was a sad loss. Then Gilbert Murray has just brought out a new version in rhyme — a mistake I think — judging by a review in *Times Literary Supplement*. I should expect to find it too much modernized and prettified, but there are sure to be felicities and he is an excellent scholar. Have I ever looked at Blackie's? I can't remember, but I have no doubt (on both scholarly and literary grounds) it is rather bad. Conington is I think the most vigorous of the other translators (somewhere about 1860–70). R. Browning, who was quite a good scholar, spoilt his work by a false doctrine of literal rendering (such as "midriff" for φρένες in the sense of brains or wits). I never heard of a good prose translation, which, if at the level of Munro's *Lucretius*, might be the best for Aeschylus as well as for Dante, of whom also no verse translation is satisfactory. On the *Eumenides* Verrall said the last and best word. There is a passable verse translation of all Aeschylus by the late Miss Swanwick, sound but rather tame.

Luxuries — yes, certainly: moreover the people who are customers for them now are the war-enriched, leaving the former rich to the mercies of super-tax.

I see there is a Nineteenth Amendment in view.[1] What would the Fathers have said? But, having gone so far, why not carry on the process to the end of a Federal code of uniform commercial law? That would seem less open to objection on political principle than XVIII and XIX.

Yours ever,
F. Pollock

Beverly Farms, August 28, 1920

Dear Pollock:

Again our letters have crossed. I received yours of August 15 just after I had answered the previous one. You say you are about to tackle Whitehead. A memorandum to get (or more probably vainly to try to get) the same book stood conspicuous on my inkstand for my next journey to town. I have finished Tourtoulon, *Principes philosophique de l'histoire du droit*, mentioned in my last, with the same pleasure throughout, though there are superfluities in the book — too many divisions, interdivisions and distinctions. A man's system is forgotten: only his *aperçus* remain. But he confirms so many of my scepticisms that he gives me much satisfaction. Now by way of reaction I am reading *A Book of English Prose* by Henley and Whibley, as one might read the *Golden Treasury*. There is a description of seeing the wind (driving the snow) by Roger Ascham that is delightful, and in model, simple English. In fact each little excerpt, chosen with an eye to interest and completeness in itself, gives pleasure. I forget what books of my summer reading I have mentioned. . . . I don't think I have spoken of Gorky's recollections of Tolstoi — adoring and in amusing contrast with the impressions of my neighbor Beveridge (ex-Senator, author of an admirable *Life of John Marshall*), who had some talk with him. I forget whether it was the book or the neighbor that

[1] The 19th amendment to the United States Constitution, which was ratified in August 1920, made provision for women's suffrage.

quoted a Russian lady (his mother-in-law?) that T. was jealous of Jesus. I think one is rather enraged at his dogmatic attitude, especially as he was ready to exhibit it on matters he knew nothing about. I can't recite on Einstein, though the same Jewish philosopher who sent me Tourtoulon and recommended Whitehead sent me two articles of his expounding Einstein's theory,[1] and a dame lent me an English pamphlet which I returned unmastered. *Le bon temps viendra.* Of course I agree with what you say as to consciousness being an epiphenomenon but I suppose those who suggest it go not on observation of self but of others — assumed to exist and to be like ourselves. As to Aeschylus it was not *Agamemnon* but *Prometheus* that I read carefully in the Greek. I have had a fancy for it ever since I was a boy. I read Gilbert Murray's translation of the *Frogs* of Aristophanes the other day, unfortunately no Greek here, and wondered at his faith in describing a scene as funny. Greek fun seems to me somewhat rudimentary, as that of the Middle Ages is like little boys' stories — that expect a laugh for dirty words. I am afraid I disagree with you as to verse translation of Dante. I thought Longfellow's quite a surprising *tour de force.* As to a Federal Code of commercial law our Court beginning with Story in *Swift* v. *Tyson* has gone, I think, indefensible lengths in disregarding local decisions upon questions arising in the U. S. Courts.

Yours ever,
O. W. Holmes

Rye, September 12, 1920

My dear Holmes:

Two letters of yours came in quick succession. This will, I suppose, find you still at Beverly Farms tho' with not many days left.

The passages about reasonable expectation as the measure of obligation in contract are not in any judgment but in essays and articles: the most material, I think, in the Wigmore cele-

[1] Morris Cohen," Einstein's Theory of Relativity," 21 *New Republic* 228 (Jan. 21, 1920); *id.*, 341 (Feb. 18, 1920).

bration volume,[1] and by Roscoe Pound. I rather think Whateley (an archbishop!) was really the first to hit that nail on the head.

Tourtoulon is quite new to me: I am asking the London Library to get the book.

From Locke to Bentham — I have been asked to review this for the new literary special issue or supplement of the *New York Evening Post*, and am waiting for a copy:[2] it is not yet accessible here.

Gorky on Tolstoy — I have seen this in magazine form and just acquired what seems to be an independent version by Leonard Woolf (married to Leslie Stephen's brilliant but eccentric daughter Virginia) and a Russian to me otherwise unknown. Tolstoy had no business to be born in Europe. He should have been an Indian sage, and then his exit to meditate in the wilderness would have been quite in the regular course and troubled nobody. So would his dogmatism: all Asiatic philosophy is dogmatic in form so far as I know; not "let us see" according to Plato's or Aristotle's way, but "thus said the Master." His talk about art and politics is of course mostly nonsense, but so is a good deal of Ruskin's and Carlyle's and (I suspect) Michelet's — not to mention learned Germans. His style is clumsy — or perhaps more justly, he had none. But the same may be said of Balzac. By the way, I have met a Balzacian here who doesn't think much of *Le Père Goriot*, thinks *La cousine Bette* too long, and puts *La Peau de Chagrin* (usually classed among *juvenilia*, exclusive of some half-dozen immature things which are printed in the collected editions but not read) in the first rank. On the second point he may have an arguable case, though such was not my impression when I read it. . . .

I have attacked Whitehead seriously and find the reasons as stiff as the conclusions are interesting, being in fact high mathematics in disguise: and some of his fundamental terms are quite hazy to me after repeated attempts to get a clear notion of them.

On more familiar ground I am much impressed by F. S. Marvin's work. . . . *The Living Past*, written before the war but

[1] *Celebration Legal Essays to Mark the 25th Year of Service of John H. Wigmore* (1919).
[2] See New York *Evening Post*, Nov. 6, 1920, p. 4.

touched up during it (3d ed. 1917), is much the best general summary "sketch of Western progress" — that is the sub-title — I have ever met with. He justly censures *int. al.*, and remedies, the neglect of Greek science in books of general history. A sequel *The Century of Hope* (2d ed. 1919), being a more detailed survey, 1815–1915, has just come from the London Library. . . .

Longfellow's Dante, a fine scholarly work certainly, but is it effective as English poetry? The difficulty is much the same with Homer: with Virgil even greater. But, using translation only as commentary on the original, I hardly ever look at a metrical version of Dante, having two or three good prose ones handy.

Yours ever,
F. P.

BEVERLY FARMS, September 26, 1920

Dear Pollock:

Your letter comes just in time (not that it wouldn't have been forwarded); we go to Boston tomorrow and on Wednesday, 29th, to Washington. By way of replication to your answer, unless I misapprehend the point, I don't see why the cases on damages do not embody the principle of reasonable expectation: he must know that the person he contracts with reasonably believes that he accepts the contract with the special condition attached to it? Willes, J., in *British Columbia Saw-Mill Co. v. Nettleship*, L. R. 3 C. P. 499, 508, cited by me in *Globe Refining Co.* v. *Landa Cotton Oil Co.* . . . 190 U. S. 540. In that I adhered as I still do to what you think heresies, but on this point I think we should agree.

Whitehead I failed to get and therefore can't recite. Marvin I read with pleasure last winter or before, probably in an earlier edition. Longfellow's Dante I used as you would a prose one, having Charles Norton's prose alongside and later using that in Dent's edition, Italian and English. Apart from the insignificant question of *variae lectiones* I thought Longfellow more useful than the prose to one who didn't know Italian — merely for purposes of accurate translation. In fact I couldn't imagine why C. N. wanted to put out his prose knowing what L. had done. I do hope you will like Laski's book as much as I do, even though you know so much more than I about the subject. Latterly, having been for a time a little pale (all right now), and Laski not being here to keep me up to improving reading I have been devouring old odds and ends that I needed to refresh myself on — *Cranford*, Walton's *Angler*, White's *Selborne*, Landor, *Gebir and Count Julian*, Lodge's *Rosalind* (basis of *As You Like It*), and one or two more serious matters. Just now I am rereading Selden's *Table Talk* with more admiration for the old man than I ever felt before. He had a sort of Aristotelian reasonableness. Landor has a lot of fair lines but the thread of events seemed to me, reading hastily, not very clear, and on the whole he seems to me rarely to hit you where you live (except in one or two little poems we all know). My excursions into innocence and fresh air were pleasant, but I look with suspicion on one who wants too much of them. As with the Psalms, one is struck with the very rudimentary life portrayed by Isaak Walton. Sing and go to bed. No compound twists. He leaves the withers of his cosmos unwrung. . . .

Soon adieu to books. My love to Lady Pollock.

Yours ever,
O. W. H.

Postal Card, Pollock to Holmes

LONDON, October 14, 1920 [1]

Landor was a great artist in prose: in verse never without distinction, still as compared with his prose rather an accomplished amateur than a master, as the excellent critic John Bailey has lately said.[2] He is one of the few great writers who really gain by judicious selection. . . .

The leading idea of reasonable expectation is certainly implicit in more than one class of authorities. Damages, construc-

[1] A postal card from Pollock, dated September 22, 1920, is omitted.
[2] See *Day-Book of Walter Savage Landor*, chosen by John Bailey (1919).

tion of promises and grants, implied conditions (as I hope to fructify in the new edition of *Contracts* now on the stocks), perhaps there are others; but it is only now becoming explicit in commentators. . . .

F. P.

LONDON, November 11, 1920

My dear Holmes:

We too have been striving with Marcel Proust — read through *Du coté de chez Swann* and felt about it much as you did; proceeded to vol. 2 and concluded that life was really too short to do more than dip into it. Now a good friend in Paris . . . has sent us vol. 3, and I expect we shall only sample that. Meanwhile my admiration of Turgenev continues to increase if possible.

I am sorry for anyone who has either to frame or construe a statutory definition of real value.

Our Court of Appeal has made a new move about restraint of trade:[1] a seller of good will is justified in taking a covenant from the buyer not to compete with him, but as to employer and the employee's freedom to compete with him after the employment is over it is generally otherwise — this, according to the C. A., is involved in recent House of Lords decisions. It makes another item in the fairly drastic revision of my old book on *Contract*, which will now be finished pretty soon.

As I write the burial of an unknown soldier in the Abbey is taking place. I really think we are becoming less Philistine. Fifty years ago such a symbolic ceremony would have been inconceivable here, and if another nation had done it we should just have said: These sentimental foreigners! . . .

Yours ever,
F. POLLOCK

[1] Attwood v. Lamont, [1920] 3 K. B. 571.

WASHINGTON, November 22, 1920

Dear Pollock:

Your letter of the 11th has just come and I this moment have finished reading it while awaiting the coming of an early conference followed by Court for the announcement of decisions, etc., and adjournment for a fortnight. Last week I polished off three opinions,[1] which was pretty sharp work while we were sitting. One rather a complex and difficult case, all involving differences among the Judges, one was given to me when I *voted* (as we say, to my regret), the other way. I stilled my scruples as I had not very strong convictions and wrote it with a "the Court's opinion" to save my conscience.[2] I often quote to the brethren Dr. Johnson's "be-rid your mind of scruples." I forget what suggested to you your mention of *real value*. We have some cases before us,[3] however, in which one side relies upon a case that I wrote on that subject, *International Harvester Co.* v. *Kentucky*, 234 U. S. 216,[4] and the other on another case of mine *Nash* v. *U. S.*, 229 at 373,[5] both of which I think pretty good, though I say it. As often happens with me they made me strike one or two brisk expressions from the former that I should have liked to keep. I must start for Court in five minutes — to be continued on my return.

5 P.M.: 'Tis o'er. My three opinions went — which was more than I ventured to hope — Brandeis writing a short dissent on one.[6] We generally agree. And now I have a fortnight ahead with nothing to do except to write such decisions as the Chief may assign to me. They can't be many and to look at a few

[1] International Bridge Co. v. New York, 254 U. S. 126; Horning v. District of Columbia, *id.* p. 135; Rock Island, Arkansas and Louisiana Rd. Co. v. United States, *id.*, p. 141 (all decided, Nov. 22, 1920).

[2] See Rock Island, Arkansas and Louisiana Rd. Co. v. United States, 254 U. S. at p. 143.

[3] See United States v. Cohen Grocery Co., 255 U. S. 81 (argued Oct. 18, 19, 1920; decided Feb. 28, 1921); Weeds, Inc. v. United States, 255 U. S. 109 (argued Oct. 19, 20, 1920; decided Feb. 28, 1921).

[4] Holding unconstitutional a statute which made unlawful any combination for the purpose or with the effect of fixing a price greater or less than the real value of the article.

[5] Holding that the Sherman Act is not unconstitutional in its requirement that a man estimate rightly "that is, as the jury subsequently estimates it, some matter of degree." (229 U. S. at 377.)

[6] Horning v. District of Columbia, 254 U.S. at 139. White, C. J., and McReynolds and Day, JJ., also dissented.

petitions for *certiorari* and motions to dismiss. I shall first devote myself to reading *Primitive Society* by Robert H. Lowie which seems to be an advance on all previous books in the same sense as Tourtoulon's *Principes philosophique de l'histoire du droit*, distrusting and even discrediting the too sweeping and easy generalizations of our earlier day. The writer seems to have made personal studies among the Indians and to be a little snubby to Morgan [7] who in his day was a real contribution I take it. I dare say that I have worked off my fundamental formula on you that the chief end of man is to frame general propositions and that no general proposition is worth a damn. We are not sure of many things and those are not so. Oh, my Frederick, it is in sooth a joy to one who has been living under extra high pressure for two weeks and has wound up by being bored and worried with a conference that lasted till near 4 P.M. to know that for a fortnight or an appreciable part of it he can take his ease. I am afraid I shall not get enough improvement out of it, but rest at least I shall try to. I am like a terrier that has been killing rats and a cat, going round on my toes and not yet available for rational discourse. But give my love to Lady Pollock. . . . Now I shall call my secretary to walk out and give me a little airing.

Yours ever,
O. W. HOLMES

LONDON, January 2, 1921

My dear Holmes:

Our only family chronicle is that we opened the new year with a party given here for Betty's young friends: in fact there were more elders than children — so did the five o'clock tea habit, as I remember, begin with parents making a pretence of visiting the children's nursery tea. There was a Punch and Judy, so much refined from the old version that Punch's old character of the triumphant unmoral superman survived only in traces, but the children liked it as well or maybe better. This

[7] Lewis Henry Morgan (1818–1881), American ethnologist.

Punch had been at the front: I suspect the humour was robuster there. But it is the standing privilege of 'motions' as the Elizabethans called the puppet shows of all kinds to gag without limit and vary the incidents at will. Indeed I think I have read of the marionettes yet flourishing in Sicily that as often as not the words are not written at all. . . .

Count Hermann Keyserling of the former Baltic Provinces of Russia — and it seems born in a family given to letters and arts — went round the world before the war, and was an Esthonian citizen before his *Reisetagebuch eines Philosophen* got into print. I met him at Oxford among philosophers in 1913 and heard he had been conversing with the sages of many schools and religions. I doubt the book coming your way and more than doubt its being translated,[1] for it is longish and not addressed to the multitude who demand facile description. But *if* you do meet with it you may find a lot of good stuff in his appreciations of Buddhist, Hindu and Confucian views of life. He gets out of his European skin for the time being as Alfred Lyall could. What he says of America at the end is hasty and superficial — he never mentions the influence of the universities or seems to be aware that there is much more respect for learning in the U. S. and Canada than in England (I don't say Scotland): indeed I think his conversation hardly got beyond the people he met on the cars. So avoid that chapter *if*, as aforesaid. Yet he sees in the (to him) disagreeable present aspect the promise of great things in the future. . . .

Yours ever,
F. Pollock

Washington, January 23, 1921

Dear F. P.:

A delightful letter from you (Jan. 2) came this week, but I have been too deep in work, and still am, to give you *quid pro quo*. I am delighted to think that you still have Punch & Judy and am impressed by your usual gift of archaeological research

[1] Keyserling's book was published in translation as *The Travel Diary of a Philosopher* in 1925.

in your exposition of the origin of 5 o'clock tea. . . . The *Reisetagebuch* will not fall in my way. I keep with reasonable closeness to my beat with serious books — if I am not contradicting myself at present by reading St. Augustine's *Confessions* when I get a chance for a chapter or two. He makes Cicero seem as of yesterday and Plato of a week ago; he is so modern by his humanity and they are so fresh to him. I expect tomorrow, for it is now the 23rd, to fire off a decision that we have a pure possessory action under the Enemy Property Custodian Act.[1] They have one, and I wrote a decision sustaining it, by survival, in Louisiana, in which no question of title can be raised.[2] Of course there are special reasons for grabbing the swag before you do anything else, in this case, but the decision, also of course, stands on a construction of the statutes. My cases have been fairly interesting, but more in the way of untying knots than of high philosophy. Brandeis wrote a good dissent, in which I concurred, in a labor case.[3] I have written so many that I was glad to have him do the job this time; I have one up my sleeve in another if it goes the way I fear.[4] He also dissented in a state case on free speech in which he had one ground worthy of serious consideration and others that I thought all wrong — while I heartily disagreed with the reasoning of the majority.[5] So I, with some doubts, concurred in the result of the decision. How eternally amazed or amused one is at the convictions of one's neighbors — imperturbedly admitting reciprocity. Well, in a week we shall have a month's recess. I am written up, so far, and have a vision of dentists, books, cutting coupons, walks with my secretary and drives in the park for a part of the time. Perhaps it is old associations, but a visit to the Zoo here always

[1] Central Trust Co. v. Garvan, 254 U. S. 554 (1921). In this case it was held that in a libel brought by the Enemy Property Custodian to secure immediate possession of enemy property, the determination of the Custodian that the property was held for the benefit of an enemy is conclusive, and that questions of title and beneficial interest could be litigated only in separate proceedings instituted after seizure by the claimant.

[2] Grant Timber & Manufacturing Co. v. Gray, 236 U. S. 133 (1915).

[3] Duplex Printing Press Co. v. Deering, 254 U. S. 443, 479 (1921).

[4] Perhaps Truax v. Corrigan, 257 U. S. 312, 342 (argued April 29, 30, 1920; restored to docket for reargument June 6, 1921; reargued Oct. 5, 6, 1921; decided Dec. 19, 1921).

[5] Gilbert v. Minnesota, 254 U. S. 325, 334 (1920). The majority of the Court, in an opinion by McKenna, J., held that a Minnesota war-time statute prohibiting the teaching and advocacy of the doctrine that men should not enlist in the United States Army or Navy was constitutional.

seems as if it were the preliminary to a lark, with now prohibited adjuncts, of a bottle of wine, and the play (I don't mean that the drama is prohibited). I am somewhat surprised to notice that after the first chill of a teetotal banquet one doesn't think of the missing drink — women still can stir up the monkies. Perhaps we shall come to Catulle Mendès' imagined time, when a high necked dress will be the culmination of indecency. I will drool no more. I am expecting momently my assignment of a case or cases to write and must clear the decks for action. My love to your wife.

Yours ever,
O. W. H.

LONDON, January 24, 1921

My dear Holmes:

We have just finished *Theodore Roosevelt and His Time*[1] — a most interesting book. It makes us think even more highly of R. than we did, and worse of some other people. The other day when we were talking of U.S. foreign policy the words d—d schoolmaster — plain English for doctrinaire — came to my lips. If by chance they fit any one concerning whom it is not fitting for a Justice of the Supreme Court to utter them, you may thank me — as a certain bishop once did a layman — for having used the appropriate language.

Roosevelt's split with Taft may have been his one bad mistake, but the causes are obscure to us here: it is not plain what Taft had been doing or omitting while R. was in Africa and Europe. R. took the measure of many European celebrities, including the Emperor William, with pretty good effect. If only he could have been your war President: he had something of a blind spot for the legal point of view and the distinction between legal and political justice, but that would not have mattered for the war. I observe that as to the *Sugar Baker's case* in New York,[2] in which you made an excellent dissenting judgment, he was perfectly right. His *amourette* with the damnable

[1] Harold Howland, *Theodore Roosevelt and His Times* (1921).

[2] Lochner v. New York, 198 U. S. 45, 74 (1905). See *supra*, vol. 1, p. 120.

heresy of "recall" went only to the point of flirtation and was dropped.

In the *Yale Law Review* I read of something called a "Hohfeld system" of classifying "jural relations."[3] I do not doubt that the late Prof. Hohfeld was a learned and ingenious man, and he seems to have had at least the merit of not inventing new words. But it is strange how many rational beings believe the ultimate truths of the universe to be reducible to patterns on a blackboard. Our geometry is *not* ultimate, we know now, *Deo gratias.*

I hardly suppose you see *Punch*: this is really an edifying dialogue.

Daughter: May I take my best doll to heaven?
Mother: No, darling.
D. May I take my second best doll?
M. No, darling.
D. Then I suppose I must go to hell and take my golliwog.

(Contrast the passage in *Aucassin & Nicolete* about all the good company being in hell.)

Yours ever,
F. POLLOCK.

WASHINGTON, February 9, 1921

Dear F. P.:

A good letter from you, just after reading *Theodore Roosevelt & His Time*, a class of work that I eschew. Of course I pretty well made up my package about him a good while ago, and I don't think I was too much disturbed by what you admit to and what was formulated by a Senator in his day, thus: "What the boys like about Roosevelt is that he doesn't care a damn for the law." It broke up our incipient friendship, however, as he looked on my dissent to the *Northern Securities case* as a political departure (or, I suspect, more truly, couldn't

[3] Arthur L. Corbin, "Jural Relations and their Classification," 30 *Yale L. J.* 226 (1921).

forgive anyone who stood in his way). We talked freely later but it never was the same after that, and if he had not been restrained by his friends, I am told that he would have made a fool of himself and would have excluded me from the White House — and as in his case about the law, so in mine about that, I never cared a damn whether I went there or not. He was very likeable, a big figure, a rather ordinary intellect, with extraordinary gifts, a shrewd and I think pretty unscrupulous politician. He played all his cards — if not more. *R. i. p.*

Hohfeld was as you surmise an ingenious gent, taking, as I judge from flying glimpses, pretty good and keen distinctions of the kind that are more needed by a lower grade of lawyer than they are by you and me. I think all those systematic schematisms rather bores; and now Kocourek in the *Illinois Law Rev.* and elsewhere adds epicycles — and I regard him civilly but as I have written don't care much for the whole machinery. I even doubt the profit of the terminology of rights (the hypostatis of a prophecy); as Hohfeld used to crack me up naturally I thought well of him, but his industry was not of a kind that I should give much time to. I took another flying glimpse at your man Vinogradoff's new book.[1] It gave me the impression of the Chinaman who ran three miles to jump over a hill — but I just looked, yawned and passed on.

Well, my Frederick, shortly after you receive this I shall have turned the eighty corner. I was so much pleased with a notice by Cohen of my book in the *New Republic*[2] that I thought I might do up the past into a package — have it insured by Cohen as valuable and pass the residue of my life in such amusement as I could find. But the moment you turn a corner you see another straight stretch ahead and there comes some further challenge to your ambition — were it only that, that I probably have mentioned to you from my youth, of being carried in a civic procession as a survivor! My love to Lady Pollock.

Yours ever,
O. W. Holmes

I take *Punch.*

[1] *Outlines of Historical Jurisprudence* (vol. 1, 1920).

[2] Holmes's, *Collected Legal Papers* was reviewed by Morris R. Cohen in 25 *New Republic* 294 (Feb. 2, 1921).

LONDON, February 24, 1921

My dear Holmes:

We congratulate you on being in the saddle and still riding straight at fourscore. My grandfather[1] was within a few months of eighty-three when he left the bench of the Exchequer, and I see no reason why you should not beat his record. Yesterday we had a friend of eighty-two calling on us — a German by birth (and his English speech still betrayeth him) but a very good Briton these many years, with sons bearing the King's Commission — his wife Belgian, so that any sub-conscious workings of a German old Adam had an effectual check ready for them. Joachim was a great friend of his, and there used to be delightful musical gatherings at his house in Hertfordshire. Also he is a connoisseur in pictures. He says the vast majority of educated Germans firmly believe (having never thought of looking at the evidence) they were engaged in a defensive war. That kind of thing gives one a sort of moral nausea.

My attempt to throw a little dry light on *Abrams* v. *U. S.*[2] has brought me:

(1) a lurid pamphlet called *Twenty Years in Prison*, issued by a seemingly not very wise Prisoner's Defense Committee in New York.[3] This came from the defendant's attorney without comment.

(2) a friendly epistle from Mr. Z. Chafee, Jr. to whose article in *Harvard Law Rev.*[4] I resorted for the facts.

(3) a rather bewildered one from dear old Elizabeth Putnam[5] who seemed to think that you and I had unaccountably become Communists (women are, I think, slower than men to take in the notion of impartial justice).

We are still turning over Wm. James's *Letters*. I think they will stand high. There seems to me just a little of the crying over spilt milk fallacy entangled with his philosophy: and

[1] Sir Jonathan Frederick Pollock (1783–1870), Lord Chief Baron, 1844–66.

[2] 36 *L. Q. Rev.* 334 (1920).

[3] Presumably *Sentenced to Twenty Years*, published by the Prisoner's Defense and Relief Committee (New York, 1919).

[4] "A Contemporary State Trial — The United States versus Jacob Abrams et al.," 33 *Harv. L. Rev.* 747 (1920).

[5] Elizabeth Cabot Putnam (1836–1922); philanthropist and sister of Doctors Charles P. and James Jackson Putnam; cousin of Holmes.

indeed few philosophers have assimilated the Horatian *vixi* and its sequel.[6] Translate, *meo periculo*, not "I have lived," but "That was life" — not perfect, but *perfective aorist* — and if you don't believe me ask a Latinist who knows the Slavonic tongues or a Slav who knows Latin. . . .

Yours ever,
F. P.

WASHINGTON, March 8, 1921

My dearly beloved F. P. and Lady Pollock:

Your telegram [1] has come this moment and I send you my thanks and love at once before doing anything else. One of the greatest abiding happinesses of my life is your friendship, as you know. It would be a good deal harder to turn the corner of eighty if you were not there. I do not attempt to write at length at this moment but this word will be enough to assure you of what you know without my writing it.

Affectionately yours,
O. W. HOLMES

LONDON, May 2, 1921 [1]

My dear Holmes:

The last sheet of the new edition of my old book on Contract is before me — I suppose it may be out in the first half of June. When you get the volume you may find some matter of

[6] ". . . ille potens sui
laetusque degit, cui licet in diem
dixisse 'vixi: cras vel atra
nube prolum pater occupato
vel sole puro; non tamen irritum,
quodcumque retro est, efficiet, neque
diffinget infectumque reddet,
quod fugiens semel hora vexit.'" — *Odes*, III, xxix, 41–48.

"Master of himself and joyful will that man live who day by day can say: 'I have lived today; tomorrow let the Father fill the heaven with murky clouds or radiant sunshine! Yet will he not render vain whatever now is past, nor will he alter and undo what once the fleeting hour has brought.'" (C. E. Bennett translation.)

[1] A cablegram dated March 8 read: "Congratulations and warm remembrances from Frederick and Georgina Pollock."

[1] A letter from Pollock, dated March 7, 1921, is omitted.

interest in the preface and in the new chapter which tries to give an orderly statement of the new doctrine about "frustration."

Here we are filling our bellies with east wind materially (but good sunshine withal) and spiritually. I confess to grave disappointment at the war having left mankind in the lump no better nor even wiser than it found them. Our coal stoppage [2] is a shocking jumble of perversity and pigheadedness on both sides, in what proportions it is hard to say, but it is certain that neither party has used reasonable diligence to explain its real position to the other or to the public. While they recriminate, the economic confusion and dislocation are getting worse every day.

That the Germans should play the part of the dishonest and cantankerous debtor who won't pay till he sees a writ or peradventure even a bailiff was only to be expected.[3] But the Allies don't make a very businesslike figure as commissioners in bankruptcy. Proceedings are actually started in some of the war crime cases. I doubt their efficacy.[4] . . .

I have been reading the great case of *Virginia* v. *W. Virginia*:[5] the final judgment in 246 U. S. seems to me between ourselves not so well expressed as it might have been. As I understand from a good little book by one Herbert Smith, Professor at McGill University, no further application was necessary.[6]

Yours ever,
F. Pollock

[2] The Government's discontinuance of control over the coal industry had led in March to a strike by the miners which continued until June 28.

[3] On January 9 the Allied Council had fixed the German reparations at £11,333,000,-000, payable in annuities for forty-two years. Germany consistently refused to comply with the order, but on May 11 it was announced by Lloyd George that the German Government had finally agreed to fulfill the obligation.

[4] During the year a number of trials of prisoners accused of war crimes by the Allies were conducted at Leipzig before the Supreme Court of Germany. The numerous aquittals and light sentences of those convicted led the French Judicial Committee which was prosecuting the cases to withdraw on July 8.

[5] 246 U. S. 565 (1918). The opinion of the Court was written by the Chief Justice. The action was brought by Virginia, seeking an order from the Supreme Court compelling the legislature of West Virginia to levy a tax to satisfy a judgment previously entered by the Supreme Court in favor of the plaintiff against the defendant. The Court, finding the issue to be one which might be resolved by Congressional action, refused at the time to grant the requested order. Holmes concurred in the decision.

[6] Herbert A. Smith, *The American Supreme Court as an International Tribunal* (1920).

WASHINGTON, May 18, 1921

Dear Pollock:

Yours of May 2 came this morning, just when I had been thinking that I should send you a line. Last week I was writing some decisions on which I became so fiercely intent that I didn't feel quite right when I had finished. But though my body possibly is weak I think this last work is up to the mark and to tell the truth am rather pleased.[1] You speak of the last phase of *Virginia* v. *West Virginia.* I never have greatly admired the Chief's mode of writing—for various reasons that I won't go into — but the poor old boy is the object of nothing but sympathy just now. He has stuck to his work (I think unwisely) in the face of illness — cataracts on his eyes that have blinded one of them, and very great deafness. But he has gone to the hospital and was to have an operation performed at 11:30 A. M. today, I was told (not on his eyes). I hope that it is not serious but feel no assurance till I hear the result. His infirmities have made the work harder for others, and I imagine that he has suffered much more than he has told. It seems an age since I last wrote. Did I mention *Moby Dick*, by Herman Melville? I remember him in my youth. It seemed to me a great book — as ten years later may some of George Borrow's things, possibly influenced by him — but I should think a much greater man. It shook me up a good deal. It is wonderful already that a book published in 1851 doesn't seem thin, now. Hawthorne did when last I read *The Scarlet Letter.* Not so *Moby Dick.* Also I forget if I have said that Wells's *Outline of History* seems to me a work of art. Inaccuracies and even hobbies don't matter much — who before ever made the story so continuous, so one in time and space, so credible? It seemed to me a book easier to undervalue than to do justice to. But of course I have had no time for reading other than most casual. At this moment I am egging on my secretary to make a little room on my shelves. What book other than yours or mine is worth the space it occupies, when a library is filled up? When

[1] On May 16 Holmes delivered the Court's opinion in Brown v. United States, 256 U. S. 335; New York Trust Co. v. Eisner, *id.* 345; American Bank and Trust Co. v. Federal Reserve Bank of Atlanta, *id.* 350.

once in a while a pestilence of gift or what not sweeps away twenty volumes it gives more joy than genius can. The glory of a library is an empty shelf. I am seeing leisure ahead, and hoping to read and write (to you). My love to Lady Pollock.

Yours ever,
O. W. H.

London, May 29, 1921

My dear Holmes:

Your letter brought me your fears about Chief Justice White's condition some days after I had learnt the end by the press messages.[1] . . . We are rather anxious to know how the vacancy may affect you. I saw a suggestion of Taft as the successor. With him I suppose you might be well content to go on. Otherwise, I don't know the possibilities or how you might view them. Meanwhile I presume it has fallen to you as the Senior Associate to say something of White in Court.[2]

We had a good time in Paris, seeing the Louvre in its revised glory (much improved by a new arrangement of the pictures), only one play, at the Vieux Colombier, where they have a building quite unlike a common theatre, no scenery to speak of, and I make bold to say the best acting in the world at this moment — and meeting old and recent friends. One meeting, excellent for body and soul, was a singularly well served lunch at the Renaissance Française club (academic-artistic) with Larnaude the Dean of my Faculty at the Sorbonne. . . .

I came away thinking that the French view of Central European politics is in the main sounder than that which prevails here. After all they have reason to know their Boche better than we do. One day we spent in going to Reims. The walls of the Cathedral are stronger than was thought — a provisional roof is on — and the fabric can on the whole be restored: much of the sculpture is irreparably damaged. For the town — in one word, the bombardments reduced it to a rubbish

[1] Mr. Chief Justice White died on May 19, 1921.

[2] Mr. Justice McKenna, who had been appointed to the Supreme Court in 1897, as the Senior Associate, on May 30, 1921, paid tribute to Chief Justice White.

heap with insignificant exceptions. Rebuilders' shanties and a few temporary buildings stand out.

I have taken up Sainte-Beuve's *Port-Royal*: it seems to me (not knowing the original authorities which, however, he quotes pretty freely) a fine piece of critical humanism, with a curious undercurrent conviction that the whole Port-Royal drama was ordained to the end of Pascal writing the *Provinciales* and settling the standard of French prose (which I am ready to admit is better before God, as Littleton saith, than defining the operation of grace). After a fine warm Whitsuntide we are shivering in a N. W. wind that seems to have traversed all the Arctic icefields.

Yours ever,
F. P.

Moby Dick never came in my way: I remember seeing something about it a while ago.

Haldane has just published a volume on Relativity[3] (in physics not law) which ought to be good. . . .

BEVERLY FARMS, June 20, 1921

Dear Pollock:

Ong Fang! as they say in France. Your letter came just as we were starting for Boston, reaching this place Saturday P. M. at 7, after a breakdown of the taxi that was taking us, and a two hours' delay. On the way on I read about 80 pages of Haldane's *Relativity*. Hard reading and I have not yet got far enough into it to criticise or indeed to talk — but Haldane seems to me a great man. His book on his part in the war was enough to convince me,[1] and the variety of his capacities certainly is remarkable. I didn't care for a Hegelian discourse of his some years ago[2] — but this seems to me likely to turn out a very different part of speech. I think I shall have some reserves as to his opinions and results but none as to his abilities. . . .

[3] Richard Burdon Haldane, *The Reign of Relativity* (1921).

[1] Richard Burdon Haldane, *Before the War* (1920).

[2] Presumably *The Pathway to Reality* (1903).

Your account of Paris is charming and makes me envious. Alas, I have played the game and am content, but I should like some more of England and Europe. I wonder if in a few years the elders will say like Talleyrand: "The charm of life before the war has not been seen since." I don't think the vacancy in the C. J.-ship will affect me much. McKenna is the senior and has the present job. If I were younger I might wonder whether they wouldn't appoint me, but I don't believe they'd think for a moment of so old a man — and I *really* don't care. My aim below has been solely to make a few competents like you say that I had hit the *ut de poitrine* in my line, and in these later years I have been satisfied. My dear love to Lady Pollock.

Yours ever,
O. W. H.

BEVERLY FARMS, July 11, 1921

Dear F. P.:

Haldane and Hegel move me to write to you, although not much about them. I read Haldane's *Relativity* with partial understanding — not complete. As in other cases the difficulty is not with the ideas but with the words. He takes a certain terminology for granted and in the philosophical as well as in the mathematical, at times I was somewhat at a loss, but with much, though not with the ultimate Hegelian conception, I found myself agreeing, and somehow the book made me like and admire him more than ever. He led me to take up Wallace's translation of Hegel's *Logic*. I have not yet quite finished the introduction. When I get to the evolution of the cosmos out of nothing I am driven back to the only thought that I remember after reading a French translation many years ago — that Hegel can't persuade me that a syllogism can wag its tail. I have not yet grasped the transit from timeless logic to phenomena in time. Meantime there have been mitigations. I read with pleasure J. A. K. Thomson's *Greeks & Barbarians*. He made me realize with what vigilance one must scrutinize the phrases of Homer, for instance, to do justice to him. Homer has been but a moderate pleasure to me and I think I may read some more of him this summer and give myself another chance. Also, not to mention lighter matters, I read Pascal's *Pensées* for the first time — at least for many years. For 150 pages I admired beyond expectation, and then was bored to the end. He moves so entirely inside the assumptions of his education, that he thinks he has transcended, and has such exploded notions of scripture that I got no nourishment. Admiral Sims's book[1] stirred my enthusiasm and made me feel more patriotic. Lansing,[2] unfinished, interested me mainly as confirming some impressions of Wilson. Thomson led me to recur to *The Mabinogion*,[3] a limited joy. As I get older, like other old men, I more [?] like the classic measure, as against the romantic extravagance. I take a little more pleasure in the *Elegy in a Country Churchyard* and a *little* less in Browning.

I am looking forward with curiosity to the new Chief Justice.[4] He marked a fundamental difference in our way of thinking by saying that this office always had been his ambition. I don't understand ambition for an office. The only one that I feel is to believe when the end comes, for till then it is always in doubt, that one has touched the superlative. No outsider can give you that, although the judgment of the competent, of course, helps to confidence — or at least to hope. Between ourselves I doubt if Mr. T. can do that. My love to Lady Pollock.

Yours ever,
O. W. H.

LONDON, August 1, 1921

My dear Holmes:

You excite my curiosity about J. A. K. Thomson, whose work is unknown to me: I have bespoken *Greeks and Barbarians* from the London Library.

Pascal's *Pensées* are bound to be a failure if treated as a

[1] W. S. Sims, *The Victory at Sea* (1920).

[2] Robert Lansing, *The Big Four and Others of the Peace Conference* (1921).

[3] Lady Charlotte Guest, *The Mabinogion*, from the Welsh of Llyfr Coch o Hergest (1877).

[4] William Howard Taft was nominated and confirmed as Chief Justice on June 30, 1921.

book: you can only dip in it on the chance, a fair sporting one, of finding a plum, and much of it is very fragmentary indeed, and the intended arrangement remains I believe conjectural. I have just been reading the *Provinciales* in connexion with *Port-Royal*: a mighty neat doing of execution. And yet — unless the Church ought to have aimed at being a little body of saints in an irreclaimably wicked world, and never tried to conquer the world — the Jesuits with all their very queer slimness were right on the main issue and the Jansenists with all their virtues wrong. In the matter of apologetic, as against heretics and infidels, I suppose they were equally and inevitably uncritical.

Yes, I think one is more inclined after threescore and ten to hold with the classics, also to take more pleasure in portraits and biographies (the few really good ones). . . .

Yours ever,
F. P.

THE OLD FLUSHING INN
RYE, SUSSEX
August 14, 1921

My dear Holmes:

We are settled here for an uneventful vacation, in a pleasant familiar place with friends about us. . . . For a time we thought we should go to the meeting of the International Law Association at The Hague at the end of this month, but we have concluded that we shall do better to go to Holland independently next spring. . . . I become less and less patient of full dress discourses and inconclusive debates in public — things you have always avoided with singular persistence and success: and the law of nations seems to me just now to be in a phase not very fit for profitable treatment in that fashion. I am rather well pleased that the Supreme Council of the Allies had to confess its impotence in the Silesian tangle and turn it over to the League of Nations,[1] whose work the Council has

[1] On August 12, 1921 the Inter-Allied Commission in Upper Silesia, following an insurrection by Poles against recognition of the plebiscite of March 20, referred the dispute to the Council of the League of Nations.

been trying to do under pretence of emergency and not doing well. The autumn session of the League ought to clear up a few things: meanwhile the settlement of the Åland islands dispute is a good clean job.

When the new edition of my *Contract* book comes to your hands (it may not have followed you from Washington) the preface will enable you to decide promptly whether you care to look at the improvements in the text. One detail not there mentioned gives me some pleasure — that I have brought *Hochster* v. *De la Tour*[2] (supposed to be anomalous by some very learned persons when it was new) into line with much earlier authority.[3] The common sense of the Common Law goes deeper than most nineteenth century judges knew.

I have started on Haldane's *Relativity* after a preparatory re-reading of H. Poincaré, *La valeur de la Science* (I don't think I read it thoroughly the first time), which I find much the best introduction to the whole business of the new physics: it makes one realize that Einstein is not a revolutionary but has put in the key stone, so to speak, of an arch that his predecessors have been building these two generations. Thus Poincaré, some twelve years ago, pointed quite plainly to a system in which the velocity of light would be the only real constant, only it was then not certain whether astronomy could or could not do without it. Haldane would be difficult reading I think for any one not already on speaking terms with both mathematico-physical and philosophical conceptions. In the main I believe his positions to be sound.

Wells has had a fierce (I understand likewise unmannerly) controversy in the *Morning Post* with Festing Jones, Samuel Butler's biographer: I have seen only Wells's parting shot and don't rightly know what the contention was. I doubt whether F. J. be man enough to take Wells down a peg, which doubtless he wants. As for Wells's opinions on things in general I have never thought them worth attention any more than Bernard Shaw's. Both are clever impostors but Shaw has the advantage of knowing it. On the things they do understand both can

[2] 2 E. & B. 678 (1853). The case is generally taken to be the earliest in which an action for anticipatory breach of contract was allowed.

[3] See *Principles of Contract* (9th ed., 1921), p. 294, footnote i.

be excellent—H. G. W. on suburban tradesmen (*e. g. Tono-Bungay* the *first* part) and Shaw on the humanities (his essay on the Sanity of Art is first-rate). What B. S. does seriously believe in is Socialism, and on that I would back him to diverge less widely from common sense than Wells. We have here a "flying squadron" of ultra-modern short stories by young or youngish men and women who think themselves as good as Maupassant or Anatole France, and almost always leave a nasty twang in your mouth. I seek refuge in Smollett, whom I never explored in my youth. His vulgarity is honest anyway. . . .

Yours ever,
F. P.

BEVERLY FARMS, August 11, 1921

Dear Pollock:

. . . I don't go with you into biographies except by accident or when F. reads one to me playing solitaire. I still have the illusion of improving my mind and have been having a philosophic debauch. I think I mentioned Hegel's *Logic* (tr. Wallace), damn him. After that Aristotle's *Metaphysics*—Clarendon press translation, no Greek along-side. I don't think it worth bothering about the Greek, for the profound insights are familiar and the rest is taken up with sophisms to which it is enough to say pooh-pooh. As usual I am amazed at the extent to which he has made the world think in his terms and also I am interested to see roots alike of Christian doctrine and Hegelian speculation. But I confess that I find reading him, like reading Hegel, a bore which I go through with to understand the history of thought, not for illumination. Otherwise it is with Bergson's *Creative Evolution* which I have just read for the third time. I don't believe it—I think he is churning the void to make cheese—but I find him full of stimulus, letting me further into truth, and making a world poem that moves me. I am waiting for the *Timaeus* and with that adieu to such bothers. Of course I tuck in other things besides the bores, but I think I mentioned the only one I care to emphasize, *The*

Mediaeval Mind by Henry Osborn Taylor — 2 vols. Macmillan—a truly first rate book, and, as I gather, by an American. Apropos of biographies, I thought Strachey's *Queen Victoria*, clever as it is, did not look as if his activities were on the up grade.

My leisure is varied by people telegraphing and coming from Pennsylvania, North Carolina, Arkansas, God knows where, as well as from Massachusetts to get writs of error allowed, the Justices of their circuit being out of the country. I seem to have denied their request often — walk with the lawyer to the station talking pleasantly, and adieu — wait for better days.

My love to Lady Pollock to whom I wrote the other day.[1]

Yours ever,
O. W. H.

Postal Card, Pollock to Holmes

August 24, 1921

Today we are midway in our time at Rye. Your last found us in better than due course, being only ten days on the way, as good as pre-war times. *Timaeus*, speaking from memory not lately refreshed, is in some parts fascinating, in others rather tedious, in none easy. . . .

What better could be said of Bergson than your praise? No philosopher can give you more than a world-poem. If he does not contradict experience or demand extravagant assumptions, and his construction hangs together, he has done all one can ask in reason. No system of the universe can be proved: there is nothing outside to prove it by. The fatal snare of system-makers is looking on the universe as a jigsaw puzzle. When they have taken it to pieces and put it together again, as they think (generally they have not), they think their way must be right: but at best they have dissected only one of its innumerable aspects (or fragments of incongruous aspects).

F. P.

[1] The letter is missing.

BEVERLY FARMS, August 27, 1921

Dear F. P.:

Your letter came this morning. . . . Poincaré's introductory books — one or two — I read years ago, but couldn't recite on them, though I know they did me good. I forget whether I spoke of Wells. I entirely agree with you as to his and B. S.'s opinions. But Wells is an artist and B. S. certainly a wit. I forget also whether I had reached my philosophical wind-up with the *Timaeus* edited and translated by Archer-Hind, with an introduction that, noticing the date,[1] seems to me remarkable. Can you tell me anything about A-H.? After that I went over Laski's new volume of essays[2] — most of which I had seen before. The new part on The Foundations of Sovereignty I thought admirable, but I wish that Figgis hadn't helped him to emphasize competing centres of power quite so much. Also my friend Einstein's (not the mathematician)[3] *Tudor Ideals*, which, while not documented as Laski's is and with lamentable defects of style, has, I think and hope, some fresh insights. It's a hard business to deal with impalpables as he does. Some little books, like Haldane's *Life of Adam Smith* — and then irresponsibility. I have just read, reread after many years, *Père Goriot*, in a translation, Oh shame, not having the French here. It makes one prefer a healthier air, but it does touch the superlative in the old man's talk about his daughter. Also as I like the melodrama, I get pleasure out of the hint at Vautrin's omnipotence — and I have just such dim and mixed impressions of Paris as fit it for a scene of romance — or perhaps instead of romance I should say, Balzac. Laski sent me the other day the *History of Conspiracy & Abuse of Legal Procedure* by P. H. Winfield which seemed an honest bit of work. Although the author is a barrister I seemed to detect an unfamiliarity with the practical everyday side of the law, at least so it struck me as I read, but I couldn't prove it without rereading. I am tempted to read nothing but light literature for a time, but I find it hard to do, just as I can't read the

[1] 1888.

[2] *The Foundations of Sovereignty and Other Essays* (1921).

[3] Lewis David Einstein.

newspapers — I feel as if I were wasting time. Perhaps I will compromise on Homer; for some reason, perhaps the vocabulary, I have found his Greek much harder than Plato's. The vacation has flown by. Why does time go so much faster for the old? Routine helps, and time goes fast when ideas take the place of events — but there is something more, I know not what.

My love to Lady Pollock.

Yours ever,
O. W. H.

London, September 18, 1921

My dear Holmes:

. . . I have been reading Aristotle too; not philosophy but the *Poetics* in my old friend Bywater's edition.

Certainly no scholar who has not made a special study of Aristotle's very peculiar style need pretend that a good translation is not a great convenience.

Archer-Hind was five years junior to me at Cambridge and died in 1910: seemingly all his published work was done before he was forty. He is recorded in the 2nd Supplement to the *Dictionary of National Biography*. He was a lively and pleasant man — a pupil of Henry Jackson.

Scrutton, L. J., has been citing your judgment in *Vegelahn* v. *Guntner* in terms of the highest praise. It is in the September *Law Reports*. . . .

F. Pollock.

P. S. Just now going back to the *Odyssey* and re-reading part of the latter half more carefully than usual I quite agree that Homer's language as distinguished from the matter is harder than Attic. For one thing, I believe the rare Homeric words were as obscure to Plato, and the current understanding of many common ones as conventional, as they are to us. But in reading Homer for pleasure one may slur over the difficulties of vocabulary (sometimes of construction and metre, too) as not affecting the general sense, which they hardly ever do: and the impression of straight-forward epic simplicity remains. . . .

Scrutton L. J.'s words [1] [1921] 3 K. B. 69, 70 are: "I respectfully concur on this point with the admirable judgment of Holmes J. in *Vegelahn* v. *Guntner* where he remarks that the unlawfulness of 'threats' depends on what you 'threaten' and of 'compulsion' on how you 'compel' . . . the statements of opinion that seem to me personally most enlightening and accurate are the judgment of Lord Herschell in *Allen* v. *Flood*, the opinion of Wright J. in the same case: the admirable judgment of Holmes J. in *Vegelahn* v. *Guntner*, and the judgment of Peterson J. in *Hodges* v. *Webb* [1920] 2 Ch. 70."

F. P.

WASHINGTON, October 2, 1921

Dear Pollock:

. . . We have been back here since last Wednesday night. I have cleared up the mass of stuff that accumulates in the summer and have begun upon the great number of applications for *certiorari* (in cases that depend on our discretion for the right to come up) that always await us — a big job. . . . Someone mentioned the case you refer to and I looked at it at the capitol yesterday and was pleased to see that Scrutton also took the same ground that I did in another case where also I dissented (opinion by Hughes) as to contracts limiting prices — *Dr. Miles Medical Co.* v. *John D. Park & Son Co.*, 220 U. S. 373, 409, 411 — or seemed to on a rapid glance. I was at the capitol for the first meeting of the J's, and I think the new C.J. promises well. Perhaps the main question as to a C. J. is his way of disposing of executive details, and Taft seems likely to take them easily and get through them without friction. In Mass. and here I have seen the difference that this makes in the wear and tear incident to the weekly meetings. I am recovering from the fatigue of the journey on, but that and an incipient cold make my hand a little more shaky than usual. In fact usually it is not so at all, I think.

I was at the Congressional Library the day before yesterday to get some etchings I left there and gave them seven volumes

[1] In Ware and DeFreville, Ltd. v. Motor Trade Association.

of my father's Ms. that I had bound up. I thought them better there than in my house, and like to contribute my mite toward making Washington a center of cultivation. With all its short comings it has some great advantages.

Homer remained on the horizon this summer. Apropos of the rare occasions when the ancients seem just like us it always has seemed to me that a wonderful example was the repentance of the lad in the (*Philoctetes*?) play of Sophocles over his deceit and the restoration of the bow. I should like to say lots more but I must go to work. This is written the moment after receiving your delightful letter. My love to Lady Pollock.

Yours ever,
O. W. Holmes

21 Hyde Park Place W.2
Sept. 26, 1921

My dear Holmes:

Premising the general truth concerning almost all cursive Ms. that if you want to read it easily it is well to have a good guess what it is about, I have known yours so long that it is hard for me to tell how it would strike a stranger, say a compositor of average ability. But I do confess that I divine rather than read the latter part of many words. *Desinit in piscem*: the bold initials tail off into a tapering serpentine compendium that — like medieval sequences of m's n's i's and u's, and the usual contractions when hastily written — might pass for any one of several combinations. The tendency of course is not confined to one type of italic hand or to one alphabet. The clear-cut final ī of the Arabic style becomes a reversed flourish in the common Indo-Persian script. باشی bāshī

Many Continental penmen wilfully turn their signature into a flourish or a tangle even when the rest of the writing is fairly plain — sometimes to the confusion of the stranger who gets a letter from them without other sufficient clue. I suppose there may be some notion of making forgery more difficult, and perhaps some influence of the no-

21 Hyde Park Place W. 2
Sept. 26 1921

My dear Holmes

Premising the general truth concerning almost all cursive MS. that if you want to read it easily it is well to have a good guess what it is about, I have known yours so long that it is hard for me to tell how it would strike a stranger, say a compositor of average ability. But I do confess that I divine rather than read the latter part of many words. Desinit in piscem: the bold initials tail off into a tapering serpentine compendium that — like mediaeval sequences of m's n's i's and u's, and the usual contractions when hastily written — might pass for any one of several combinations. The tendency of course is not confined to one type of italic hand or to one alphabet. The clear-cut final ī of the Arabic style باشی bāshī becomes a reversed flourish in the common Indo-Persian script. باشی

Many Continental penmen wilfully turn their signature into a flourish or a tarial *paraphe*, which used to be an elegant geometrical design but has degenerated. . . .

Yours ever,
F. P.

SUPREME COURT OF THE UNITED STATES
WASHINGTON, D.C. Oct. 13, 1921

Dear Pollock:

Your letter as to handwriting provokes a line following recent letters. I never did hold it, as our statists do, a baseness to write fair (I suppose on the theory that it showed time taken from the sword for the pen). On the contrary I used rather to pride myself on writing legal documents before the times of modern apparatus. Somewhat in this manner, only more elaborate. But as I noticed once in a book that studied design in New Guinea (Haddon, *Evolution in Art*) degeneration in one direction may mean development in another, and rudimentary human hands or frigate birds etc. become beautiful and complex arabesques. So, as the copy book fades personality becomes more distinct and sometimes appearance is improved. Your *desinit in piscem* made me chuckle. . . .

Yours ever,
O. W. H.

LONDON, October 27, 1921

My dear Holmes:

I am really indebted to you for telling me of J. A. K. Thomson's *Greeks & Barbarians*: I have now got it, after some waiting, from the London Library, and it is a delightful book: the scholarship so far as I can see quite sound. I have no notion who or what he is. Nearing the end of the *Odyssey*, I am struck by the frequency of interpolated passages of anything from half a dozen to twenty or thirty lines, some of them such obvious misfits that the Greek critics spotted them 2000 years ago. Were these foisted in from other poems of later date or the invention of reciters? These being discounted, the standing

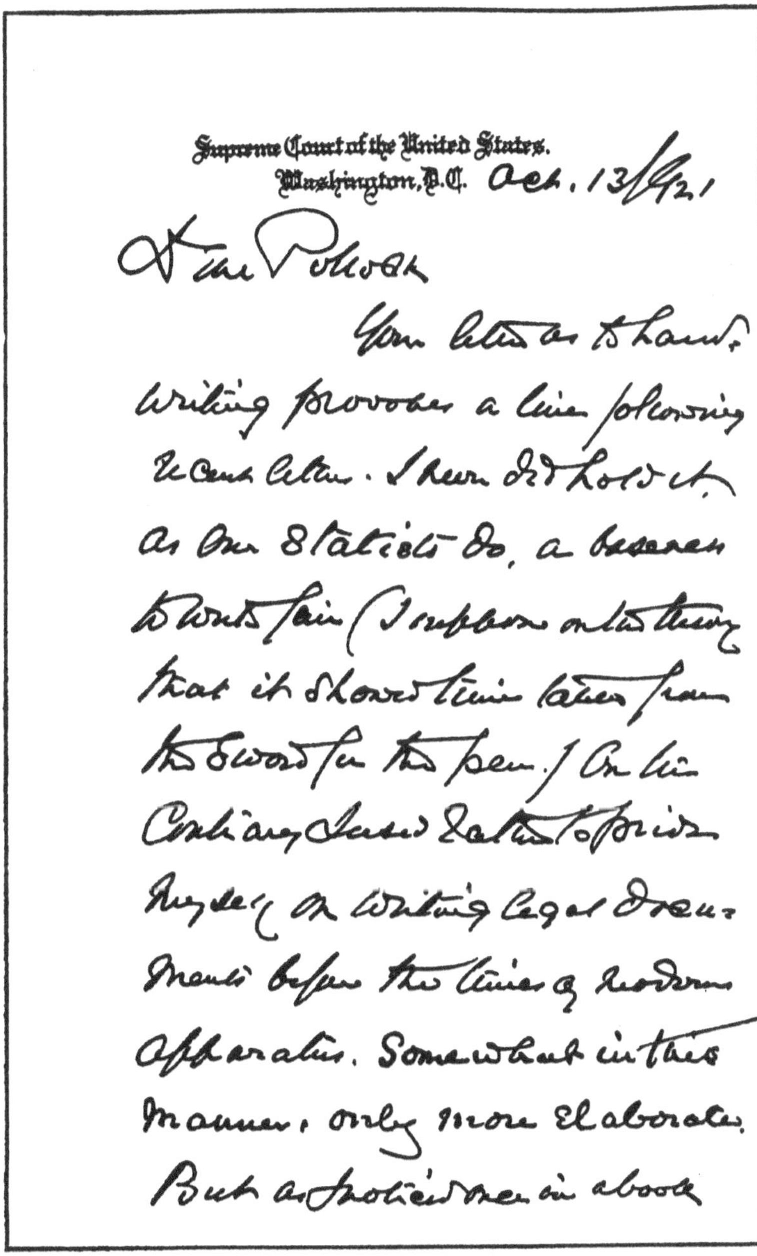

Supreme Court of the United States.
Washington, D.C. Oct. 13/21

Dear Pollock

Your letter as to hand-writing provokes a line following the last letter. I never did hold it, as our statists do, a baseness to write fair (I suppose on the theory that it showed time taken from the sword for the pen.) On the contrary I used rather to pride myself on writing legal documents before the time of modern apparatus. Somewhat in this manner, only more elaborate. But as noticed once in a book

question whether the poet (ποιητής — constructor, not necessarily first author) of the *Iliad* and the *Odyssey* can have been the same person seems rather nice. . . .

I am thoroughly ashamed of my fellow M.A.'s of Cambridge for their stupidity in refusing to admit women to the university.[1] Now I suppose it will come to parliamentary compulsion.

The House of Lords has greatly fluttered the dovecots of the bookmakers by holding that under a crabbed Act of 1835 payment of bets made by cheque can be recovered back.[2] All because the 18th century judges had not the courage to lay down that no action would lie on a wager, as they very well might have done. Statutes have made a horrid mess of it.

Yours ever,
F. Pollock

Washington, November 15, 1921

Dear Pollock:

Good for *Greeks and Barbarians*. I am glad you like it. . . . Here the quiet has been interrupted by the unknown soldier ceremonies which moved me deeply and unexpectedly, though I was persuaded not to go to Arlington which was the most impressive moment. I am glad I was prudent, and I spare you some reflection I was led to make upon the whole matter, but I have some tall talk in my head. Also I was delighted at the opening of the Limitation of Armament Conference — both by Hughes's dignity and what he said.[1] It showed that we mean business and I hope for results — which I hardly had before. I am overwhelmed with people having introductions and asking what are you going to do for me, in the form when can I see you. Yesterday P. M. (Monday when we are open to

[1] On October 20, 1921, the Senate of Cambridge University voted by a majority of 214 against the admission of members of Newnham and Girton Colleges to limited membership in the University. It was voted, however, that titular degrees might be conferred on women by diploma.

[2] Sutters v. Briggs, [1922] 1 A. C. 1.

[1] On November 12 the Conference on the Limitation of Armaments opened in Washington. Charles Evans Hughes, Secretary of State, and United States Commissioner to the Conference, served as its chairman.

all comers) among others Sir John Salmond [2] called and I had a pleasant talk with him. I was much interested by what he said about New Zealand, which had been held up as the Garden of Eden, and which he said was simply ordinary men wanting to make some money — a piece of England. I noted too that some Canadians insisted on their being Canadians not Englishmen — though part of the Empire (and I didn't doubt enthusiastic for that). . . . Now by the blessing of the Lord I hope to settle down to quiet except such personal civilities as may take a little time. I forget whether I notified you that (by way of exception) I gave an introduction to you to Pound. He is a remarkable man who is doing much good (*me judice*) to the world reputation [?] of law, is personally retiring, but who ought while he is in England to see what he wants to of Oxford and Cambridge and, if it might be, to talk with some of the legal lights. It is jaw, not the lighter joys, that I hope he will get. I don't believe he aspires to general society. I do not mean to bother you except in an exceptional case.

I forget too whether I have expressed my gratification at your note on *Vegelahn* v. *Guntner*.[3] We have a case before us now awaiting discussion to which I expect to be in a minority which involves the old questions,[4] and I was mighty glad to be able to refer to the recent English backing.

How is Lady Pollock? Please give her my love. Now I scrabble off to Court.

Yours ever,
O. W. H.

[2] Judge of the Supreme Court of New Zealand, 1920–1924, and member of the British delegation to the Washington Arms Conference, 1921.

[3] In the October issue of the Law Quarterly Review, Pollock, in noting Ware and DeFreville, Ltd. v. Motor Trade Association, [1921] 3 K. B. 40, had said of Holmes's dissenting opinion in Vegelahn v. Guntner: "This is one of the judgments which, like more than one of Lord Bowen's, appear, if we may be allowed so familiar an expression, to improve in bottle." 37 *L. Q. Rev.* 395, 398 (1921).

[4] Probably Truax v. Corrigan, 257 U. S. 312, 342 (argued April 29, 30, 1920; reargued Oct. 5, 6, 1921; decided Dec. 19, 1921).

VII

1922-1924

LONDON, January 5, 1922

My dear Holmes:

We are sorry to hear of a cough troubling you.[1] I have a bit of a throat irritation still hanging about me since my bad cold of a month ago, and not the better for the rapid changes of weather — almost up to the Atlantic coast standard. . . . In one point I have the advantage of you. Long ago a very shrewd doctor advised that tobacco was rather good than bad for my particular kind of cough, provided one likes it, which with a heavy cold or a distinct super-normal temperature one does not. . . .

In the December number of the *Law Reports*, K. B. 560, is the case of one *Polemis*[2] in which the Court of Appeal affirmed the opinion of Beven and Jeremiah Smith[3] against that of Salmond and myself,[4] *viz.* that when negligence or wrongful action is once found, liability for consequences is not limited by the test of what a reasonable man in the defendant's place could be expected to foresee. The facts raised the question quite squarely and were pretty strong, as you will see. Judging by the amount in dispute it may well go to the House of Lords. The decision of the Court of Appeal seems to me wrong in principle and inconvenient as multiplying distinctions without necessity: but it is unanimous. I think the L. JJ. hardly real-

[1] No letter from Holmes mentioning such a matter has been found.

[2] *In re* Polemis and Furness Withy and Co., [1921] 3 K. B. 560. See Pollock's note on the case, 38 *L. Q. Rev.* 165 (1922).

[3] 1 Beven, *Negligence* (3rd ed., 1908) pp. 88–90; Jeremiah Smith, "Legal Cause in Actions of Tort," 25 *Harv. L. Rev.* 103 (1911), reprinted in *Select Essays in the Law of Torts* (1924) p. 649.

[4] Sir John Salmond, *Law of Torts* (5th ed., 1920) p. 132; Pollock, *Law of Torts* (11th ed., 1920), pp. 39–40.

ized that they were following important but still not decisive *dicta* without due regard to at least one or two considered decisions which in effect, though not naming them, they overruled. If it stands, some pages of Pollock on *Torts* will have to be rewritten.

I wish you could have met Balfour at Washington: he seems to have been in excellent form and quite the right man for the work.[5]

Do Irishmen talk in America as much as they do when they go on the loose in Dublin? The Dáil (pronounced almost like *Doyle*) Eireann is still outpouring — and suggests as not the worst possible solution a provisional administration governing and the Dáil talking for an indefinite time.

I turn to *Law Report* proofs.

Yours ever,
F. POLLOCK

WASHINGTON, January 23, 1922

Dear Pollock:

The forty-eight hours that have elapsed since I received your letter have changed the tone of my thoughts, since today brings news of Bryce's death.[1] Thus breaks one of the oldest associations that I had with living men. Ah, my dear boy, please make sure that you survive me and don't leave me in the greater solitude. We intimately mixed, rather than chemically combined, but the mixture was so intimate that the loss is great to me as, no doubt, to you. I am glad that we didn't miss a visit from him last summer and had some last familiar talks. I felt a little shy about asking them, thinking that they would be bored with many invitations, but found that they were glad to come as we were glad to have them — many old memories come back but I will say no more.

I must look at the case you mention on damages. I am not

[5] Arthur J. Balfour was the head of the British delegation to the Washington Arms Conference.

[1] On January 22, 1922.

quite sure from your letter which way the decision went. My recollection is that I wrote a decision in Mass. that the tort once established the tort-feasor took the risk of the consequences.[2] I know J. Smith discoursed later on the theme but I never studied carefully his elaborate lucubrations. . . . Apropos of Ireland I had a long letter from Dicey bewailing the situation more, I should think, than you would or than I should so far as I understand it. I wrote a line to Balfour a day or two ago telling him that I should much have liked to have an evening of talk on friends and philosophy apart from politics but that I had assumed that he was too busy. A big dinner was no object, but I guess he has been going to them a good deal. I, not. It is time for me to go to Court where I hope to fire off an opinion.[3] I think I still have my teeth in that way. We have had some brisk differences, amiable but marked, and I have dissented two or three times[4] — but things are going very pleasantly. Please give my love to Lady Pollock and keep well. I assume that the cough is not a serious matter. It is disgusting to see how mine has changed since I stopped smoking in the evening. And I don't believe your doctor, even while I don't admit, at least to my wife, that tobacco was the trouble with me.

Yours ever,
O. W. H.

London, February 13, 1922

My dear Holmes:

Yes, Bryce leaves a gap in our lives, all the more because he was so active to the last that one hardly thought of him as an old man, though he did look older in the last year or two. But what an ideal end for a good man's long life: it appears he went off in his sleep without any illness or even a premonition beyond feeling rather tired. *Hoc est nimirum magis e vita feliciter egredi*

[2] Perhaps Spade v. Lynn and Boston Rd. Co., 172 Mass. 488, 491 (1899).

[3] North Dakota v. Chicago and Northwestern Ry. Co., 257 U. S. 485 (1922).

[4] See Citizens National Bank v. Durr, 257 U. S. 99, 110; Truax v. Corrigan, *id.*, 312, 342; American Column and Lumber Co. v. United States, *id.*, 377, 412; Federal Trade Commission v. Beech-Nut Packing Co., *id.*. 441, 456.

quam mori, as Velleius Paterculus says of Metellus the conqueror of Macedonia. Prothero has bespoken an article from me for the *Quarterly*.[1] . . . So far the next few weeks I shall be immersed in Bryce's books and pamphlets, including British Academy addresses practically unknown to the general public but fully up to his best mark. The high uniform excellence of his work almost conceals both the art and the learning. Yet, going back to *Transcaucasia and Ararat* (1877) one can hardly believe it was produced by a man not yet middle aged. It took a great scholar as well as a very competent mountaineer to look down from Ararat on the whole drama of the Roman empire in Asia. His accuracy seems to me quite extraordinary for an author covering so much ground — think of Maine for instance in comparison with him. It is also singularly free from parade; his command of authorities has to be discovered in the footnotes. Younger men may perhaps think the style oldfashioned: it is a very good style nevertheless. . . .

Dicey is very sad over Ireland I fear. Of course there will be various troubles before things settle down: one can't play tricks with law and order for nothing, and governments of both parties have been doing it for years.

Yours ever,
F. POLLOCK

WASHINGTON, February 26, 1922

My dear Pollock:

Your letter of the 13th comes this morning — welcome as ever. I don't doubt that you will say the right things about Bryce — character, loveableness and great powers make a good theme. I have suspected that he was too industrious and that the steady flow of his production diluted the sting of personality, but I have not read enough of his later works to have any great confidence that I am right and I don't doubt that all that you say is true. His knowledge was amazing in its variety as well as its extent. To me who always drop a fact as soon as I can it was incomprehensible. . . .

[1] Pollock's article on Bryce appeared in 237 *Quarterly Review* 400 (April 1922).

Our adjournment has come to end and tomorrow we begin again. I have four cases to fire off,[1] and think I shall express a dissent upon a matter that has been settled without to my mind adequate consideration of the question.[2] The U. S. Statutes require letters, etc., to be sent by post, which apart from the requirement is practically the only means of communication at a distance. The Postmaster General stops letters and circulars that he (*i. e.* generally, I suppose, some understaffer) decides to be fraudulent, etc. etc.. The Constitution, 1st Amendment, forbids any law abridging the freedom of speech and I can't believe that the stoppage is lawful. I think in fact it has been an instrument of more or less tyranny and used to stop communications that would seem all right to a different mode of thought.

As a result of a decision from which I dissented[3] it turned out that I, in common with other U. S. judges, had paid considerably too large an income tax. The U. S. now actually has refunded it and I celebrated the fact by buying a few prints out of the odd hundreds of dollars received. It is a pleasure even in old age to get a new thing once in a while, and a print is what I buy more readily than anything else. My library is so crowded that generally I would rather have the space than a new book; a print takes less room and has a personal smack, not to speak of the pleasant roots of the old ones in the past. I always say that society is founded on the death of men — if you don't kill the weakest one way you kill them another — and the romance of life is largely founded on the same fact, so that, as I once put it in a speech, the memorial tablets of a war are as good as an addition of two hundred years in which men have lived and died in the place. So a two hundred years old print has a charm different from one of yesterday. It is queer that second rate but good impressions of great things like Vandyke's etchings sell for less than recently published works of men without a spark of originality. I bought one of the Mantegna series which sells for less because thought not from his

[1] Gooch v. Oregon Short Line Rd. Co., 258 U. S. 22; New York, New Haven and Hartford Rd. Co. v. United States, *id.*, 32; Burrill v. Locomobile Co., *id.*, 34; (J. L. Whiting–J. J. Adams Co. v. Burrill, *id.*, 39); Jones v. United States, *id.*, 40.

[2] Leach v. Carlile, 258 U. S. 138, 140.

[3] Evans v. Gore, 253 U. S. 245, 264 (1920).

hand, and a ripping proof of the thing I most like by your man Palmer. The influence of Blake inspired what to me is a mysterious and magical work — though a misuse of etching. Also one by 's Gravesande; do you know him? He had a touch of genius; a Legros, and two American things — so I am an aesthete for the moment. I got time to read a few books — one on the excavations in Crete,[4] Pound's *Spirit of the Common Law*, *Essays* of Nevinson [5] that he gave me, etc., etc., but less than I hoped. Now for harness again. My love to Lady Pollock.

Yours ever,
O. W. H.

LONDON, March 9, 1922

My dear Holmes:

I am glad to hear the recovery of tax from the U. S. has encouraged you to buy some prints — you don't say what the Palmer is. 's Gravesande I seem to have heard of, but I know next to nothing about etchers or engravers either. . . .

Prothero has the ms. of my article on Bryce and is pleased with it. To my mind it is rather a patchwork affair, being done as it had to be at odd times: I hope I may have concealed the joins with tolerable success.

I am not familiar with our Post Office statutes, but power to stop anything that looks fraudulent to the postmaster seems to me rather tall, and I don't think we go so far. . . .

Yours ever,
F. P.

WASHINGTON, March 29, 1922

Dear F. P.:

This will be but a poor bulletin as I have been and am living in a mosquito swarm of little things that must be done,

[4] Ronald M. Burrows, *The Discoveries in Crete* (1907).
[5] H. W. Nevinson, *Essays in Freedom and Rebellion* (1921).

with, as I wrote to L. C.[1] this morning, two or three big wasps of duties that from time to time sting. However, I am getting along. On Monday I fired off a decision cutting the turn table cases (children hurt when playing on them) down to somewhat more precise limits.[2] My brother Clarke uttered a larmoyant dissent that seemed to me more sentiment and rhetoric than reasoning, but the C. J. and Day agreed with him. I cannot but suspect, on reasoning of their own. We are adjourned for a fortnight and I am struggling desperately to get a little leisure for a book or two and a morning with prints in the Congressional Library, but I haven't got there yet. . I have had some letters and one or two notices in the papers that have touched me deeply. They have said what I longed to hear said and would almost willingly have died to hear twenty years ago.

Not that you, my dear friend, did not say things that made life seem worth living; but when I was offered this place, going on twenty years ago, the newspaper talk, which was unusually friendly, made me unhappy. There wasn't a line of critical understanding, so far as I knew or saw. But don't think your friend is getting a swelled head. It would prevent it, if imminent, merely to be on this bench.

I am feeling in very good shape but I was wondering this afternoon if a man hasn't passed the line and run his race at 80 and whether the subsequent cantering is not simply a way of quieting down. I don't feel so—and I passed 81 on the 8th.

My love to Lady Pollock.

Yours ever,
O. W. H.

[1] Perhaps Lucy (Mrs. W. K.) Clifford.

[2] United Zinc and Chemical Co. v. Britt, 258 U. S. 268 (1922). The majority of the Court held that the Chemical Company was not liable for the death of children who trespassed on the company's land and were killed by going into innocuous looking but poisoned water kept there by the Company. There was no evidence that the children were induced to enter upon the land because they saw the water or that other children were in the habit of trespassing on the property.

LONDON, April 10, 1922

My dear Holmes:

Thanks for your advices to both of us. Please let me have the judgments in your case on infantile trespassers or licensees when printed. If I live to do another edition of *Torts*, of which there is a reasonable prospect, the life of an edition being from two to three years, I shall have to consider them carefully. Some of our authorities here proceed on rather strained findings of fact on the point of a tacit invitation, which in one or two cases the Court thought barely admissible. Such findings, of course, decide nothing in law, but ordinary practitioners and even able writers often fail to see this. . . .

As for *anno Domini*, Bryce was 83 when he produced *Modern Democracies* — of secondary rank among his works but quite enough to have made a younger man's reputation. You and I have sufficient critical faculty, I think, to be safe in going on as long as we feel like it. The second edition of my *League of Nations* is announced, and the volume of *Essays in the Law* at the last stage of passing through the press.

And now Dicey is gone,[1] having lived even longer than Bryce and left notable work, but though I esteem the work highly I loved the man more, oddities and all (among others an invincible ignorance of the points of the compass). In the 1860's he and Bryce were university Liberals together, but his ideas remained fixed on all material points while Bryce's mind was open to the last. If the New York *Nation* has anything good about Dicey (as it ought) please let me know. I have done a rather careful notice of Laski's last book for the April *L. Q. R.*[2] The twist he got from Figgis is still doing him harm, I fear.

Yours ever,
F. P.

I wonder whether any echoes of Coué's auto-suggestion campaign have reached you: we are interested in it, and have met him all to ourselves. . . . He is quite genuine and simple, not

[1] Albert Venn Dicey died on April 7, 1922.

[2] *The Foundations of Sovereignty and Other Essays* (1921), reviewed, 38 *L. Q. Rev.* 242. See *supra*, p. 77.

the least puffed up, and his method is a scientific simplification of what has been obscurely known and practised for ages. Not that I look for much personal profit from it, being already a born optimist as my grandfather was.

LONDON, May 8, 1922

My dear Holmes:

Thanks for the judgments in the *United Zinc Co.'s case.*[1] Your opinion seems clearly right. A mere apprehension of possible trespass will not make a licence. *Cp., Jenkins* v. *G. W. R.* [1912]1 K. B. 525. I fail to understand the dissenting opinion unless the dissentients assume that a child of tender years cannot in any case be a trespasser. Would they hold even an express warning sufficient?

My wife and I are reading Lord Byron's letters, mainly in Lord Ernle's edition published twenty and odd years ago. All the contemporary evidence appears to us dead against Mrs. Beecher Stowe's legend[2] — not only the contents and tone of Augusta Leigh's correspondence with B. but the well attested fact that she had no personal attractions. If the story rested on good positive testimony one could only say that extremely improbable things do happen sometimes. In truth, however, there is really nothing but a belief formed at some uncertain time, it seems long after (certainly not at the date of separation) by Lady B. — *ex relat.* Mrs. B. S. and perhaps not unimproved in the relation. The only *pièce de conviction* alleged is a mutilated letter or draft of one addressed to — someone whose initial was A, and that is all. It is plain that no one suspected any such thing at the time: what the real decisive ground of Lady B.'s refusal to live with B. may have been remaining and apparently will remain unknown. B. had the makings of a really great man spoilt.

At last we have sunshine and warmth here after the wintriest

[1] 258 U. S. 268 (1922).

[2] Harriet Beecher Stowe (1811-1896), in her article, "The True Story of Lady Byron's Life," in the *Atlantic Monthly* for September 1869, and in her book, *Lady Byron Vindicated* (1870), had charged Lord Byron with incestuous relations with his sister, Mrs. Leigh.

early spring within recent memory. I am trying to catch the learned Roscoe Pound through Brown Shipley & Co. — he left a card last week without any address.

Yours ever,
F. P.

WASHINGTON, May 21, 1922

Dear Pollock:

This ought to be a specially good moment for writing to you. The last week I wrote and distributed five opinions on pretty important cases [1] by Thursday noon and then spent a day in considering the applications for *certiorari* (where the right to come to our Court is a matter of our discretion), etc., so that I was pretty tired; but as the opinions have all been returned by at least a majority, approved, I feel like a terrier that has killed a cat. Perhaps I should explain that we print our opinions and send them round to the other J's. as a preliminary to their being passed at the next conference. But in spite of now having reached leisure the reaction and the weather leave me a little languid. In the last evenings for an hour after dinner before I rejoin my wife I have been reading Saintsbury's *Letter Book* with much pleasure. Do repeat my thanks to Lady Pollock. I don't think Saintsbury a good writer but I find what he has to say agreeable and interesting and the letters delightful. But my time for reading has been little and when I say an hour after dinner I exaggerate. For beside the law there are odds and ends to be attended to and tucked in as the hour for moving to Boston and Beverly Farms draws near. Our passage is engaged for June 7. Then as usual the last half of the week at the Touraine and then Beverly Farms. In the summer I always expect to improve my mind, but a reference of Saintsbury's led me to take down a cheap edition of Pepys's *Diary* and I think that as a preface to more serious employment I must get from the Athenaeum or buy the later unexpurgated

[1] Probably in Morrisdale Coal Co. v. United States, 259 U. S. 188; Pine Hill Coal Co. v. United States, *id.*, p. 191; Santa Fe Pacific Rd. Co. v. Fall, *id.*, p. 197; Federal Baseball Club v. National League, *id.*, p. 200; Mutual Life Insurance Co. v. Liebing, *id.*, p. 209 (all decided May 29, 1922).

edition and read it through. When you open Pepys you get one leg on the fly paper at once and it is hard to get away. A while ago I read George Willis, *The Philosophy of Speech* with pleasure. I should suppose that he was very bold in linguistic hypotheses. He tumbles all the languages round in his lap like puppies but you don't have to believe a man implicitly to be stimulated. Quiller-Couch on *The Art of Writing* which I read just before, barely repaid the reading — not much more. But a book that I read earlier and think that I have not mentioned heretofore, W. Lippmann on *Public Opinion*, seems to me really extraordinary. Perhaps he doesn't get anywhere in particular but there are few living I think who so discern and articulate the nuances of the human mind. There are some other things in this year's list worth mentioning but I won't write a catalogue. I must say a word for Radcliffe *Fishing from the Earliest Times* which filled a day when I was shut up by the doctor, with joy. Did you ever read anything by Francis Hackett who lately has left the *New Republic*? I think that in literary matters he has more power to utter the unutterable than anyone I can think of, but the gift hardly if at all appears in his *Story of the Irish Nation*, which seems to be written with enforced simplicity. One discounts somewhat any partisan account, but he tells a moving story well. One who is interested in the writer can say that, without accepting his point of view. . . . We are very happy with the present Chief, as I may have told you. He is good humored, laughs readily, not quite rapid enough, but keeping things moving pleasantly. His writing varies; he has done some things that I don't care for but others that I think touch a pretty high level. A slight difference at times is good, and I thought the other day that he expressed the movement of interstate commerce in a large and rather masterly way.[2] Well, *sat prata biberunt* as the Latin Grammar says. Goodbye for the moment. My love to your wife.

Yours ever,
O. W. Holmes

In answer to your last, I have gathered that Pound had been much delighted at his experiences and that you had done much

[2] Perhaps in Stafford v. Wallace, 258 U. S. 495 (decided May 1, 1922).

for him, which rejoices me. As to Ld. Byron, the life of him in 2 vols. by Miss —— [3] published some years ago seemed to treat the charge as now established. I thought it was regarded so since a publication by B.'s grandson — [4] but I remember a notice that treats the question as open and inclines to your view. I don't care a d. whether it is true or not. I doubt if I should say a very great man. Laski was much pleased by your notice.

LONDON, June 8, 1922

My dear Holmes:

From your last (May 21) I collect that it is time to write to you at Beverly Farms — where you will have no more opinions to compose for a season.

We had a most interesting visit to Brussels for the 150th Anniversary of the Royal Academy of Belgium. I saw Maria Theresa's charter, in French, which seemed to me hardly the proper tongue of the Holy Roman Empire. Met divers learned French as well as Belgian colleagues, such as the venerable Lyon-Caen, who is still quite lively though senior to both of us, had some words with Cardinal Mercier, a mighty fine presence of a man very fit to rebuke kings and kaisers — if all Princes of the Church were such it would go near to make one a Papist — and we were presented to H. M. of Belgium *et ux.* in a marvellous greenhouse of palms and blazing flowers of azaleas and many other sorts out at Laeken — the only drawback being that it was main hot. When we were at the solemn meeting of the Academy I discovered that, with Kenyon and another, I was representing the British Academy of which I had no previous notice: so I had done well to bring my Privy Councillor's togs (not so much hotter than ordinary clothes as you might think, for though the coat is buttoned up one wears a soft shirt and no collar). Brussels, otherwise, is a very pleasant capital, spacious and abounding in greenery. No time to see pictures or the like. . . .

[3] Ethel Colburn Mayne.

[4] *Astarte* (1905), by Ralph Milbanke, Earl of Lovelace.

Too late for today's mail, so I shall finish this at home at leisure.[1] The next thing I did was to satisfy myself at the Fencing Club that my fingers were still in good order and condition. — If the literal prophecy-mongers knew anything of swordsmanship they would find a miraculous prevision of the modern French masters' *doigté* in the Psalmists verse "teacheth my hands to war and my fingers to fight": I have heard much worse examples seriously propounded. —

Sunday 11*th*. We have been reading a brilliant satirical novel by Robert Grant (still living I hope) . . . the life history of a conceited half educated woman (middle Western States) in the generation following the Civil War who thought herself an earnest-minded champion of American ideals and was in fact vulgarly ambitious: the title *Unleavened Bread*. I should think that type is less common now. Here it was to be found lately, in a more offensive form, among the shriller sort of female suffragists and the like. Probably it now finds a refuge among pacifists. . . .

Francis Hackett, Geo. Willis — *connais pas*. Lippmann on *Public Opinion*, which I had not heard of, is announced for publication here. My volume of *Essays* seems to hang fire in the press or at the binders: it will not be out till after Midsummer.

Yours ever,
F. P.

I hope decent Americans understand that when Lloyd George asked Randolph W. Hearst to lunch[2] he may have honestly thought to please the people of the U. S. by doing honour to an eminent American journalist: for his ignorance is enormous and his information very odd.

[1] The letter was written on notepaper of The Athenaeum.

[2] On June 1, 1922, the Prime Minister, Lloyd George, entertained Mr. and Mrs. William Randolph Hearst at a luncheon at 10 Downing Street.

THE COREY HILL HOSPITAL,
BROOKLINE,
June 23, 1922

Dear old F. P.:

This will be an unexpected document. Just as we had (privately) reached our golden wedding, and I was preparing to go to Amherst for a degree the lightning struck and I was told that I must come here instead for an operation — serious, but the Doctor says more than nine out of ten chances of coming through. Now I am preparing — which will take from two to six weeks according [to] circumstances. Everybody is wonderfully kind and so far the thing has kept out of the papers. If I could see you I would talk literature, but my thoughts are easily confused as I haven't slept much and so only this bulletin. You mignt tell Mrs. Clifford. My love to Lady Pollock.

Yours ever,
O. W. H.

LONDON, July 6, 1922

My dear Holmes:

This is a wicked stroke in Fortune's tyrannous game, but we trust you are too tough for her — by 100 to 1 if as your medico says the average of success in the like case is 10 for 1, for your resisting power of both mind & body is a long way above the average, and you may honestly say as often as you please but especially the last thing at night "It's coming all right" (Coué's formula: I warrant the repetition of "*tous les jours, a tous points de vue, cela va de mieux en mieux*" a good accelerator of sleep).

General news may seem to you "a little flat and dead" as reading of good books of morality did to Bacon (an aphorism I shall quote to the Moral Education Congress at Geneva). So I will only mention that our Bench & Bar dined Taft C. J. in the Middle Temple Hall last night with becoming but not excessive festivity and he made a mighty good speech.

We shall hope for good news of you by the time we settle at Rye for the long vacation.

Yours ever,
F. P.

BEVERLY FARMS, September 4, 1922

Dear { Pollock
Lady Pollock:

Such a dear letter from you this morning.[1] F. refers to his cabled prophecy. It went to my heart and certainly has come true so far. I say so far because of course I have a longish job to regain my strength, although it seems to be coming back as fast as could be expected. I cautiously do a little more all the time. I don't bother about responsibilities or outside matters but take a drive, walk a very little, lie upon a lounge and read Shakespeare. I try to do it free from religion which he is to most who speak English. I forget whether I fired off my first remark — that some of the plays seemed to me inert matter that was carried to the sky by two or three little electric sentences — or an old one with a slight variation, that as Stillman[2] said about Turner and nature, the bard makes word fugues about life rather than pictures it, often with questionable regard to dramatic fitness. It is not fresh in my mind but I hardly think a Scotch soldier fighting for his life and told that his right hand, his wife, was gone, would vent the magnificent discourse of Macbeth. Shakespeare could talk better than Macbeth and much to our satisfaction lets us have the best he can. A larger part of the plays than I expected seems to me dead — I mean portions of the plays severally not individual plays — though I whisper that, bar Bottom and a few touches, *A Midsummer Night's Dream* seems to me rather slow. And I thought the best thing in *The Taming of the Shrew* was what the editor of the excellent little edition I am reading, Israel Gollancz, repudiates as undramatic and not Shakespeare when at the end of an act Sly joins the compliments to the play and adds "would 'twere done." As I have told you before I think the best edition I know is the reprint by two American women of the First Folio, *verbatim et literatim*, giving the variations of the quartos etc. and confining all suggested and largely repudiated amend-

[1] To a letter from Lady Pollock, dated August 23, 1922, Pollock added a brief postscript which is omitted. In that postscript he had said: "I am quite stuck up by my cocksure prophecy being completely justified." There is also omitted a brief penciled note from Holmes dated July 18, 1922.

[2] William James Stillman (1828–1901).

ments to notes at the end — one little volume for each play.[3] Of course I don't speak of Furness upon whose mighty labors I never have impinged. But this edition by Gollancz is very good, and handy for the sea shore. I expect to go back to Washington on time. Thanks to you two dears once more from your affectionate

O. W. Holmes

London, September 19, 1922

My dear Holmes:

We are delighted to have your good report, which finds us at Salcombe, S. Devon, in the last days of our vacation — we leave tomorrow — our daughter and granddaughter are still at a modern farmhouse a few miles off — our son-in-law Orlo Williams is off for a North Italian holiday. Yesterday we took them to Dartmouth, a lovely drive mostly in sight of the sea. Do you know that least English-looking of English harbours? it might almost be the head of an Italian lake: the quay reminds me somewhat of Geneva, which I lately revisited after half a century for the Moral Education Congress.

Now as to the matter that is or seems inert in Shakespeare's plays there be divers distinctions.

1. Some really dull stuff is not Shakespeare at all but the residual *corpus vile* of older plays which he either patched up (as *King Henry VI*) or recast (as *King John*) — sometimes, I doubt not, in haste and with a final rather grumbling "guess it'll have to do." Then in the historical plays there are chunks of versified chronicle (*e.g.* opening of *Henry V*), mistakes and all — this a nut the Baconians have never tried to crack: and those are dull enough to us, but apparently Elizabethan audiences wanted the history set out. Shakespeare was a thorough playwright, whatever else he was, and was not gratuitously dull.

2. Several of the comedies are slow to read but come out all right on the stage: such are *Midsummer Night's Dream*, and emphatically *The Taming of the Shrew* (I saw Ada Rehan in it),

[3] Presumably the Pembroke Edition, by Charlotte Porter and Helen A. Clarke, 13 volumes, 1903–1908.

which is dull and intricate on paper but in action is a rattling good piece, the under-plot falling into its proper place quite naturally. The critics are now coming to understand that Shakespeare wrote to be acted, and on the stage of his day, whose peculiarities were already extinct when his plays were revived in the Restoration time and Pepys on the whole did not think much of them.

3. As to the persons not talking as they would in real life — of course not. Did Molière's marquises and exquisites talk Alexandrines? Nay more: ten minutes of the best actual modern talk — say the Saturday Club's — would be intolerable if transferred literally to the prose comedy of manners. And the real Tony Lumpkin, or Cloten in *Cymbeline*, would be a very tedious lout. All art is a matter of conventional selection and presentation; dramatic art, I conceive, most so. Even Bernard Shaw, who is very nearly a great dramatist, becomes dull when he wilfully neglects the canons of stagecraft.

4. But I think it is true that in the very latest plays, when Shakespeare had gone back to Stratford and ceased to be in active touch with the stage, he rather neglected stage effect and let his poetry run away with him. *Cymbeline* is distinctly not a good acting play (I don't think it was Irving's fault). *The Winter's Tale* drags (I have seen it both in German and in English, with much the same impression). *The Tempest* is beautiful and interesting, but rather a dramatic fantasy than a proper play: and there I like to think that Shakespeare perceived — or his old comrades even told him? — that *Cymbeline* did not quite go, and said, "Well, I can't repeat my old comic manner; there can be no more *Twelfth Nights*: but how about challenging the Court masque-makers at their own game?"

Further it is to be remembered that the text we read in modern editions is (except where the first Folio is the sole ultimate authority) a conflation of the folio and quarto texts and therefore does not represent, as it stands, any Shakespearian acting copy. I don't know the American reprint you mention: the principle seems very sound.

As to corruption and emendations, no one who is acquainted with the general carelessness of 16th–17th century printers, not to mention the scribes of prompt copies, will doubt that the corruption is extensive, or waste time in trying to make sense out of obvious nonsense by forced constructions. In some cases the correction is obvious, but in many one can't get beyond approximation to what W. S. probably meant to say. Some emendations have to be received to enable the actors to speak intelligibly. As to perhaps the most famous of all, Theobald's "a' babbled of green fields," I doubt not Shakespeare ought to have written it but am not convinced that he did. But many conjectures are due to simple ignorance of Elizabethan idiom.

As to the search for political or personal motives, allegories, symbolism (apart from the manifest allusions to Queen Elizabeth and such like) I confess myself extremely sceptical: nor am I greatly interested in the puzzle of the *Sonnets*. W. S. would surely not risk a scandal even "among his private friends" and must have been careful so to embroider the substratum of fact, whatever it was, that they could not make one. So there you have the articles of my Shakespearian faith, which I have never set down before for anyone.

The industrious and ingenious Laski has brought out a handy selection of Burke's letters. So far I find the ministerial intrigues of the third quarter of the 18th century pretty tiresome — but one will come to America and the French Revolution. . . .

Yours ever,
F. P.

WASHINGTON, October 15, 1922

Dear F. P.:

Forgive me if I fail to write for a time. Our house is in confusion, putting in an elevator, and I have to live for a week or more longer at the Powhatan hard by. This wastes much time. The work is very pressing and I am not yet very strong — in the body. The total is that I am distracted. It is the first moment of feeling like an old man, but don't tell this, for I hope to pop up all right as soon as I get a little more settled. Give my love to Lady Pollock.

Yours ever,
O. W. HOLMES

WASHINGTON, November 19, 1922

Dear Pollock:

. . . A while ago I wrote as if writing were impossible; it was the discouragement of having to live in a hotel and lose much time in the adjustment between two places, coupled with the pressure of beginning work. Now I am back in my house and although at this moment I have two decisions to write I am much more serene. I still am rather weak in the joints and perhaps am more tired than I used to be when I come from Court. I drive each way and walk but little. But everything seems to be going as well as possible. I simply avoid all extra fatigue or tasks. Putting in an elevator to save going up the steep front stairs to library and bedroom displaced some of my folios and left less room for them, but I have sent off the 9th English edition of the *Encyclopaedia Britannica* and Rees's *Cyclopaedia* dear to my boyhood and got more room. The title *Low Countries*, *Engravers of the* was my delight in my teens, and I can recite the abbreviations on the back from *Dec — Deg* to *Yam — Zol.* For some reason the first few volumes didn't fix themselves in my memory. I kept them from filial piety, but now have sent them to the Pittsfield Library to which long ago I sent a lot of my father's books. Last year I sent his MSs. and autographs etc. to the Congressional Library and in this way gradually am cutting down, and giving permanent place to things of interest. I am not contemplating death and still aim some years ahead, but I had to contemplate it last summer. It isn't the same thing to an old man that is it to a young one — he has had his whack and can't complain. Metchnikof's suggestion of a parallel between the destiny and desires of living creatures illustrated by the *éphémères*[1] — which I saw once at Niagara Falls — seems to hold good, but living is very pleasant and I mean to do as much of it as I can. What a divine gift is fire. In the clearing up that I have nearly finished I have cut short a thousand hesitations and shut out many fool vistas of possible interest by burning odds and ends. Civilization is the process of reducing the infinite to the finite. I could dilate, but refrain. I have enhanced the circulation in the extremities as

[1] See Ilya Metchnikoff, *The Nature of Man* (1903).

one does by cutting one's nails. But I must stop and go to work. This is merely a wiggle of your friend to show that he is still alive.

Yours ever,
O. W. H.

My love to Lady Pollock.

LONDON, November 13, 1922

My dear Holmes:

We have been to see *Julius Caesar* done at the "Old Vic" — the one house where Shakespeare is regularly played without stars and without modern frills of pomp and decoration — on the whole with better intentions than success, yet well enough to be worth seeing: which reminds me that if you want some real light on W. S. and his art you should get John Masefield's *William Shakespeare*, a short and cheap book in the Home University series, Henry Holt & Co. of New York the American agents. It is worth a cartload of the ordinary commentators' stuff, the author being himself no mean dramatic poet, and a competent student of the Elizabethan drama wholly free from pedantry. . . .

Is it not strange that the two greatest classics of our tongue, Shakespeare and the English Bible, are just the two books that editorial stupidity, bad arrangement and perverse tradition have made the hardest for the general reader to enjoy with understanding? But so it is, and I don't know whether the nonsense of Shakespearian or of scriptural expositors is the worse.

So far as I have observed there are none but official mourners at the funeral of our adventurous and irresponsible Coalition government.[1]

Yours ever,
F. P.

[1] On October 19 the Conservative members of Parliament voted to withdraw from the Coalition Government. Immediately thereafter Lloyd George resigned as Prime Minister. The personnel of Mr. Bonar Law's government was announced on October 25, and on the 26th the King dissolved Parliament and ordered a new Parliament to assemble on November 20.

WASHINGTON, November 26, 1922

Dear Pollock:

Your letter, 13th, comes this morning. I should think it must have crossed one of mine. I am much obliged for the mention of Masefield's book on W. S. I will get it, but I don't bother about the bard just now, as I am full of law. At our conference yesterday two cases of mine were hung up for further consideration, Brandeis wanting to write against one[1] — that I don't care about — and everybody seeming to have misgivings about another on the police power[2] which I believe to be a compact statement of the real facts of the law and as such sure to rouse opposition for want of the customary soft phrases. But as I couldn't get at what the trouble was, or rather troubles were, for different men had different difficulties, I told them I would put my head under my wing and go to sleep until somebody wrote something. This morning (Sunday) I have two more that I think will make less trouble. We are back in our house now and I have just come up in the elevator for which we waited. I don't feel any trouble in walking up stairs and the doctor has knocked off the digitalis that I was given until lately. I rather think that everything is or is on the way to being all right, though I still am not very strong in the joints. What you say about the commentators on Shakespeare and the Bible is true of course, but I often have thought that the translation, which I suspect of being also stupid at times, owes to imperfect understanding what poetry often owes to rhyme. The suggestion of a rhyme interrupts the logical flow of thought and gives the magic touch of chance. The translators when they didn't exactly know what the old Jew was driving at had a general notion that it was something damned splendid and wrote taller talk than the honest Hebrew ever dreamed of. I *guess* that if we could read the Old Testament as it was meant we always should see how rational men could talk like that even if we didn't believe it. But of course a poet can get a good way into the inane when he is on the tripod. I daresay I have said

[1] Probably Portsmouth Harbor Land and Hotel Co. v. United States, 260 U. S. 327 (argued Nov. 15, 1922; decided Dec. 4, 1922), Brandeis and Sutherland, JJ., dissenting.

[2] Probably Pennsylvania Coal Co. v. Mahon, 260 U. S. 393 (argued November 14; decided December 11, 1922). Brandeis, J., wrote a dissenting opinion.

this all before, for it is an old hobby. The only serious book — no — *pièce de résistance* — that I have read is Warren on the Supreme Court (3 vols.).[3] It is very good, interesting and able, as well as the result of careful search. A good pendant to Beveridge's *Marshall*, and to me quite as instructive. At odd minutes I am reading Owen Wister's *Neighbors Henceforth* — so far an account of his travels in France within a year of the end of the war. I find it very moving, and knowing Wister understand the personality it expresses — a little too savage for now. I received a day or two ago an invitation to renew my subscription to the *Archiv für wirtschaftsphilosophie*, which formerly I took out of regard for old Kohler.[4] Oddly I had just taken out the old numbers to be given away if anyone would take them. I shouldn't read the periodical if I took it. I don't want it and I don't know whether simply not to answer, to write a polite refusal, or to subscribe. I must go to work. Please give my love to Lady Pollock. From what my wife tells me of the papers I should judge that old Clemenceau wasn't making much of a fist of his harmonizing pilgrimage.[5]

Yours ever,
O. W. H.

LINCOLN'S INN, LONDON
December 19, 1922

My dear Holmes:

Our chief professional event here has been the celebration, a fortnight ago, of the 500th anniversary — not of this Honourable Society's existence, which dates from some unknown time in the 14th century — but of the first entry in the "Black Book" which has been a continuous record ever since 1422.

[3] Charles Warren, *The Supreme Court in United States History* (1922).

[4] Josef Kohler (1849–1919); German jurist, teacher of law at the Universities of Würzburg and Berlin. Kohler had been one of the editors of the *Archiv für Rechts- und Wirtschaftsphilosophie*.

[5] On November 11 the former prime minister of France, Georges Clemenceau, sailed for the United States. His motive was to encourage American participation in the settlement of international questions. His most important speeches were delivered in New York and Boston.

When it was last really black I don't know: the present binding is irreverent common calf of late 18th or early 19th century. We had a mighty fine commemoration banquet in hall, and a notable speech from Merry del Val the Spanish ambassador whose English is perfect (when he quoted a few words of his national tongue Darling, J. said privily, "How nicely he speaks Spanish"): and some days earlier a service in our (not very imposing) chapel, where the King and Queen attended.

If you want to be woke up about the book of Genesis look at Lenormant's French translation — not that I have done so lately. A new edition of *Torts* is called for. With some grumbling I have turned several pages inside out in consequence of the Court of Appeal's decision a year ago in *Polemis' case*, which I think wrong.

Yours ever,
F. P.

WASHINGTON, December 31, 1922

Dear Pollock:

A happy New Year to you and yours. It promises to begin happily at this end. I have just finished reading your *Essays in the Law* — or rather rereading, for the most part, and have done it with admiration of the learning mastered and vitalized and the happy and luminous exposition. I tell you what: for a young fellow you are doing well. My reading was delayed by my work, but I have had time not only to read that but to do a bigger chore (do you have the word?), in the form of Frazer's *Golden Bough* in the one volume edition, pitilessly compact print, ideas that had become familiar to me, Salomon Reinach *et al.*, and the immense mass of facts that mostly vanish from my mind — but a book to be read for the Day of Judgment. I should suspect that his latent motive was to show that all the great doctrines of Christianity were survivals or transfigurations of universal superstitions of the most primitive times. Perhaps I should put it stronger than suspect. . . . I forget whether I have told you that the 8th and 15th respectively were the 20th anniversary of my taking my seat here and the

40th of my going upon the Massachusetts bench, and that I was surprised to receive a number of letters — increased by a puff in the *New Republic*,[1] that made me repeat that when you get to the top of a hill there is nothing left but to come down. I used to think that the main-spring was broken by 80, although my father kept on writing. I hope I was wrong for I am keeping on in the same way. I like it and want to produce as long as I can. I enclose one of my last decisions that you may judge whether there is any falling off.[2] It was unpopular in Pennsylvania of course. Brandeis's dissent speaks as if what I call average reciprocity of advantage were made the general ground by me. Not so. I use that only to explain a particular case. My ground is that the public only got on to this land by paying for it and that if they saw fit to pay only for a surface right they can't enlarge it because they need it now any more than they could have taken the right of being there in the first place. Perhaps it would have been well if I had emphasized more the distinction between the rights of the public in places where their right to be there is unqualified and their right where they only get any *locus standi* by a transaction that renounced what they now claim. However, I don't know that this kind of question will interest you — as you don't have to deal with it. Anything interests when you do have to — and understand. Please give my love to Lady Pollock.

Yours ever,
O. W. H.

LONDON, January 12, 1923

My dear Holmes:

We are very glad you are restored to full activity, as I see by the opinion you have delivered. May you emulate Frederic Harrison in perpetual youth: we have just seen him at Bath, *aet.* 91 and nothing senile about him except that I believe he

[1] 33 *New Republic* 84 (Dec. 20, 1922).

[2] Pennsylvania Coal Co. v. Mahon, 260 U. S. 393 (1922). In this case the Court held that as against the owner of certain mining rights, a statute of Pennsylvania which forbade mining in such a way as to cause subsidence of streets and houses, was a violation of the due process and contract clauses of the Federal Constitution.

takes less exercise than ten years ago. He carried me to the meeting of a local society where we discussed English versification, led by Prof. Sonnenschein, a very good scholar, and agreed that almost all writers on the matter have been led astray by false analogies taken from Latin or Greek metre. . . .

A Parisian friend writes to me in effect that it is much pleasanter to differ with Bonar Law than to agree with Lloyd George.

Yours ever,
F. P.

WASHINGTON, January 25, 1923

Dear Pollock:

Nothing special to report in answer to your line of the 12th. On Monday we have an adjournment which will be welcome after four weeks of sitting, but my cases are all written up to date. One on burning themes [1] may go over for one of the JJ. or two, to consider whether it shall be swallowed according to the majority or whether, as a child put it, they will swallow *up*. I am afraid I shan't be able to keep the pace with F. Harrison, but as I still feel the shock of the operation last summer I won't lose hope. Everyone tells me that it takes many months to feel quite normal, and I certainly have improved since I have been here and have done my full share of work, though very little else. I get no exercise while we are sitting, but when the adjournment comes I shall trot round a little with my secretary.[2] I need it. He is a pleasant though somewhat silent companion, and a sharp little devil. He has made useful suggestions to me more than once. I like these young chaps from the Law School. As you know I get a new one every year and try to know the fashions. I wonder if there is a great difference in the way of thinking of the young. From time to time I meet young men

[1] Probably Moore v. Dempsey, 261 U. S. 86 (argued Jan. 9; decided Feb. 19, 1923), the majority of the Court concurred in Holmes's opinion holding that a conviction for murder secured at a trial which was dominated by threats of mob violence did not constitute due process of law. McReynolds, J., wrote a dissenting opinion in which Sutherland, J., concurred.

[2] Robert M. Benjamin.

from both sides of the water who profess to think patriotism an empty superstition or even a noxious humbug. But it strikes me as little more than an example of experimenting in negations — now in vogue. At this point I went to Court and now am just back from the barber. I do like the flourish of the negroes. I am told that there are boot blacking places here where they give you a shine to music! They have curled my moustache to beat the Kaiser and cut my hair (not quite) to rival Bond Street. So I am feeling very fine *pro tem*. To be continued in our next. My love to Lady Pollock.

Yours ever,
O. W. H.

LONDON, February 5, 1923
(thought I should have to hustle off a scrap on Monday, but mail day is Tuesday this week)

My dear Holmes:

We are glad to have continuing good news of you, though we note you still have some leeway to make up. . . .

Revision of *Torts* just done.[1] *United Zinc Co.* v. *Van Britt*[2] [*sic*] is quoted with provisional reference by date only: I doubt whether the full report will be to hand in time to refer to in the proof. It may disclose more difference on the evidence than appears on the judgments alone: otherwise the dissenting opinion appears to me, with all respect for your Chief, rather wild. In your later case of the *Pennsylvania Coal Co.* it seems to me, though I always feel diffident about these constitutional questions, that if Brandeis' dissent were right the Fourteenth Amendment would be eviscerated: and your opinion exposes the fallacy of stretching police power to that extent in a very convincing fashion. There was no such case on the facts, I suppose, as that the Coal Co. threatened and intended to let down the whole city of Philadelphia and had refused all offers of reasonable compensation. That the destruction of this or that dwelling house taken by itself is necessarily a bad thing is very

[1] The 12th edition was published in 1923.
[2] United Zinc Co. v. Britt, 258 U. S. 268. See *supra*, pp. 92, 93.

far from obvious: I know many by sight which I would gladly see devoured by a mine, a dragon or anything else. . . .

Frazer's universal theories were needful, I presume, to tie up his most interesting collections of the facts into manageable bundles — but I don't believe in them. He constantly omits to consider whether his key is the only one that fits, or whether it is a matter of one key at all. But he tells a story mighty well, and in working out details within an appropriate field he is excellent. . . .

Yours ever,
F. P.

LONDON, February 16, 1923

My dear Holmes:

These last few days I have been considering a monstrous clever book by Dean Roscoe Pound of the Harvard Law School called *Interpretations of Legal History* — a sort of funeral march with divers variations at the supposed death and burial of the historical school supposed to have dominated English legal science *throughout the* (*19th*) *century*. Now I should have said — subject to a further reservation or two — the last third or so of the century. Very few people knew much here of the historical school before *Ancient Law* was published (1861); J. S. Willes I should think the only man on the Bench who did. It puzzles me to think where Pound got his impression: but he mixes up the historical school with *Rylands* v. *Fletcher*[1] — "status to contract" (to my mind an *economic* fad, not historical or metaphysical at all) — and other matters "the connexion of which with the plot one sees" *not*. (Do you know that pleasing poem of Calverley's?) I am sure P. greatly overrates the influence of academic theories and formulas here; *quaere* also in America tho' I can't pretend to criticize him there. Well, anyhow I have to write something on him for the *L. Q. R.*[2] He seems to have read every mortal thing published in English, French

[1] L. R. 3 H. L. 330 (1818), imposing absolute liability, regardless of fault, on the owner of a reservoir which flooded the mines of the plaintiff.

[2] Pollock, "A Plea for Historical Interpretation," 39 *L. Q. Rev.* 163 (April 1923).

and German about the philosophy of law (as to Italian I am not sure) besides a vast mass of reported cases. Once or twice he reads into English decisions ideas that are not really there, but he is vastly ingenious. Most likely you won't have the time to look at the book, but I should like to know at your leisure whether you have ever felt — as a member of the Supreme Court — conscious of any definite attitude towards the "historical school," be the same German, English (not *British* — it is otherwise in Scots law schools, I think) or American. . . .

Yours ever,
F. P.

WASHINGTON, February 24, 1923

Dear Pollock:

Wonderful man to know what is mail day. I have lived steadily on the pre-war tradition that a mail boat sails on Saturday. Whether it does or not I have no information since about 1914. . . . I am just back from a conference. We now have a full court again with Sutherland, Butler, and Sanford *vice* Clarke, Day and Pitney.[1] I am not sure that it should not be Pitney & Day. Mrs. Pitney telephoned to me to call on her husband tomorrow. I dread it, as I believe he is emotional and does not realize how seriously ill he is. When he first came on the bench he used to get on my nerves, as he talked too much from the bench and in conference, but he improved in that and I came to appreciate his great faithfulness to duty, his industry and his candor. He had not wings and was not a thunderbolt, but he was a very honest hard working Judge and a useful critic. The new men all impress me favorably though I don't expect to be astonished. The meetings are perhaps pleasanter than I ever have known them — thanks largely to

[1] Mr. Justice Clarke resigned from the Court in September, 1922; Mr. Justice Day retired in November, and Mr. Justice Pitney in December, 1922. George Sutherland was nominated and confirmed in September 1922 to succeed Mr. Justice Clarke, and Pierce Butler took his seat on the Bench on January 2, 1923, succeeding Mr. Justice Day. Edward T. Sanford was nominated and confirmed as successor of Mr. Justice Pitney and took his seat on February 19, 1923.

the C. J. but also to the disappearance of men with the habit of some of our older generation, that regarded a difference of opinion as a cockfight and often left a good deal to be desired in point of manners.

I think Pound's book *Interpretations of Legal History* (Camb. Univ. Press) the best thing I have read of his — a larger masterly panoramic view of the whole show. I thought at first that he overticketed and pigeonholed, but it helps clearness and remembering and I am inclined only to praise. The eminent in the law have been gathering here, yearning for the upward and onward — specifically the restatement of the law,[2] I presume by members of their body. On earnest exhortation I showed up for a few minutes yesterday to the extent of looking in while Root was delivering a somewhat flamboyant address;[3] but I am an aged sceptic and was pleased at Brandeis's remark, "Why I am restating the law every day."

In a few minutes I expect two or three of the pundits to look in on me — Wigmore with Kocourek, Learned Hand, J. (a good U. S. District Judge, whom I should like to see on our bench), and I know not if anyone else. I think of nothing else of momentary interest except that I have been listening in the evenings to two or three thrillers, the last, *Bull Dog Drummond.* Wilkie Collins was right that what men want is a story. Also on Sunday I read, I believe for the first time (bar abridgments for boys), *Gulliver's Travels.* I think that there, as in *Polite Conversation*, you see incipient insanity in the intensity of his insistence on the baseness as on the banality of man.

Yours ever,
O. W. H.

Please give my love to Lady Pollock. I think I grow stronger, though not yet *in statu quo ante.*

[2] The American Law Institute was organized on February 23, 1923, at a meeting in Washington. Its purpose was to mitigate the uncertainty and complexity of American law by the preparation and publication of Restatements of certain basic topics of the law. Elihu Root was Chairman of the organization.

See 1 *Am. L. Inst. Proc.* (1923), p. 48.

WASHINGTON, March 10, 1923

Dear Pollock:

You are dear things and I send you my thanks and love for your cable.[1] The year starts well, but the week has been, like many other of my weeks, a spasm shot with anxiety till, say, Wednesday evening, then, my cases written and the work outside the Court got into shape, a gradual collapse into languor and content. I must answer F. P. as to Pound's book. I made a cricitism somewhat similar to his — that Pound had overticketed and pigeonholed, (perhaps under German influence). I don't think things so formulable, and I agree with F. as to the historical school. I don't believe most judges knew or cared a sixpence for any school. But I thought that Pound's geography was or might be an aid to clear thinking and to memory, and I did regard the performance as rather a mighty production of a panoramic view — the best thing I have read of Pound's. His vast learning has seemed to me perhaps to prevent any great poignancy in his thought. He has not the sting of genius, but he seems to me big and to have a great and impressive grasp. The number of things that chap knows drives me silly. I speak *ex rel.* as I never had more than a few words with him. He had a reputation as a botanist before he came to Harvard College. He was said to be an authority on I know not what Latin texts. He wrote a history of Freemasonry, spent vacations in studying the topography of the battles of the Civil War, and, I was told, when he first came there, was put into a dining club to equalize a baseball man because he knew all the scores for years. I never saw anyone so well read in the philosophy of law and I am told he can hold his own against seasoned heads over the wine cup. Laski could tell you more, probably. Oh yes — he was a Judge for a while in the highest Court of I forget the State.[2] He was Chairman I think of the Republican State Committee. Oh dear me, it makes me tired to try to remember the titles of what he knows. . . .

I have just received, years after the publication I think,

[1] Holmes was eighty-two on March 8. The cable referred to is missing.

[2] From 1901–1903 Pound was Commissioner of Appeals on the Supreme Court of Nebraska.

vol. 4 of Salomon Reinach *Cultes, Mythes et Religions.* Perhaps he believes a little more in totems etc., etc. than would a sceptic, but I think the other volumes golden cisterns of delight unless my memory is all wrong. Goodbye my dears — from the height of 82.

Yours as always,
O. W. Holmes

London, June 5, 1923[1]

My dear Holmes:

The enclosed note will show you that in four weeks my brains have pretty well picked up again, but I am a long way yet from being my own man otherwise. The day of resuming proper clothes is not yet in sight but I am allowed to be out of bed for a gradually increasing time every morning. Meanwhile routine work goes of itself in my clerk's skilled hands and I put in my blue pencil just enough to show that I am alive. . . .

I hope you read Montaigne in an edition worthy of him, with good paper and spacious print and the old spelling untouched of course. Since Montaigne and Bacon it seems to me there have been very few essayists who were also great humanists addressing the whole world of letters. Lamb needs a commentator at Edinburgh and Sainte-Beuve, I suspect, at Marseilles. Emerson meant to be universal but does not in fact get beyond the English-speaking world. If I had to pick one of the lot for a stand-by it would be Montaigne.

Jowett's real personal genius was his unique faculty for making his pupils show themselves to the world for all they were worth or a little bit more. . . .

Yours ever,
F. P.

[1] On May 11 Pollock was injured when struck by a cyclist near his house in Hyde Park Place. A postal card and a short note from Pollock, dated April 17 and May 28, 1923, respectively, are omitted. Any intervening letters from Holmes are missing.

[*Enclosure*]

Minimum Wage Board of D. C.
v.
Children's Hospital, D. C.[2]

I agree with you and the C. J.:

1. Because I radically dissent from the position of the majority that "In principle there can be no difference between the case of selling labor and the case of selling goods." (p. 16 of print.)

Every actionable promise no doubt involves exchange in a large economic sense — parting, for something that may be called in the like sense a price, with some disposing power of the promisor's: and there are economic generalities applicable to all or most business contracts.

Nevertheless the power of disposing of one's own bodily or mental activity is very different from the power of dealing with money or corporeal chattels: and a contract for work and labour is not either in common sense or in the Common Law a sub-species of the contract of sale.

2. Because, although the decisions of the Court cannot be reconciled, the weight of recent authority appears to be on your side. In particular the distinction attempted by the majority between the present case and *Muller* v. *Oregon*[3] (so far as I can tell without seeing the full report thereof) looks really too thin to be tenable.

The wisdom of the Act of Congress may well be open to grave doubt: but that, as you have said, was not the question before the Court.

F. P.

WASHINGTON, June 10, 1923

Dear Pollock:

It is a joy to see your noble fist again and to know that no permanent harm was done. It is hard for old sportsmen to avoid the perils of the highway. I have come devilish near to running into an automobile. Keep the aquiline orb peeled. However, you are not old yet. Age begins with 80. Tomorrow morning we come in for our last opinions and adjourn for the summer.... I shall have a dissent in two suits by *Pennsylvania* and *Ohio* vs. *West Virginia* to prevent the enforcement of a W. V. statute intended to give a preference to the inhabitants of W. V. in the

[2] Adkins v. Children's Hospital, 261 U. S. 525 (1923). Mr. Justice Sutherland for a majority of the Court wrote an opinion in this case holding that a statute providing for minimum wages for women employed in the District of Columbia was unconstitutional. Chief Justice Taft wrote a dissenting opinion in which Sanford, J., concurred, and Holmes wrote another. Brandeis, J., took no part in the decision.

[3] 208 U. S. 412 (1908).

use of the natural gas produced in the State.[1] As the case has not yet been decided I say no more. Otherwise I have nothing. My cases all have been written and delivered. I am pleased to think that I have done my full share of work — the doctor thinks it remarkable that I was able to — but as I don't know how narrow the margin may be I have not volunteered as I generally do to take some extra cases and relieve those who are hard pressed, and generally I have avoided all additional taxes. As a result I feel in good case, though none of us knows how tired he may be. I told you I believe that late in life I have discovered Montaigne and have read him with enormous delight. The beast knows a lot of things that I had fondly hoped had been reserved for me. . . . I got a letter this morning from a girl asking what were the requirements for a stenographer. I told her that I never employed one. If it weren't for my wife I doubt if I should have any modern improvements. She put in electricity, the telephone, and now the elevator — and the queer thing is that she never will go to the telephone or use the lift. Our women go north this evening and leave us as usual with a female caretaker who will get our breakfasts, and two colored men. I rather like the change for a few days.

Don't overtax yourself while you are getting thoroughly well and give my love to your wife who I dare say has felt the burden of your accident quite as much as you. . . .

Yours ever,
O. W. Holmes

London, July 19, 1923

My dear Holmes:

Thanks for your praise of idleness from Beverly Farms.[1] Ste-Beuve's *Causeries* — I forget how many volumes — are a pretty good budget for one vacation. I have never done more than dip into them, many of the essays being minute studies of

[1] Pennsylvania v. West Virginia; Ohio v. West Virginia, 262 U. S. 553, 600. A majority of the Court found the West Virginia statute unconstitutional.

[1] The letter referred to is missing. In Holmes's Journal it appears that in the summer of 1923 he read the twelve volumes of Sainte-Beuve's *Causeries du lundi*.

persons and things rather outside my interests. But his book on Port-Royal, which I read through two years ago, is a really great piece of work: though it leaves one feeling that Jansenists, like Protestant Puritans, must have been rather provoking to live with notwithstanding — or partly because of — their extreme virtue: and thinking that notwithstanding their highly censurable methods the Jesuits were right, against the Jansenist position, on the practical issue that if the Church is to conquer the world it can't afford to limit its membership to Saints.

The reason why I was a long time laid up was that such is the approved treatment of the rattle to a man's brain-pan known as concussion in medical terms of art. Complete rest at first is enjoined. For a week or so I was not allowed even to see print or writing or hear a letter read out, and only one visitor a day was admitted besides the family and my clerk. Then for a time I might look on picture books with an undertaking not to read much of the print, and I think it was four weeks before I was trusted with the handling of a newspaper and its large proportion of small print. Now I am *homo sapiens* again but not yet fully *homo bipes ambulans* to the extent of more than a mile or so. Tomorrow we go to our own (the Sussex Public House Trust Co.'s) Inn at Burford Bridge for a week, and I hope the air of Box Hill and the blessing of George Meredith (which surely should abide there for all faithful tramps) may finish the job.

Frankfurter of the Harvard Law School has been celebrating your judgments, I see, in the *Harvard Law Review* that I received a day or two ago.[2] It is a useful kind of bibliography. Do you remember the story of the lady who asked Lord Wensleydale what he had published and was referred by him to *Meeson & Welsby's Reports* at large? Meanwhile I groan over the amount of merely ephemeral stuff (revenue and War regulation cases etc.) we have to print in the *Law Reports*.

Next month we go to France, with the luxury of a travelling maid, suggested by the thoughtful Jack. . . .

Yours ever,

F. P.

[2] Felix Frankfurter, "Twenty Years of Mr. Justice Holmes's Constitutional Opinions," 36 *Harv. L. Rev.* 909 (1923).

BEVERLY FARMS, August 2, 1923

Dear F. P.:

It is a great satisfaction to get a letter from you feeling re-established except as to legs. I am with you on that. I don't work mine very much. A mile is the maximum. I don't know whether it is heart or what (the doctor in Washington said I had a good pump) but I don't find it wise to press exercise as much as I should like. Even a short walk takes time however, and what with that and drives about (there are wondrous sights on this cape) and solitaire and snoozes I don't have such a lot of time for reading. I haven't quite finished the 7th Vol. of Sainte-Beuve even now. If I didn't avoid mental improvement this summer I might have taken his *Port-Royal* instead. But he is just what I want; you finish a subject by the time you have had enough of it; most of those he talks about I want to know better than I do, and it is an added pleasure when you don't admire excessively the man you read. I have told you I think of a young Chinaman who writes to me from Berlin.[1] His professor Stammler is deeply occupied with the forms of thought — like a true German. I wrote the other day, though not to Mr. Wu, that infinite meditation upon a pint pot wouldn't give one a gill of beer, and that I was more concerned with the contents than the forms. I think you will agree. The other day Laski wrote glorifying your saint Miss Austin [*sic*]. I must get *Pride and Prejudice*: but have I dared confess to you that the last time I tackled her I found her — let me whisper it very softly — a bore?

I envy you your environment and possible, I suppose before this actual, journey to France. The old world is the place for those who are more interested in the works of man than in those of God, but I am very happy here, and as even the old is relative I can get the mystery of the past if I go to Boston and look at the steps that lead from Bosworth Street — formerly Montgomery Place — to Province Street. By there I was born and they have not changed, and with memory they call up a Boston of two centuries ago. Two centuries are not as good as two

[1] John C. H. Wu. A number of Holmes's letters to Wu appeared in 1 *Tien Hsia Monthly* 251–302 (1935) and are reprinted in Shriver, 151–206.

milleniums — but beyond an early point a man can't count the difference. They say that crows can't count above three. A billion and a million miles or dollars are much the same for ordinary thought — and so of years. Fare thee well for the moment. My love to Lady Pollock.

Yours ever,
O. W. H.

WASHINGTON, October 12, 1923

Dear Pollock:

It is long since a letter has passed. I don't count postal cards though they are better than nothing.[1] But last night came your book.[2] Twelfth edition! Pretty good for you — I hope with due return of cash. I am in no condition to write having been hard driven ever since I got here and now having a cold on top, although otherwise in good shape. To make up (in volume) I will enclose an introduction that I wrote last winter for Wigmore's collection of extracts called *The Rational Basis of Legal Institutions* — the pros and cons on property, contract, inheritance, marriage, criminal law.[3] It says nothing perhaps that I haven't said before, and is my last appearance in public except in the reports. . . . I read Sir J. Reynolds: *Discourses on Art* coming on here with amusement and satisfaction. Had I the energy I would discourse in my turn on the notion that prevailed for 200 years (*quaere*, originating in the Court of Louis XIV?) that only the general was elegant and local color vulgar. I could give many illustrations — one in Johnson's preliminary remarks in his edition of Dryden, another in Sir Joshua, Legouvé in his *Sixty Years* says that when his father in one of his plays makes a character answer the question what o'clock, "*Minuit*," they feared there would be a riot in the theatre. I suppose it was expected that the answer should be, "The hour when graves give up their dead." I sup-

[1] A postal card from Pollock in France and dated August 20, 1923, is omitted.

[2] His *Law of Torts*.

[3] "Law and the Social Factor," an Introduction to *Rational Basis of Legal Institutions* (Modern Legal Philosophy Series) 1913, by various authors.

pose the French abstract figures of Commerce, etc. etc. in their sculpture — perhaps even St. Gaudens' Angel leading Sherman or floating above Bob Shaw are echoes. — Sir Joshua had the sound notion of trying to see the universal in the particular, but with the unfortunate result that he put Rembrandt and the Venetians in the second rank.

I must be off to Court. Please give my love to Lady Pollock.

I read only *belles lettres*, etc. in the summer — bar Charles Pierce, *Chance, Love & Logic*, edited by my friend the real philosopher M. Cohen.

Yours ever,
O. W. H.

LONDON, October 25, 1923[1]

My dear Holmes:

This is but a scrap. We are glad to have a good account of you. It has taken me some three weeks to get arrears cleared off — not including certain sets of books I should like not to cumber my limited shelf-room, but there is no market for them.

We had a vacation of wonderful fine weather and various interests: talking League of Nations with French lawyers and scholars next door to St. Bernard's abbey at Pontigny, luxuriating in a smart hotel at Fontainebleau (the house we had known and liked was full) and improving our acquaintance with the forest, and three weeks' delightful idleness at a small *plage* on the Gironde estuary where no strangers go, with motor excursions to Saintes (once a notable Roman station), La Rochelle, etc. Did you ever go to Marennes? Guess not, then you don't know how good mussels can be. Not to mention huge prawns. Bordeaux being the other side of the river is practically a long way from St. Palais-sur-mer but there seemed to be a good few Bordeaux (and Cognac) business folk there. Incidentally we fell in love with romanesque churches, which made me all the readier to take a young friend to St. Bartholomew the Great Last Sunday. . . .

Yours ever,
F. P.

[1] A letter from Pollock, mailed at Malta, and dated September 13, 1923, is omitted.

. . . Just now I have a very mean opinion of both politicians and newspaper owners. Mussolini [2] is a man at any rate, and Masaryk [3] I think a wise man. . . .

WASHINGTON, November 5, 1923

Dear Pollock:

Your letter has just arrived and allows me to infer that you are as well as ever and feel no traces of your accident. I hope this is true? How I envy your being able to go to a thousand interesting places that echo of the past. I love the old. I like to have books in my library that were on shelves before America was discovered. I prefer prints that go back two or three hundred years and show one the same human feeling that we have today. Apart from "the grand old masters" I have hanging here a little Ostade that brought tears to my eyes until I became accustomed to it. A little peasant family sitting around a table with a bowl of porridge over which the father is saying grace — the little boy standing with the same reverential shoulders that one sees in Millet's *Angelus*, but with no self-consciousness or melodrama. . . . Last spring I got a rather below par impression of Rembrandt's portrait of himself in a felt hat — after he got religion — that I long had wanted and that I think very fine. My colleague Butler always reminds me of it in the modeling of his face. . . .

I am making the most I can of a few hours of leisure, and re-reading Zimmern's *Greek Commonwealth* [1] which I think is a wonderful and inspiring book. I grieve that Zimmern should be detached from such themes and turned to modern affairs. He is always delicate and fine but I feel as if the world wasn't getting his best from him. If I have time I will read a play of Euripides. But leisure only means a chance to do other jobs that demand attention. Do you ever see my young(ish) friend Laski? He is a *heluo librorum*, reads a paragraph at a time and

[2] Since October 1922 Benito Mussolini had been virtual dictator of Italy.

[3] In October President Thomas G. Masaryk of Czechoslovakia visited England.

[1] Sir Alfred Zimmern, historian and political economist, was a personal friend of Holmes. The third edition of his *Greek Commonwealth* was published in 1922.

remembers it. I read much more slowly and forget. One does not forget the limits — one remembers that Hegel or Marx could not affect this mind beyond such and such points — but the articulation of their arguments or systems disappears.

I have interrupted myself at this point to consider a case in which Brandeis wants me to be ready with a dissent,[a] because it weighs on my mind, and so I am no longer the careless and happy boy that began this. Please give my love to Lady Pollock. I drop with a shriek of adieu into the gulf. . . .

Yours ever,
O. W. H.

LONDON, November 15, 1923

My dear Holmes:

. . . For a lively play of Euripides I recommend *The Bacchae*: what E. was driving at is much disputed, but a rattling good plot it is, and well edited, Sandys 1885, a learned Frenchman Dalmeyda, 1908, besides Gilbert Murray's version and essays by Verrall (who made new plots to several Greek plays — too ingenious to be true in my opinion) and Norwood.

My estimate of politicians grows meaner year by year. You will have seen (if you observe our news) that a surprise general election is upon us.[1] The one thing the Government has certainly achieved is to reconcile Asquith and Lloyd George, which nothing else could have done. In the main it is a good thing if we get back to solid and definite parties, but I fear the *Tertius gaudens* this time may be the Labour Party with its frank and blatant policy of plunder as a bait to the Have-nots. There will not be a serious contest in any constituency I can vote for, so I need not decide whether I would vote for a Protectionist to keep out a Labour man. Our Prime Minister seems to me to be approaching the dominant position of your President, whether for better or worse I know not. . . .

[a] Probably in Craig v. Hecht, 263 U. S. 255, 280 (argued Oct. 17; decided Nov. 19, 1923). Brandeis, J., concurred in Holmes's dissenting opinion.

[1] On October 30 Stanley Baldwin had declared for a protective tariff. He told Parliament on November 13 it would be dissolved three days later. Soon after the election of December 6, Baldwin resigned, and Ramsay MacDonald came in as Prime Minister.

Of Laski I have seen nothing in the flesh since he lunched with me at the Athenaeum not long after he settled here, but I keep an eye on his work and I think he is improving in width of outlook and sense of proportion. . . .

Winston Churchill's second volume on the war [2] comes down to the evacuation of Gallipoli. As an *apologia* it leaves on the whole a good impression: no doubt he was sometimes wrong, but never without good company that I can see; at all events he saw that hesitation and fumbling are the deadliest sins in conducting war. His one sign of bad temper is the depreciation of Allenby's feat in Palestine. . . .

Yours ever,
F. P.

WASHINGTON, November 24, 1923

Dear F. P.:

Your letter is delightful and I devote the quarter hour I have before dinner to you instead of to slumber as I had intended, after one of our tiring judicial conferences, to discuss the cases of the week. We have some interesting questions up but my soul is calmer than once it was. I forget what started Euripides between us. I don't think I could have read the *Medea* when I last wrote, as I did the other day, after rereading Zimmern's *Greek Commonwealth* and I am pretty sure I didn't make the reflections that connected themselves with others on the Bard that I may have uttered to you. Shakespeare it always seems to me is so full of the mystery of life that anything pulls the trigger and he goes off with splendid talk that one wouldn't for the world give up but that seems to me often to disregard dramatic probability or reason, *e.g.*, Richard II or Macbeth when told of his wife's death, or a broken line from Percy when run through the guts. Euripides — I suggest tentatively for I know next to nothing of him — will wind up a feeling or even a passionate burst with something at least approaching an axiom of mundane experience, that, as I wrote to Laski, settles the stirred coffee grounds of emotion

[2] *The World Crisis, 1915* (1923).

with a dash of cold water. I submit myself for your correction. I should think he had more human pathos than the others. (Did it ever strike you that *Antony & Cleopatra* had more of that than perhaps any other of S.'s plays?) I remember from school days what I will venture to write as I remember it — Hecuba's τύραννος ἦν ποτ', [ἀλλὰ] νῦν δούλη σέθεν.[1] Since I wrote the last words I have received my assignment of a case to write; an unusual proceeding under the Sherman Act against a combination of manufacturers and employees — for once together — it is alleged in restraint of trade. I expect some pleasure in writing it.[2] . . .

I don't read biographies, as a rule, or Life & Letters, or books about the war. I have to confine myself to my subjects, with excursions into literature, as last summer, for levity. I have taken up for odd moments Vol. 1 of Ferrero's *Greatness and Decline of Rome*, though it is of the genus general history for which I don't care much, it is so unquantified in premises and conclusions. He led me this A. M. to verify a statement in Pliny, *Historiae Naturalis* that human sacrifices were only abolished in Rome less than 100 years B. C. Now I must go and play our evening solitaire. My love to Lady Pollock.

Yours ever,
O. W. H.

LONDON, February 11, 1924

My dear Holmes:

The most material professional news is that preparations for welcoming the American Bar Association in July are well in hand. The Bench and Bar will give a banquet in Westminster Hall: the Inns will probably give garden parties: and the freemasons of the company — something like twenty per cent. of the whole, and including at least one illustrious Brother, your Chief to wit — will be received by their Brethren of the

[1] "A queen was I, time was, but now thy slave." Euripides, *Hecuba*, line 809; Arthur S. Way, tr.

[2] National Association of Window Glass Manufacturers v. United States, 263 U. S. 403.

profession in due form, perhaps in Lincoln's Inn Hall. Your humble servant was the first to interview the high authorities of Freemasons' Hall and secure their approval. The Canadians, who will be about 200, claim the right of being not guests but joint hosts with our Bar, which is pretty of them. *Quae omnia bene eveniant.*

In a month's time I am to lecture to the Law Faculty of the University of London on "Learning the Law":[1] trying to put it from the learner's point of view and so keep clear of the regular scholastic grooves. There may not be much in it when it is done but I hope to make it fairly interesting. Both from my own experience and from information I believe students' main trouble is to make out the connexion of the book-law they are examined in with the live business of the Courts. Whose fault this is, if any one's in particular, and what is the remedy, is rather hard to say. If one could send them all on circuit as judges' marshals — that was how I learnt a lot of common law from James Shaw Willes. But obviously there are not enough judges to go round, were they all as wise as Willes.

It is amusing to see our Labour Ministers getting their necks into the collar. I don't trust Ramsay Macdonald further than I can see him,[2] but he is a clever opportunist and therefore won't do anything very rash. Will his extreme followers jib? (There are signs of it at Glasgow.)

Also to see a Woodrow Wilson legend in the making: what sort of legend will come out? A New York *Herald* man rang me up before the poor man's breath was out of his body and wanted an appreciation.[3] I told him my opinion of W.'s policy (since the war I mean) would not be fit for publication. Still a *legenda aurea* is possible, and the gross bad manners of the Germans may help it. The Lord in his mercy made those very able people even more stupid. Otherwise our Lady the Common Law and all that she stands for might have been in a bad way. The thing I can't stomach about W. is his appropriation of the League of Nations idea from Taft and Root without a word of

[1] Reprinted, 40 *L. Q. Rev.* 287 (1924).
[2] Ramsay MacDonald was Prime Minister from January to November 1924.
[3] Woodrow Wilson died February 3, 1924.

acknowledgment that I ever heard of: a mean kind of vanity.

Do you know Flaubert's letters? I find them mighty good to return to for an odd quarter of an hour the first thing in the morning when I wake in time. He was a very human creature and a good friend as well as a great artist. I have been drawn in black and white by an ingenious and agreeable young limner from your parts, Tittle by name.[4] He should have had an ancestor Colonus Tittle of Poyntz Manor, who *m.* Serifa daughter of Minimus Jott Esq. and had issue:

1. Scribonius, *m.* Hon. Virgula Penwell *d.* of Lord Ampersand. Her uncle Col. Penwell of the Hon. E. I. Co's service was famous for his romantic adventure with the heroic Nugta Begum of Qalampur. A collateral relative Quiller J. Penwell of Philadelphia owns the ancient Spanish estate of Teldes y Cedillas, California.
2. Hyphena . . . etc., etc. (she *m.* Brevier Forme Esq.).

Yours ever,
F. POLLOCK

WASHINGTON, March 7, 1924

Dear Pollock:

Your letter is most welcome. I have delayed a day or two in answering because of work and but for the hope of catching an earlier boat should delay one day more that I might write on reaching the august age of 83. I wish you well with your lectures — I quite understand the difficulties of connecting the books with life. I remember a chap who had just left the Law School writing to another that he had seen a real writ (or deed, I forget). I know Flaubert's letters well — and remember his queer fancy for writing dirty words to women — a trifle to recall as against so much admirable discourse. Also I think I remember Tittle as having spent an

[4] Walter Tittle's pencil drawing of Pollock was reproduced to accompany his article "Portraits in Pencil and Pen," in the *Century Magazine*, October 1924. Subsequently a pencil drawing of Holmes, also by Mr. Tittle, was printed with an article, "Glimpses of Interesting Americans," in the *Century Magazine*, June 1925.

evening in this library showing his etchings. Which reminds me that I have just received an etching [1] of myself from a photograph that I think is the best thing there is of me — (bar a painting). I am much pleased with your genealogical tree for Tittle. I have been following the usual routine, writing an opinion on Sundays and sitting in Court during the week. I have on the stocks two neat cases: one as to trademark for a perfume, which awaits the oscillations of McKenna to determine whether it shall be the judgment of the Court or of four,[2] and on the liability of a telegraph co. under the restrictions on its blanks — that I expect will go next Monday.[3] I think I haven't written since the last adjournment when I read Rousseau's *Confessions* with great interest. He seemed to me a martyr to free speech who was too ingenuous to realize what was the matter and crazy enough to think the trouble was with his friends. Also I somewhat laboriously reread part 1 of *Faust* — Margaret pure pathos and quite perfect, the rest a hodge podge with fine things — and the immense indication of the unconscious humor of the book of Job. The great Panjandrum is made uneasy when he catches the cold eye of the appraising intellect. My wife reads to me at night while I play solitaire. *Inter alia* a mighty good book by Beebe telling of a scientific visit to the Galápagos. She is now reading a life of Wilberforce.[4] It has amused me in times past to see that saint one of the most determined opponents of any mitigation in the laws against combinations of laborers, etc. If I had time I should like to speak of a study of the Town (or Country?) Laborer in which he figures [5] — a book cracked up by Graham Wallas but as to which I thought there were grave reserves to be made. I am still keeping quiet and going nowhere. When do you touch 80? Old age does not begin till then. Time is like judicial legislation. It works interstitially — but from six months to six months it shows results. I wish I could write

[1] By Franklin T. Wood.

[2] Prestonettes, Inc. v. Coty, 264 U. S. 359. McReynolds, J., dissented without opinion.

[3] Western Union Telegraph Co. v. Czizek, 264 U. S. 281. McKenna, J., dissented without opinion.

[4] Probably Reginald Coupland's *Wilberforce* (1924).

[5] J. L. Hammond and Barbara Hammond, *The Town Labourer*, 1760–1832 (1917), read by Holmes in 1918.

more but I must get ready for Court. My love to Lady Pollock.

Yours ever,
O. W. Holmes

London, March 24, 1924 [1]

My dear Holmes:

When I am 80, *viz.* Dec. 10, 1925, if I so long live, I hope I may be as young as you are now, but I guess it will then be time to give up the *Law Reports* to a successor who may or may not have patience to correct the journalese jargon of shorthand notes expanded by illiterate shorthand writers (though I fear some of it is what the judges really say in unwritten judgments). Strange that newspaper reporters have invented a dialect nobody speaks and no self-respecting author writes. Diplomatic French is the nearest thing I know to it in foreign parts.

Did you ever see *Faust*, Part 1, on the stage? I did when I knew just enough German to follow it — with a reading party, so called, at Dresden, myself being an unattached graduate — the effect is tremendous. We all came away without speaking a word. Part 2 (which in spite of apparent incoherence follows the legend much more closely) is acted sometimes, not often. Helena and the last scene the best, I think. Carlyle thereon (when he still wrote English) is excellent. But perhaps the poetical gem of the whole thing is the opening song of the archangels in Part 1. Shelley (a much more serious scholar than most critics have perceived) translated it. Of the whole, Bayard Taylor's version is far and away the best: I examined more than one in my reviewing days. Bayard Taylor turns up in some new Thackeray letters, in Hester Ritchie's memoir of her mother. The title is *Letters of Anne Thackeray Ritchie*; nevertheless W. M. T.'s fill about one third of the volume. A few with amusing sketches are facsimiled. The letters would bear a little weeding but are good.

A team and bus strike has made London streets look spacious:

[1] A short note from Holmes dated March 17, 1924, expressing thanks for birthday wishes, is omitted.

it will end in a general public control which we ought to have had years ago. Certainly the war has not made public men either wiser or better: I did hope it would teach them a little wisdom. What we have is polish without backbone like Asquith or energy without knowledge or principle like Lloyd George (who is lying low just now). If only Winston Churchill had ballast he would be worth the lot, but his genius is too flighty. . . .

Ten days ago I gave my lecture to about three men six women and seven boys (some Indian students probably hoping for examination tips). Such is the usual University College audience. I don't know yet when or where it will get printed.[2] . . .

Yours ever,
F. POLLOCK

We have just got out of a long spell of E. wind — the last fortnight of it mercifully fine: one gets accustomed to having one's bronchial tubes full of London smoke but I don't think it a good custom.

WASHINGTON, April 6, 1924

Dear Pollock:

A good letter from you came yesterday to cheer me on my return from conference preliminary to sitting again on Monday. Apropos of "journalese jargon" of which you speak I remember once saying: profanity is vitriol, slang is vinegar, but reporters' English is rancid butter. I don't know that you have the thing to which I refer in England — an intrusion into the language of sentiment, as when they call a house a home. It abounds here. No, I never saw *Faust* (*i. e.* Goethe's) on the stage. I agree that B. Taylor's translation is much the best, but he does take the edge off and the poetry out of many passages. As to part 2, I wait for better days — though I have read it. . . .

I have taken a very little turn at the classics while I had some leisure. I found that I had Seneca and turned over his pages

[2] See *supra*, p. 127.

for a few hours, got some really good things and said goodbye — too much crumbs. Then a little Plutarch in translation and then the *Menaechmi* of Plautus, as I didn't remember ever having read one of his plays — the Latin easy to my surprise — the fun rudimentary, not to my ditto. Then I took up Tacitus (for [?] the Day of Judgment), as I never had read anything but his short pieces. I read two books of the *History*, all I had time for, with great delight. The intense compactness of his writing is a lesson. I must add him to Rousseau's *Confessions* as one that is as good as ever was. I think I have not written all this to you before, but my memory wobbles. Have I uttered the fundamental blasphemy, that once said, set the spirit free? The Literature of the past is a bore — when one has said that frankly to oneself then one can proceed to qualify and make exceptions. Now I have opened Santayana *Scepticism and Animal Faith*. He is not a bore, but I think he improvises and obscures the foundations of his thought with too many tickling words. *Au fond*, unless I mistake, he takes much the same view that I have taken *en passant* in one or two of my things. His philosophy is much nearer to my way of thinking than James's or Royce's. But my moments of reading will be cut off for a month now.

I was amused by a question of taste yesterday. In one of my opinions I give a short account of a statute and say that there are amplifications "to stop rat holes" that need not be stated as the plaintiffs admit that they are within the Statute.[1] The C. J. criticised. I said our reports were dull because we had the notion that judicial dignity required solemn fluffy speech, as, when I grew up, everybody wore black frock coats and black cravats (I didn't say that to them). I didn't care for the phrase but do for the principle. I don't follow politics — we are investigating everybody and I dare say fostering a belief too readily accepted that public men generally are corrupt.[2] My love to Lady Pollock.

Yours ever,
O. W. Holmes

[1] Dillingham v. McLaughlin, 264 U. S. 370, 372.

[2] The principal Congressional investigations of the time were the Teapot Dome inquiry and the investigation into the Department of Justice under Attorney General Daugherty.

LONDON, April 27, 1924

My dear Holmes:

Yes — the Home is sickening. . . . My special aversion here is "rang out." Nobody is allowed, even in the *Times*, to fire or hear a shot. However that can hardly get into the *Law Reports*.

Certainly 19/20ths of literature is — as such — a bore. But why past more than present? Only because of the trouble, in the case of many old authors, of knowing what the man is talking about: which is more than it is worth unless he is a really great author, or one is out for detailed information for some extra-literary purpose. A minor Dante would be an intolerable bore. The theme seems to invite meditation in a 17th century manner (sample herewith).

Judicial dignity: does your Chief know Knight Bruce's judgments?[1] . . .

Yours ever,
F. P.

[*Enclosure*]

Of Tediousness in Books

That of the multitude of books the more part are tedious is matter of common observation. Of the *Antients* and the *Moderns* which may bear the palm for tediousness is a question peradventure insoluble — for whereas we know by report that many great works of ancient authors have perished, we can but guess by conjecture (for our partial consolation) the bulk and mortal sum of tediousness, in elucubrations of Greek Rhetoricians and the like (of whom he who will may sample an abridgment in *Seneca*), which our studies have escaped. What soporfic rolls, perchance yet decipherable, may lie buried in Herculaneum, I willingly leave to the industry of posterity. *Sufficit diei malitia sua.* Now there are differences in tedium, according as the book is for pleasure or for profit. Writings for a profitable intent be commonly tedious by prolix and disorderly presentment of the matter; and, seeing that by the judgment of wise men there is no book so inept or inartificial but some man may some time find his profit therein. This fault, howsoever grave in its kind, is yet venial, and expiable in the purgatory of an upper shelf. But he that sets forth to beget pleasure in the reader must pretend to hit the mark by mastery of his form; which if he miss (save if he redeem himself, as some do, by some casual felicities *nantes in gurgite vasto*, which may precariously survive in other men's posies and commonplace books), it is fatal and in-

[1] Sir James Lewis Knight Bruce (1791–1866); Lord Justice of Appeal in Chancery, 1851–1866. His judicial opinions were characterized by an easy-going humor and informal sarcasm. See 22 *Law Mag. and Rev.* 278 (1867).

expiable, being as it were a sin against the holy spirit of humane letters. Into this slough do fall the inglorious company of imitative poets: of whom examples are too numerous to need voucher. In mixt kinds of writing both kinds of tedium may be proportionably and intricately mixt; which to pursue would itself be a warning. For the rest, this plague hath a facile remedy; for no man is constrained to read more of a book than he list. Except it be in the way of his trade, or for passing of an examination; and then he hath no shift but to remember that *Job* was before him.

St. Leonards-on-Sea, April 20, 1924

My dear Holmes:

We are here for Easter week. . . .

I have received (rather late) an off-print of a criticism (very late methinks) of Dicey's theory of jurisdiction in Conflict of Laws by the very learned Pillet of Paris;[1] have not compared it with Dicey's text but I rather think P. is right in failing to find much bottom to D.'s substitute for the old fudge about "comity."

Dicey, as a good Benthamite, always shied at cosmopolitan elements in law and tried to avoid any explicit admission of them — though one would think it a sound utilitarian position that uniformity in the treatment of extraterritorial problems of succession, legitimacy, etc., is desirable. If you think Pillet's paper would interest you, I have the disposal of some copies. One will go by my advice to Roscoe Pound.

Yours ever,
F. P.

Washington, May 5, 1924

Dear Pollock:

A line from you came last week when I hardly knew which way to turn I was so busy with the last week of our regular sittings, although we don't adjourn till June 9. This morning we come in for opinions and to hear one short argument, and then it looks like leisure, as I have written the case assigned to me on Saturday — but the Chief may ask me to relieve one of the brethren who has been overloaded. In answer to your

[1] Antoine Pillet, "Sur un point peu aperçu de la Doctrine de Dicey," 4 *Revue de Droit International*, 3me serie (1923), p. 345.

suggestion, I should a little and reasonably like to see Pillet — whom I know not — on Dicey. I guess that Dicey was all right in his meaning, which I take to be only, as I said in *The Western Maid*, 257 U. S. 419, 432, "there is no mystic overlaw to which even the United States must bow." In that case we held that a vessel, a military transport I believe, that had wrongly collided with another while belonging to U. S. and that couldn't be sued while belonging to the U. S. couldn't be sued after it was sold — much to the wrath of some admiralty men — *inter alios* Hough a good old admiralty judge — who wrote an amusing article, *Harv. Law Rev.*, March 1924,[1] to me unconvincing — in which he seemed to think I had forgotten *The China*[2] about [which] I discoursed in the Common Law and quoted:

"It aint so much as wot 'e said
As the narsty w'y 'e said it."

I quote as he quoted though the *as* seems wrong in the first line. Your courts decided the same way a little later.[3] The good Hough says that I refine on the meaning of a word unknown to the admiralty law — *tort* — that the admiralty only knows *collision*, that as I conclude that there was no tort I conclude that there was no collision! This suggests several reflections too obvious to write out.

Later: Well, we have adjourned for a week and I actually have taken a walk this afternoon and gazed at other idle persons amusing themselves with baseball at the rear of the White House. The spring is and has been lovely. In my back yard, there was first a magnolia with a mass of flowers, then a double flowering apple tree — a mass of pink — now a wistaria hanging the adjoining wall with purple blossoms and by and by I hope the divine polonia.[4] Already I begin to wonder what book I shall read, but I dare say I am premature. I think the first thing to do is to sleep long and late. My love to Lady Pollock.

Yours ever,
O. W. H.

[1] Charles Merrill Hough, "Admiralty Jurisdiction — of Late Years," 37 *Harv. L. Rev.* 529.
[2] 7 Wallace 53 (1868).
[3] The Sylvan Arrow, [1923] P. 220.
[4] *Paulownia tomentosa.*

WASHINGTON, May 11, 1924

Dear F. P.:

Would that you were going to receive such an altogether delightful letter as that which has come from you with . . . the fortifying 17th Century discourse on the tedium of literature. But I don't give up the discriminative *past*, because in addition to all the omnipresent difficulties there is the different emotional emphasis, when you get even 50 years back. Our continuous sittings are ended. My opinions are written and, all but two, delivered — one of them assigned to me yesterday P. M.[1] The other,[2] to which I am as profoundly indifferent as I could be to anything that I had tried to do, does not hit the views of the majority and the Chief has taken [it] to see if he can tinker a compromise. It is a matter, although not a case, on which the Alabama Courts have the last word — and that no one wanted to write about. I told the boys that if someone would take it to write the other way it would give me a chance to say what I really thought in the way of theory instead of guessing the meaning of muddle-headed cases.

I suppose one or two more things may drift in for me before we depart, but I am shy of offering to take extras for fear that I may be overdoing — beyond my strength.

I haven't yet tasted real leisure. There are jobs to attend to even where there is no case to be written, but I told my secretary that I expected to be looking for a handle to the void. I have finished [?] up so many things that it really seems as if I soon might sit with drooping jaw as empty as Wordsworth and "listen to the flapping of the flame." (I wonder if this will get a rise out of the true child of culture whom I address.) And yet I should feel as if I wasted time if I read the newspapers! As I look back I don't seem to think that I have had any cases of special interest this term or can pride myself on anything more than perhaps a little subtilty in dealing with one or two delicate matters. Brandeis wrote a good dissent, showing profound study of the art of bread making,

[1] Presumably Davis v. Corona Coal Co., 265 U. S. 219 (argued May 5; decided May 26, 1924).

[2] Opelika v. Opelika Sewer Co., 265 U. S. 215 (decided May 26, 1924). The decision was unanimous.

to uphold the constitutionality of a state law fixing the weight of loaves, against all but me, I think. I concurred with him.[3] The 14th Amendment is a roguish thing. Naturally I have read little: a good little book on Taxation by the Secretary of the Treasury[4] — but I believe Congress has turned him and his ideas down. I think they seemed right to me.

My love to the Lady.

Yours ever,
O. W. H.

WASHINGTON, June 11, 1924

Dear Pollock:

Pillet's pamphlet came a day or two ago and I snatch a few moments of the afternoon of our departure for Boston & Beverly Farms to say a word. *Imprimis*: naturally I think that our mode of proceeding by cases rather than by discussion of generalities leads to more accurate generalities, and I don't think that we need fear comparison with the continentals for philosophical views of the law. I half infer that Pillet thinks that there is a *droit international privé* which means something more than what the tribunal having to deal with a case will apply (assuming of course that the Court has the sovereign power of its country behind it). If he does think so I think it is a humbug. Of course there is a tendency in civilized countries to accept some principles that are not those of local dealings when they have to do with exceptional cases. A court might hold that the competence of a Frenchman to make a given marriage within its jurisdiction that would be valid between its own citizens depended for recognition by the Court concerned upon what the law of France, or for the matter of that, upon what the law of his domicile would have been if the marriage had been celebrated in France or the domicile. But it would be because the Court speaking for the Sovereign damn chose to — however excellent the reasons.

[3] Burns Baking Co. v. Bryan, 264 U. S. 504, 517.

[4] Andrew W. Mellon, *Taxation, the People's Business* (1924). The principal thesis of the volume was that the surtax rates should be reduced.

I don't find much beyond a yearning in the virtuous Pillet, that goes beyond Dicey as I take Dicey from him. I have no time to look into the matter. Dicey went further than I should in emphasizing local policy. Take a liability in tort accruing in Mexico. I should say that it gave rise to an *obligatio* that civilized courts will recognize, though different from the local run, unless one could clearly say that the local policy was opposed to and not only different from that of Mexico.[1] We used to fight about it. I mean Dicey and I. This is merely the pop of a soda cork. Adieu. May our journey tonight not be as uncomfortable as I expect it to be.

Yours ever,
O. W. H.

LONDON, June 30, 1924[1]

My dear Holmes:

Concerning Pillet I agree with you generally as you will see when I send you a mail or two later a spare clean proof of my note in the July *L. Q. R.*[2] Dicey never intended his rule or maxim to be a universal solvent of particular problems, any more than Bentham supposed the principle of greatest happiness to be itself capable of deciding what did make for the greatest happiness in a given case. But seemingly no Continental jurist will believe that any writer (whatever he may protest) does not intend to lay down a complete deductive system. Bentham by the way once or twice works out the conflict of convenience and inconvenience to an even balance and escapes a deadlock by falling back on the presumption that in case of doubt the less "Thou shalt not" the better. ("Teach your grandmother, Jerry!" says our Lady the Common Law.)

A second couple of young pigeons is hatched in my chambers

[1] See Holmes's opinion in Slater v. Mexican National Railroad Company, 194 U. S. 120 (1904).

[1] A brief note from Holmes, dated June 4, 1924, and one from Pollock, dated June 16, 1924, are omitted.

[2] 40 *L. Q. Rev.* 271 (1924).

and looks like thriving. They go through a stage of looking awkward when their quills are grown but not feathered — otherwise in the villatic fowl, I think.

Yours ever,
F. P.

BEVERLY FARMS, July 18, 1924

Dear Pollock:

The hatching of pigeons in your chambers needs explanation. "How — How — How — the Devil got the apple in?" I . . . should be in repose but for Oswald Spengler, *Der Untergang des Abendlandes* that I have been toiling through with a dictionary. The book is pretty thick with suggestion, and the writer seemingly at home in the higher mathematics, music and art, but I suspect less so in the physical sciences. His thesis that every *Kult*, the Greek, the Arabian, the Egyptian, the Chinese, that of the *Abendland*, is the incommunicable result of a special way of seeing and feeling life, that there is no eternal truth, no universal morality, no ever abiding questions, but that each *Kult* has its day — and, being an organism, its end. Ours reached its climax in the calculus and the music of Parsifal. I don't value his conclusion, but do his *aperçus*. Isn't that so of all theorists and system makers? He not only suggests new things but makes me realize more fully what I believed before, *e. g.*, how little we understand the Greeks, their drama, their philosophy, the meaning of their key words. But, oh, to have unloaded upon one as a job — a duty — a task of which you count the pages! Yet when one suspects that a man knows something about life that one hasn't heard before one is uneasy until one has found out what he has to say. It is long since I have got so much from a book as this, and if I heard that the swine were dead I should thank God. However only 53 pages more. My love to Lady Pollock.

Yours ever,
O. W. H.

LONDON, July 17, 1924

My dear Holmes:

. . . We are now in a spell of settled fine weather with days occasionally rather too hot for pleasure: so the prospects are good for the coming week of dinner and garden parties to be given to the Canadian and American Bar Associations, of which the best summary account will be in the words of the *Morte d' Arthur* on an incursion of seven kings and their hosts: "And the number was hideous to behold."

The *Russell case* in the House of Lords [1] will hardly interest you, tho' perhaps the question decided may be open in some States. I think the majority did not give proper weight to the constant practice of the Court, which surely ought to turn the scale where reported authority is ambiguous. . . .

Two pair of pigeons have now grown up in these chambers — the second now all but full-grown. It should be a good omen.

Yours ever,
F. P.

BEVERLY FARMS, July 27, 1924

Dear Pollock:

. . . Again I ask further explanation of the mystery of pigeons in your chambers. I am getting the vacation feeling — I have nearly washed out the ever imminent sense that I am neglecting some legal or spiritual duty to others or myself when I idle. For a new *pièce de résistance* I have the Loeb Thucydides — my last Day of Judgment book — but I must read him or part of him before I die. Also Tolstoy *La Guerre et la Paix;* neither seems pressing, but still I like to keep something moving. I really am more serene of mind than I often am. I know not of the *Russell case* that you mention. I should think our Bar Association incursion would be a bore to most concerned. My love to Lady Pollock.

Yours ever,
O. W. H.

[1] Russell v. Russell, [1924] A. C. 687. In this decision it was held by the House of Lords, Lord Sumner and Lord Carson dissenting, that the rule forbidding a spouse to

LONDON, July 24, 1924

My dear Holmes:

I have just met your colleague Sanford at a lunch given by the members of the Harvard Law School Association present here, and rebuked him for talking of being old at 60.

Also the learned and ingenious Roscoe Pound.

Were you aware of a libel action of *O'Dwyer* v. *Sankaran Nair* in our Courts? Issue: whether excesses had been committed in repressing disorder in the Punjab under the general instructions of the plaintiff as Lieutenant Governor, and if so, whether he was answerable therefor.[1] Evidence of excesses — by no means wholly credible — was produced for the defendant, but nothing whatever to show that O'Dwyer specifically authorized any such things (rather the contrary) or that his orders could not have been executed otherwise. Verdict for plaintiff — one juryman dissenting. That juryman was, if you please, Harold Laski. People here say he is a Communist, which I can hardly believe considering his historical learning. But anyhow I don't understand in what school he learnt to give a verdict dead against the evidence. (In the result, the parties agreed to accept the verdict of the majority). . . .

Yours ever,
F. P.

BEVERLY FARMS, August 9, 1924

Dear Pollock:

Laski in his letters to me has said nothing about the case after the first stages when he seemed much interested. He never told me what it was. I don't for a moment believe that he is a Communist, but I think his experience with Figgis gave an unfortunate turn to his speculations on government. I doubt if he has much practical experience, and don't feel sure of his

give evidence of non-intercourse, where access is possible, to bastardize a child born in wedlock, is applicable in divorce proceedings for adultery.

[1] The plaintiff in this case, Sir Michael O'Dwyer, was assassinated by an Indian nationalist on March 13, 1940.

judgment on practical matters. But he is a devoted scholar and an independent mind and I am glad to have him go ahead with his books. He will forward thought even if he goes wrong. I have finished my last chore, Thucydides, whom I hitherto have shirked barring the short passages I read in school or college. I read books 1, 2 and 7 in the Greek, for the rest I mainly contented myself with the translation, as I didn't care to spend more time on it. It isn't the kind of thing I like to read — just as I hate to read of our Civil War — and apart from its being the first of its kind, a most important fact, no doubt, I think it is overvalued in England. Of course there are brave and fine things in it, and sayings of eternal truth, but I can get more of them for the same money in modern books. I am struck again as in the Greek choruses by the absence of our notion of manners. They say what they think with no polite veils. Nikias by way of compliment tells his allies that they are distinguished for imitating the Athenians more exactly than any others! I like the absence of the hypocritic Christian unction. They say outright that of course the crowd that has the force means to have the top — and everybody understands it. But I had enough of his for the most part tuppenny skirmishes, and reflected with satisfaction that meantime Socrates was jawing away and that after Athens fell it became the leader of the world in philosophy. I shall bother no more about improving my mind this vacation. I have begun *La Guerre et la Paix* which was interrupted years ago. I am motored an hour or more *per diem* and take naps. All goes well so far. This month I always fear. Love to the Lady.

Yours ever,
O. W. H.

[Undated]

My dear Holmes:

The pigeons are grown up and flown. The parent birds (part of a flock that constantly haunts our precincts) came in very simply at a little swing window, which is always open, in the book-cupboard and made their nest inside on the sill.

A strenuous week of entertainments has passed off well in spite of broken weather and our guests from both Canada and the U. S. are departing well pleased. The evening reception at the House of Lords — the whole suite and Westminster Hall being open and pretty well filled — was a really fine sight.

Law Merchant: I don't see what you object to,[1] my very point being that as Michael Foster said the custom of merchants is in law the custom of England, and so is "private international law." Then I have noted elsewhere (more than once I think), that the L. M. coming under the roof of our lady the Common Law had to pay footing by adapting itself to Common Law categories and especially to the doctrine of consideration.

There must be some fine confused feeding in *Der Untergang des Abendlandes.* But as to the *Untergang* business, while all things doubtless come to an end it's a wise lane that knows its own turning, and it seems to me that when people are at the turning they hardly ever know it. Was Jerome or Claudian or Sidonius or even Augustine aware that the Western Empire was breaking up? Not being versed in those authors I don't know. The French Revolution was foreseen from St-Simon downward (he saw clearly, tho' all the more clearly because he had a personal dislike to Louis XIV, that the rotten system of finance must end in a crash if not mended betimes), but not as to its date and still less as to its consequences. Also I don't believe in *incommunicable* tradition. Of course learning habits is not the same as being bred in them: but they can be learnt.

There is another clever paradoxical book of similar type by one Vaihinger — *Die Philosophie von Als Ob* — which I know only by the review of a translation in the *Times Literary Supplement.* The ingenious author has a kind of super-pragmatic thesis that all our truths are only fiction. The grain of justification I conceive is that we have to pick out of infinite activities and relations outside ourselves those which appear to matter

[1] In his note concerning Professor Pillet's pamphlet, Pollock had briefly mentioned the cosmopolitan character of the law merchant as administered in the English courts of common law. 40 *L. Q. Rev.* 271–272. It seems probable that in a letter of Holmes to Pollock, now missing, there was some mention of Pollock's comment.

to us, and sort them for our own purposes at our own peril, and at any moment we may find that something we have neglected does matter in some unexpected way. But selection is not fiction. . . .

Divers learned friends make a good report of you.

Yours ever,
F. POLLOCK.

OAKLEY, SURREY
August 14, 1924

My dear Holmes:

Don't read Tolstoy in French if you can get Mrs. Garnett's English version, which is much better both by reason of the translator's special competence and because the rather loose-jointed Russian construction goes much more naturally into English. The same holds for Turgenev except where the author himself revised — or even in some cases wrote — the French translation. Older English versions, of American origin I think, are inferior. You may find it useful to practise the art of skipping a little: Tolstoy had no more style than Balzac and could be tedious: Turgenev was perhaps not such a big man but an incomparably better artist (as Vinogradoff told me long ago before I thought I should ever know a word of Russian).

We have had a farewell visit here from my learned friend Cornelia Sorabji who is returning to practice in India after being called to the Bar here. I wish you could know her — one of the very rare people (Alfred Lyall the only other I can name) who have both a Western and an Eastern mind. She has very little to learn about India or at any rate the northern half of it and not much about Europe, and has a wonderful range of acquaintance with persons and things. We are not to meet again for two years. As for you and me we have waited more than ten, but there is already talk of a return visit of the profession to America, which should give me — if still active enough — a good reason for crossing the ocean once more.

Without a definite occasion I can't manage it in all my circumstances.

I am beginning to think how long I ought to keep on with the *Law Reports*: not that I feel less capable, but I don't want to stay till people say I am too old. If only I could have a successor warranted to correct bad English as rigorously as I do. Why judicial language (in unwritten judgments) runs to a kind of journalistic jargon which no human being speaks and only second-rate newspaper men write — that is one of the mysteries of iniquity. . . .

Yours ever,
F. P.

RED LION INN, OAKLEY
August 24, 1924

My dear Holmes:

Thucydides (Thicksides we familiarly called him) was one of the authors we were expected to know pretty well at Cambridge: I read him through in my under-graduate days and still have my notes on the Syracusan expedition (a great tragic narrative that, surely). In later years I have hardly looked at him again except for Pericles' funeral oration, which I like to believe in the main truly reported, as T. most likely heard it (one of the greatest things again in all the books of the world, and full of political wisdom). As for the other discussions I suppose T. condensed and improved them somewhat as a good modern reporter deals with the arguments in a case (*N. B.*, I think ours do this better than yours: having no printed briefs to rely on they are bound really to follow the oral argument in court): disarming critics beforehand with his *τοιάδε*. I had forgotten poor Nikias' fatuous compliment to the allies. But it is modern enough — just the kind of thing English publicists were saying to all Europe from the middle of the 18th to the middle of the 19th century. Irishmen and Indians took them at their word with sufficiently surprising results, matter for some future Thucydides.

Nikias is otherwise like many modern failures. Cleon of

course is an everlasting type: not such a bad specimen either, for he did bring off a campaign whereas Lloyd George did his best to lose one (1918). . . .

Yours ever,
F. P.

FAIRDENE NURSING HOME
DORKING, SURREY
September 3, 1924

My dear Holmes:

Today we should have been on the North Sea, my wife and I . . . bound for Gothenburg and Stockholm. But the Red Lion at Oakley hath a few square feet of old and worn stone paving at the back door opening on the garden, and on that pavement, being mighty wet, I slipped on Friday forenoon and came down with what I thought was a shrewd knock above the left knee: but in fact, it seems, there was an automatic effort of the great front muscle of the thigh to recover the balance, the tendon attaching the kneecap to it gave way under the strain and the kneecap was left out of action tho' not broken (two very small fragments torn off). Such is the X-ray record (by an enlightened chemist in Dorking) as construed by a London orthopædic specialist confirming the opinion of the very capable Dorking medico. . . .

The result of the consultation is that about the end of the vacation I may be restored to the use of a "serviceable" knee, *i. e.*, somewhat less than good as new. My return to the Fencing Club as an active member looks rather precarious. We can go home to London whenever our house is delivered from that annual occupation by cleaners which to our sex is mysterious. I think you would like Johnson's and Boswell's accounts of their Hebridean tour (excellently edited in one vol. at the Clarendon Press), if you don't know them already. . . .

Yours ever,
F. P.

London, November 6, 1924[1]

My dear Holmes:

I am on my feet again, with my left leg in a most elegant contraption of light steel guides and leather, and a graduated joint to allow of increased bending by stages: it was put on yesterday: as the leg is kept quite straight at first I stump about the room a little and clumsily. But 'tis a beginning.

Law Merchant: Schedule of contributions:

I. Substantive law.

Negotiability.

You may say negotiability was always implicit in current coin. But coined money was treated as a thing *sui generis* in all civil laws.

The C. L. boggled a long time at any sort of transfer of credit (save by operation of law, like an executor's succession). For a long time equity allowed an assignee to sue in his own name only if the assignor refused to assist.

Then, in earlier days, I suspect much of the *ius gentium* was Mediterranean merchants' custom, (this now seems rather generally accepted).

II. Procedure: Stoppage *in transitu* (which Equity very nearly appropriated before the Common Law discovered it). Here there was no power in any Court (now it is by quite modern statute), to make a recusant party execute a conveyance. Equity of course would not meddle with a legal estate. Once I met in an abstract of title with two Lancashire women who went to gaol and stayed there eleven years rather than obey the order of the Court to convey some property.

I am reading again Dorothy Osborne's letters as a contrast to Pepys. *Quaere*: whether the correspondence of educated writers like D. O. had not much to do with the formation of modern English prose. What an adorable woman — and humourist.

It is pretty to observe that your Presidential and our General Election have come within a week, and both more decisive than any one expected.[2] We are well pleased with ours. I

[1] A letter from Pollock, dated September 28, 1924. is omitted.

[2] On November 4, Calvin Coolidge, who had succeeded to the Presidency on the

went near to think R. M. a shifty knave but did not know he could be such a fool. But that is what clever knaves often are.

Yours ever,
F. P.

WASHINGTON, November 17, 1924

Dear Pollock:

I am delighted to hear that you are beginning to stump about, as I felt a little anxious. We began another sitting to-day. I fired off five opinions [1] and a dissent [2] (having with me Taft, McKenna & Brandeis) and start with a clean slate. But I hasten to get off a word before I am caught in a whirlpool that I feel coming.

I don't think you make much [of] a fist in your list of contributions attributable to the law merchant. It certainly didn't originate the transfer of a contract — witness the learning [?] of covenants — and what its own theory or mode of reaching the results may have been never has seemed to me to have been fully cleared up by what I have read in Brunner's or elsewhere. I suspect that privity played a part and perhaps *per contra* the notion that the obligation inhered in the parchment, which has had real consequences in later law.

I have been having my eyes opened by two big and ugly volumes issued by the Encyclopaedia Britannica Co. called *These Eventful Years;* all the mighty of the earth write about the war and nations, and economic and social problems, and then I think about whatever else is needed to give a picture of the life of this century. I am dragged along unwillingly, because it is not the kind of book that I naturally should read, but I am dragged and thrilled and stimulated. However, no more reading for me, for a month.

death of Warren G. Harding in August 1923, was elected President of the United States. On October 9 the British Parliament had been prorogued and a general election followed on October 29, resulting in a Conservative victory and the resignation on November 4 of the Labour Cabinet headed by Ramsay MacDonald.

[1] Avent v. United States, 266 U. S. 127; Mackenzie v. Englehard Co., *id.* p. 131; Fernandez and Bros. v. Ojeda, *id.* p. 144; Davis v. Kennedy, *id.* p. 147; Duckett and Co. v. United States, *id.* p. 149 (all decided Nov. 17, 1924).

[2] Panama Railroad Co. v. Rock, 266 U. S. 209, 215.

Not to know augurs myself unknown, but I don't know what Dorothy Osborne's letters are, though the name is familiar. If this is a disgrace don't give me away.

Why should those letters not have counted in forming English style? I always supposed that the exigencies of the Court in France counted in teaching the French how to talk and to write. *Sat prata biberunt.* My secretary has piled a lot of records by my side and to them I turn. My love to Lady Pollock.

Yours ever,
O. W. Holmes

London, November 30, 1924

My dear Holmes:

The beginning of information about Dorothy Osborne is Macaulay's *Essay on Sir William Temple.* If that excites your curiosity then there are the letters edited by Judge (of County Courts) Parry: see that you use the second and much improved issue (1903 is the date of both editions I think).

I was so bombarded with advertisements of *These Eventful Years* that I got sick of the title — to say nothing of Tirpitz, the man of all whom we ought to have hanged, being a contributor. He murdered not only many innocent non-combatants but the ancient comradeship of the sea which in all former wars held even between enemies.

You don't think I regard the Law Merchant as a finished system standing over against the general law and custom of the realm? Not that, but a store of half manufactured material which the general law assimilated and worked up. We did it more thoroughly than the civilians: on the Continent you still find, with the notable exception of Switzerland, separate codes, courts (in the French system at any rate) and procedure for civil and commercial law.

That we *might* have developed a legal theory of *credit* — that is the main thing to my mind — without the merchants is surely but pious conjecture.

Now I am allowed to come downstairs; out of doors, perhaps, in a week or so.

Yours ever,
F. P.

We have laughed much over *Leave it to Psmith.* Now I fall back on Labiche's farces when I want a frivolous half hour. . . .

WASHINGTON, December 12, 1924

Dear Pollock:

Your letter came just as I was thinking a little anxiously that I hadn't heard how your leg was getting on. Your news sounds good. All is well here. We adjourn for three weeks on Monday after having to go to the House (of Representatives) to listen to a long eulogy of Wilson and then returning to court to deliver opinions and receive motions before going home. I shall have a long, serious, but I think both interesting and easy case to write[1] with I know not yet what else — as I am just back from conference — and only the C. J. knows what else he will assign to me beyond the big one that he has told me to expect. I went to poor Pitney's funeral a morning or two ago.[2] He has painfully lingered with hardening of arteries and broken faculties and speech. He could not touch the superlative, and when he first came on the bench riled me by excessive discourse. But he took his work seriously, was untiring in industry, had had some experience of life, and as Brandeis always said and, I came to think, truly had intellectual honesty that sometimes brought him out against his prejudices and first judgment. So they drop off, and I still remain like the Wandering Jew. I wish I could flatter myself that I put you on to *Leave it to Psmith*: Do you know Leacock? I believe his serious job is in the way of political philosophy or economics, but he has written many, too many perhaps, funny books. They vary but some of them have made me roar, and always, his is cultivated fun, even when disguised [?]. I stick to *These*

[1] Probably Sanitary District of Chicago v. United States, 266 U. S. 405 (argued Dec. 8, 9, 1924; decided January 5, 1925).

[2] Mr. Justice Pitney died December 9, 1924.

Eventful Years, an ugly book with a repellent title, but I have found it thrilling. Work has arrested me before I have finished Vol. 2. Perhaps you who have read the papers and, in the loathly phrase of the reporters, kept abreast of the times, would be less moved by it, but I feel as if I were making up for all my omissions of the last quarter-century. As I wrote to the Editor (*not* for publication): it is a swan in duck's clothing. I never should have looked into it if it hadn't been sent to me, but I always let those who send them understand that they can have the book back, but in no circumstances will get a *quid pro quo* in advertisable phrases. When the concomitant letter indicates that expectation I send the book back.

You and Lady Pollock have my best wishes for this year and the next. May the Christmas of '25 find us in as good shape as now.

Yours ever,
O. W. H.

VIII

1925-1929

WASHINGTON, February 10, 1925

Dear Pollock:

It seems long since the winged word has flown between us. Lo, an adjournment for this month and my work is done unless I take over some extras, so for the moment I am a gent. of leisure. I never had read anything of Bradley's so I got his *Essays on Truth & Reality* and perused them. It seems to me that Hegel has been a blight wherever he has passed: if people once have got into that system they continue to swing round and round in his circles and not to get any forrarder. I feel that with Bradley as I have with Haldane. But he is a keen logician and makes a good deal of common writing and thinking seem thin. Whatever the different way of getting there, I am thoroughly with him on the inseparability of the individual from the cosmos. But his cosmos has got its tail in its mouth and is self-supporting as a row of men sitting in each other's laps in a circle, whereas mine is an I know not what, beyond my capacity to predicate (wherein I fear we are not quite at one). Meantime how are you? Is the leg all right now? I have made what to my regret many people here call in′-quĭries but have only inference to go on.

Accident has just led me to reread *Troilus and Cressida* — hardly enough esteemed I should think in popular speech, but illustrating what seems to me very characteristic of the bard, *viz.*, when anything suggests to him his magnificent tall talk about life or the ultimate mysteries he fires it off bang, without the slightest regard to dramatic fitness, and as we would rather hear Shakespeare talk than Richard II or Achilles or Macbeth it goes — we accept it as all right and are grateful. If we can have nectar we don't mind the cup, to talk like an earlier generation.

My messenger waiteth to go home, so with this tweak at my fellow monkey's tail I shut up. My love to Lady Pollock....

Yours ever,
O. W. H.

LONDON, February 24, 1925

My dear Holmes:

Thanks for yours not yet ten days old....

Long ago I reviewed a volume of Bradley's Essays, when I was less favourably disposed to him than I should be now. I never fairly tackled *Appearance and Reality*. Who invented "the Absolute"? — an inept term to my mind. All experience is absolute in the sense that (1) it is incontrovertibly there, (2) though it may have ascertainable (and similar experiences may have similar constant) relations to other forms of experience, *its quality as we feel it* is an irreducible fact. My sensation *red* goes along with impact of a light-wave of certain length on my retina: the sensation *violet* with another length. But why *red* (as felt) answers to this end of the spectrum and *violet* to that nobody knows. If those ultimate facts are not absolute, what is?

In the greater metaphysical questions I find no use for any such word. Bradley (I rather think) was so much afraid of disparaging the absoluteness of his Absolute that he reduced it to having less than any assignable reality (an old schoolman's trick at that). Still I believe he had much of the root of the matter. I conceive the individual as distinguishable but not (as the theologians vainly talk with their separate creation of souls) separable from the Cosmos, and of course not capable of imagining, though it may be of conceiving the whole as a whole. The doctrine of the Trinity is a daring effort to construct an Absolute-Relative.

Most philosophers have their own 14^h at which they expect to find noon, and when they don't they sit down and cry or else fudge the clock.

As to my very finite and relative leg, I am still hobbling but hobble a little better every week, and the doctor has not looked in these ten days. My young man does massage with much zeal and moderate skill, and I shall need two or three months' patience yet.

Shakespeare was in a mighty bad temper when he wrote *Troilus & Cressida*, and meant it to be a frankly arbitrary satire, not respecting even legend, and wilfully flouting history, for he really must have known that Aristotle came after the Trojan war as well as that King William came before King Richard (you know that tale of him and Burbage?)[1] However, his depreciation of the Greek heroes merely follows medieval romances: see, S. Lee's *Life of Shakespeare.* But it remains an enigmatic play.

Yours ever,
F. P.

LONDON, February 10, 1925

My dear Holmes:

. . . We are reading for the first time some of A. K. Green's detective stories (you may remember she was a favourite author of Dicey's); she excels in making false clues, but the supposed real facts and the ultimate explanations are rather too elaborate to be credible. The manner (apt to be tedious in narrative) is much like Wilkie Collins; it may be only the general fashion of the time.

Have your courts ever been infested with the "rolled-up" form of defence in libel suits: facts true (not specifying them) and comment fair? After giving much trouble ever since it was invented (1890) it seems to be pretty well discredited by recent

[1] In *The Diary of John Manningham* (Bruce, ed., 1868) p. 39, there appeared the following entry: "March 13, 1601. Upon a tyme when Burbidge played Richard III there was a citizen grone soe farr in liking with him, that before shee went from the play shee appointed him to come that night unto hir, by the name of Richard the Third. Shakespeare, overhearing their conclusion went before, was intertained and at his game ere Burbidge came. Then message being brought that Richard the Third was at the dore, Shakespeare caused returne to be made that William the Conqueror was before Richard the Third. Shakespeare's name Willm."

remarks in the House of Lords.[1] I always thought that if intended as justification it must be bad for uncertainty, and so it can only be "fair comment" with a strictly superfluous inducement: which is now confirmed in the House of Lords. But perhaps it never got across the Atlantic. . . .

Yours ever,
F. P.

WASHINGTON, February 20, 1925

Dear Pollock:

Your letter must have crossed one from me to you. I don't know about the bother you mention in libel suits. They were not common in Massachusetts and still rarer before us though I once had pleasure in giving a unanimous decision, *Peck-Tribune Co.*, 214 U. S. 185, that in principle backed up a dissent of mine in Massachusetts, *Hanson* v. *Globe Newspaper Co.*, 159 Mass. 293, in which I thought the majority failed to grasp the first principles of liability in tort.[1] A judge of the Court of Appeals of the District has just sent me a decision[2] in which they followed my decision seemingly in ignorance of *Peck-Tribune Co.* and quote English cases that later they said had adopted the same views that I did. The article in the *Globe* described the plaintiff H. P. Hanson as in the prisoner's dock, whereas the real man was A. P. H. Hanson. The majority held the defendant not liable as they intended the latter. In the *Peck case* a certificate to the merits of Duffy's Par Malt Whiskey by Mrs. A. Schuman was surmounted by a portrait of the plaintiff who was not Mrs. Schuman and was a teetotaler — we overruled the lower U. S. Courts and held she could recover. We also dismissed the suggestion that there was no consensus of opinion that drinking whiskey was disreputable (this was long before the 18th amendment), answering that liability was not a question of majority vote. . . .

[1] Sutherland v. Stopes, [1925] A. C. 47; noted by Pollock in 41 *L. Q. Rev.* 126 (April 1925).

[1] See *supra*, Vol. I, p. 46; Vol. II, pp. 19, 29, 30.

[2] Presumably Washington Post v. Kennedy, 3 Fed. 2nd 207 (1925).

I have just read the *Memorials of Dicey*. What a dear, naif, ingenuous creature he was, and how modest as to his own powers.

Probably I mentioned Bradley's book on Truth & Reality the other day. Little as I agree with anyone who has begun to circle in the Hegelian System, he makes ordinary writing seem thin. Did I also mention having renewed my youth over Lamb's *Dramatic Poets*. Some fine things, and a lot of good language, but the lot of them seem to want the subtlety to which we are accustomed and which Shakespeare had. Now I am again recurring to my youth by reading about engraving and etching — putting the glass to my Dürers and other old prints. But as I write, there comes a longish opinion from the C. J. to which I must turn my critical attention. Wherefore my love to Lady Pollock and the lad.

Adieu for the moment.

Yours ever,
O. W. H.

London, March 20, 1925

My dear Holmes:

The news of London is that Madame Tussaud's is nearly burnt out — it was last night. I wonder whether the fact appears (a) in any American journal at all (b) if yea whether west of the Hudson River. When I was a small boy I was taken (not many times) to the show in its old quarters in Baker Street. I was never inside the new building.

An epidemic of scandalous lawsuits appears to be following on the flu. — not only one but both parties apparently wanting to hang out all their dirty linen, so that it is rather hard for the judge to stop irrelevant or barely relevant cross-examination when counsel do not object. At Lincoln's Inn, where we don't touch that sort of work, we shrug a disapproving shoulder. Another notable English philosopher is dead, James Ward: I knew him pretty well but had not the time to read his books at large. I think he would please you better than Bradley.

My progress continues: the rather martinet young orderly

now takes my arm only crossing the street or on uneven ground, and after Easter I hope to exchange him for an ordinary valet (the medical training has of course to be paid for) — not that I like being valeted either more or less. Lady Bryce has told me it was she who sent you the Dicey book. I am glad you like it.

Yours ever,
F. P.

Item: I have been nibbling through 3 vols. of Holdsworth's *History of English Law*, a great monument of industry & accuracy but I fear not very readable, though there are quite good bits.

WASHINGTON, March 27, 1925

Dear Pollock:

Your requiem over Madame Tussaud comes today. It was in the papers, as my wife mentioned it to me. I went, it must have been, to the old show in my early days in London, and to a new one the last time, I think, that I was there. It seemed a little squalid to me when revisited, and I am afraid I failed to realize how many really interesting relics were there. I think a book-selling shop to which Colvin [1] sent me was in the neighborhood, where I hesitated over an extra fine Beaumont and Fletcher at 60 odd pound, thought I had better refresh my knowledge before I bought, so spent a shilling for a volume that I read on my way back across the ocean and was glad that I had saved my money. We are adjourned again just now and my work is done. I was a little under the weather for a week or more and perhaps from the season am still languid although all right. I don't feel much inclination to improving my mind and saving my immortal soul. Perhaps I may follow your suggestion of Holdsworth but I doubt it. I have been reading half a dozen of the French plays published by *L'Illustration* with pleasure and satiety. *Aimer*, *Amants*, *L'Amour* were three! *Chifforton*, *Ysabeau*, *L'Age de Raison* (a tender little touch of bourgeois dim romance), *Un ami de jeunesse*, *Trois Types*.

[1] Probably Sir Sidney Colvin (1845–1927), biographer and art critic.

I have had about enough, but they are good stop gaps for vacuity. I glanced into Ovid a week ago but decided that he could wait as poetry till I turned to Seneca for prose. I think it easy to waste time mumbling over the old when there is so much new waiting, if one only could think what, at the right moment.

I must to the tavern for our Sunday supper and so stop and will post this. My love to Lady Pollock.

Yours ever,
O. W. H.

WASHINGTON, May 2, 1925 [1]

Dear Pollock:

. . . I have been pretty hard at work as the term draws toward a close. The last arguments tomorrow. My work is well up and I am hoping to have some leisure before we head for Beverly Farms. But probably your experience is like mine in being dreadfully driven in leisure moments. The other day Frankfurter sent me Bertrand Russell's *What I Believe*—in most of which I believe with B. R. By the by do you know him? and do you like him? He called on me last year and we had a talk that made me wish for more. But I think he is something of a sentimentalist, and does not talk well of war. Also I gather that he has a kind of respect for human criticism of or rebellion at the Cosmos, which to my mind is simply damning the weather, evidence that the speaker is ill-adjusted and not otherwise to be taken seriously. But I read little in the busy time. I did take down the *Anatomy of Melancholy* the other day and opening it at random found discourse on love, portions in discreet Latin, that suggested an explanation why old files [?] like to read him. I always had assumed that he was one of those amiable bores who belong to a more leisurely time than ours. Also I have lying on my desk Tawney's edition of *A Discourse upon Usury*.[2] Tawney's introduction so far as I have read is

[1] Two letters from Pollock dated April 9 and May 3, 1925, are omitted.
[2] By Thomas Wilson.

learned and instructive. Perhaps I mentioned lately taking up Bodin's answer to the fallacies of somebody I forget whom,[3] and giving him credit for seeming to have realized that money no more has a stable value than anything else. But after 20 more or less dull pages, not easy to my eyes in my copy, I said why mumble over what now is a common-place much better stated in later books, and arguments of detail forgotten as soon as read with no present interest etc. So I put it back on the shelves. Another warning not to waste too much time on the past, unless you are going to talk about it — unless that is, it is a subject for you and not read as a contribution. . . .

Apropos of Swift,[4] is not his *Polite Conversation* a diabolical work? — stamping as banal things that even now one might find oneself saying without a blush.

My homage to your beloved Lady.

Yours ever,
O. W. H.

London, May 18, 1925

My dear Holmes:

Your last comes just in time. We are off on our fortnight's cruise tomorrow and shall have no post till the first week in June.

Bertrand Russell: I used to know him a little but have not seen him for a long time. As *mathematician*, one of the first half-dozen in the world, but I have philosophic doubts about his enterprise of reducing even arithmetic to pure logic, and so I believe had H. Poincaré, one of the few competent critics. He thinks he has *proved* (with a new symbolical-logical calculus) that $1 + 1 = 2$. As *philosopher*, wrong to my mind but brilliant, certainly clever enough to know that one may think oneself a valiant fellow for throwing stones at God Almighty's windows, or a sage for being cocksure there are no

[3] Probably *Réponse aux paradoxes de M. de Malestroit, touchant le fait des monnaies et l'encherissement de toutes choses* (1568).

[4] In his letter of April 9, 1925, which is omitted, Pollock had stated that he was reading selections from Swift: "a very human man as well as a great writer and I prefer an unsolved mystery to believing that he really committed any dishonourable action."

such windows nor any house at all, but not both at once. I can hardly think he would give himself away so easily. As *citizen*, thoroughly bad. He did much mischief, which still works, among young people at Cambridge during the war, and was mixed up with the sort of pacifists who did not stick at falsifying evidence. Incidentally, he got himself locked up for a short time. Note that the high average ability of the Russell family is often alloyed with a strain of crankiness and self-conceit. Odo R. (first Lord Ampthill) and his less known but really not less distinguished brother Lord Arthur were free from this.

When I looked into Bodin long ago I confined myself to his theory of the State. He was quite capable of being acute in economics.

It so happens I have just been reading Swift's *Polite Conversation* again. He was too great an artist I think to keep his Sparkish, Neverout & Co. — not forgetting Miss Notable — on a dead level of foolishness, and allowed them to rise now and then to such small talk as is harmless in moderation and may be useful by way of conjunction between better things. But I think there was a real opinion among refined people that proverbs were in themselves vulgar even when to the point: *cp.* Lord Chesterfield, and Saintsbury's judicious introduction to Swift's dialogues. . . .

Burton: I have the second edition, 1625, cheek by jowl with Hobbes' *Leviathan* and Harrington's *Oceana*; read all or most of it about forty years ago — not a bore in print anyhow, for you can take him up and drop him anywhere. I doubt whether he talked like that at all.

Yours ever,
F. P.

WASHINGTON, May 17, 1925

Dear Pollock:

It is hard to write to one who is wandering one knows not where in Southern Seas.[1] But as in battle sometimes two bul-

[1] Pollcck, at this time, was on a cruise to the Canary Islands.

lets meet and coalesce I fire into the air trusting to the remote chance. . . . My wife has just read to me in the evenings a novel by Francis Hackett, called *That Nice Young Couple*, which excited some interest in me. F. H. at one time wrote for the *New Republic* and I thought there had more power to utter the unutterable than anyone. There is something of that gift here, and vivid observation, but the book raised a question in my mind whether it was an Irish characteristic to speak of things that we generally prefer to leave unmentioned. I think of Joyce and George Moore — perhaps it is only their influence — and it is by no means as marked here as with those men, only once in a while you wonder why he wanted to put that in. . . . This morning my wife tells me the paper announces that my retirement is fixed for the beginning of next term. I am not given to base suspicions, but former rumors came from Boston. The present Chief Justice of Mass., Rugg,[2] wants my place. He is a friend, I think a classmate of the President, and recently was at the White House, but didn't call on me. I can't help wondering if the wish was father to the thought — all this strictly between ourselves. But I shall hold on unless something gives way. As old Fuller said to me when he was C. J., "I am not to be paragraphed out of my place." Rugg is a respectable, hard-working, rather long-winded man, who, I believe, has made his own way very creditably, but from the talk of the bar and what I have read of his writing I should think not the equal of his predecessor Knowlton [3] who in his day was most anxious for my appointment and showed it with a *naïveté* that made me smile. He knew that the outgoing governor would appoint him to my place and wanted to fasten it before the new governor came in.[4] He wrote me a long letter to show that I ought to resign when Roosevelt offered me the place here without waiting to see if the Senate would confirm me: that it was due to Mr. Roosevelt. So I wrote to Roosevelt who said of course don't resign until you are confirmed. I hope this

[2] Arthur Prentice Rugg (1862–1938); Associate Justice, Supreme Judicial Court of Massachusetts, 1906–11; Chief Justice, 1911–38.

[3] Marcus Perrin Knowlton (1839–1918); Associate Justice, Supreme Judicial Court of Massachusetts, 1887–1902; Chief Justice, 1902–11.

[4] The outgoing Governor, Winthrop Murray Crane, appointed Knowlton to fill the office of Chief Justice before the new Governor, John L. Bates, took office in 1903.

personal gossip doesn't bore you. I think it an amusing touch of human nature.

I am in good shape. My work is done except such things as may turn up before the final adjournment. All my cases are disposed of except two given to me since the last court day and they are written and agreed to. . . . My love to the dear lady.

Yours ever,
O. W. H.

WASHINGTON, June 2, 1925

Dear Pollock:

. . . How can a man talk with one whose whereabouts are unknown, who but for cannibalism having gone out of fashion, might be gracing a banquet in the South Seas, or, again, teaching Gandhi religion, or whispering nothings in a Parisian ear. I believe it is since I last wrote that I read Morgan's book about Morley [1] which I thought rather charming, and I am sure it is since then that I read Morley on Compromise. Rather a work of the time and place of its writing it seemed to me. But I must to solitaire. It is half past nine. Since I began this and after dinner we went round by the river side to get a little air and see the wonderful look by night.

June 3. Still roasting. I am bothered by a case in which conscience and judgment are a little in doubt concerning the constitutionality under the 14th amendment of a State law punishing the publication of a manifesto advocating the forcible over-throw of government.[2] x x x Such is the effect of putting a doubt into words that I turned aside from this letter and wrote my views which now are waiting to go to the printer. The theme is one on which I have written majority and minority opinions heretofore and to which I thought I could add about ten words to what I have said before. So the result is that you get nothing from me this time except wishes for a pleasant

[1] John Hartman Morgan, *John, Viscount Morley* (1924).

[2] Gitlow v. New York, 268 U. S. 652 (1925). The majority of the Court, in an opinion by Sanford J., held that the New York Criminal Anarchy statute was constitutionally applicable to the defendant's publication. Holmes wrote a dissenting opinion in which Brandeis, J., concurred.

journey and successful return which I suppose is approaching. I have been and still am bothered about getting the accommodations that I want for Boston but in one way or another expect to get through on or about the 10th and go to Beverly Farms at the end of the week. Please give my love to Lady Pollock.

Yours ever,
O. H. W.

BEVERLY FARMS, June 18, 1925

Dear Pollock:

It is a pleasure to know that you are on *terra firma*, and I thank you for seven pages.[1] As I believe I have said before, I take no stock in B. Russell's defiance of the sky. I think the proper attitude is that we know nothing of cosmic values and bow our heads — seeing reason enough for doing all we can and not demanding the plan of campaign of the General — or even asking whether there is any general or any plan. It's enough for me that this universe can produce intelligence, ideals, etc. — *et superest ager*. It seems to me most probable that our ultimates are not cosmic ultimates but something less. We got here Saturday last and I am just about recovered from the devastating heat of Washington and trying for irresponsible leisure.

My last performance during the term, on the last day, was a dissent (in which Brandeis joined) in favor of the rights of an anarchist (so-called) to talk drool in favor of the proletarian dictatorship.[2] But the prevailing notion of free speech seems to be that you may say what you choose if you don't shock *me*. Laski put me on to Sainte-Beuve's *Port-Royal* as to which as yet I am not enthusiastic. I don't know what Ste-B. believed or disbelieved but his talk about Grace sounds hypocritical to me and I dislike him. But I don't mean to bother about improving my mind if I can help it.

Love to the Lady.

Yours ever,
O. W. H.

[1] This letter is missing. A brief note from Pollock, dated June 8, 1925, is omitted.
[2] Gitlow v. New York; see Holmes to Pollock, June 2, 1925.

LONDON, July 30, 1925[1]

My dear Holmes:

I don't see why *Port-Royal* should be the more tedious or the less interesting to you because you heartily dislike Louis XIV (in which you are fully supported, if need be, by the contemporary authority of Saint-Simon). But certainly there do be *longueurs* even in the immortal *Provinciales*. Perhaps the Lord ordained it all that Pascal might not shirk his part in creating modern French prose: anyhow there have been worse arguments in the matter of final causes. As for the Jansenist and many other controversies, the mischief was done when, the Church having become respectable, theology fell into the hands of men trained in the logic-chopping of the Graeco-Roman schools. Augustine and his successors turned the logic-chopping loose on points they deemed essential to salvation. When people began to think you could be damned merely for an erroneous opinion I don't know. The Jews B. C. did not I believe worry about speculative opinion so long as there was no incitement to actual disobedience of the Law. Indeed I believe Catholics, *so long as they are at all times ready and willing to submit to the authority of the Church*, have always had more speculative freedom than Protestants commonly know — and before 1870 more than most orthodox Protestants. But now the Jesuits have got it reduced to the crudest terms: Kiss the Pope's toe and ask no questions in this world if you would not kiss the Devil's — in the next. And I suppose biblical letter-worship may be a little better than that, though not much....

Yours ever,
F. P.

[1] Letters from Pollock, dated June 22 and July 13, 1925, are omitted. It seems probable that a letter from Holmes is missing.

THE DRUMMOND ARMS, ALBURY
GUILDFORD, SURREY
August 3, 1925

My dear Holmes:

As to Socialist Utopias I wholly agree.[1] Mankind being what they are they would work out (if at all) only to a pretty despotic oligarchy, none the better for a disguise of philanthropic formulas, and administered mainly in the interest of the official ring — if in an illusion of honest conceit so much the worse. But if mankind became different the machine would not be wanted. So, as dreams go, I prefer the idyllic anarchy of William Morris's *News from Nowhere*. Therefore I shall read Laski's book by deputy, to wit H. J. Randall, a really learned solicitor (uncommon variety) who has already criticized divers works of legal-political speculation for the *L. Q. R.* No relation to the lately deceased editor.[2] If he reports it very well written I may then look at it myself for curiosity.[3] . . .

Meanwhile the *Times Literary Supplement*[4] treats the *Grammar of Politics* with respect though it censures the arrangement as inconvenient. Apparently he (Laski) is not a Socialist of any definite school. The element of truth in Socialism is to my mind something the Common Law knew long before any modern Socialists were born: Monopolies are in principle odious, and when they are necessary they must be under public control: whether the control shall be central or local, direct as in the post-office, or indirect by way of regulated franchises, is a matter of means and economic expediency (thus electric supply now seems capable of centralization on a great scale and with advantage, and our numerous railway companies are now amalgamated in a few groups). Our lady the Common Law is a very wise old lady though she still has something to learn in telling what she knows.

We have just tided over our coal mining crisis,[5] to the disgust

[1] No letter from Holmes discussing such matters has been found.

[2] A. E. Randall (1862–1925).

[3] In Holmes's Journal it appears that at approximately this time he had finished Laski's *A Grammar of Politics* (1925). The book was reviewed by Randall in 42 *L. Q. Rev.* 111 (1926).

[4] July 30, 1925, p. 503.

[5] On July 31, after a special meeting of the Cabinet to deal with the threatened stop-

of the Germans, who looked to make great profit out of a stoppage here: a fact which coal owners and miners ought alike to take to heart, but both sides are horribly pig-headed and I doubt the honesty of some of the trade union leaders. Bolshevik agents are no doubt doing their best to make trouble and they have no lack of money or unscrupulous agitators. There seems to me quite an appreciable chance that the civilized world may have to fight the Bolsheviks one day — it would have been comparatively easy to suppress them immediately after the war, but we puttered about giving subsidies to incompetent partisan traders whom the Bolsheviks mopped up in detail.

The ex-cemetery of St. George's Hanover Sq.[6] is now divided between allotments and sports (lawn tennis, cricket nets for practice bowling, a rudimentary bowling green which needs proper turf, and a strip at the end just long enough to give a refuge to the Toxophilite Society turned out of Regent's Park by lawn tennis courts). So there is no hay. Our cat spends most of his time there. . . .

Yours ever,
F. P.

Drummond Arms, Albury
August 22, 1925

My dear Holmes:

Your two letters of 8th and 13th have come almost together;[1] the later one having it seems just caught a fast mail. . . .

An intelligent monopolist may doubtless be a benefactor, and so may an intelligent despot. But intelligence cannot be warranted, therefore despotism and monopoly are both objectionable in principle. Surely there is no doubt about the attitude of the Common Law or the popular feeling it represented. Con-

page of all movement of coal, an offer was made by the Prime Minister, Stanley Baldwin, to the operators and unions for a Government inquiry into the grievances and a grant for the time being of a government subsidy for the maintenance of wages in the industry. The offer was accepted and the stoppage forestalled.

[6] The rear windows of Pollock's house at 21 Hyde Park Place overlooked this spot.

[1] These letters are both missing.

sider how all the chandlers of a ward in Norwich were fined by a local court for making a ring in the price of candles: cited under restraint of trade in P. on *Contract.*[2]

I wonder why no Roman publicist under the Empire tried to devise a plan for making monarchy fool-proof. Gibbon observes that any fixed rule of succession, even hereditary, would have been better than being at the mercy of the Praetorians. As it is, the only great elective monarchy in the world is the Papacy, and the results have not been wholly satisfactory. . . .

I have just read Petronius, *Cena Trimalchionis*, and Seneca, *Apokolocyntosis* (a skit on the death of the Emperor Claudius), edited in a handy volume at the Oxford University Press. The vulgar Latin of the former is curious; about 50 A. D. people were already using the medieval construction with *quod* or *quia* instead of the classical *oratio obliqua*: the vocabulary full of strange words, partly slang and partly affected. The moral is that vulgar new rich people have always been much the same, perhaps rather more so *temp.* Nero.

As for the Seneca it is one of the few contemporary political documents, but as satirical literature not a patch on Byron's *Vision of Judgment.* Whereas P. may be reckoned an ancestor of the 'picaresque' novelists.

Scott and Cervantes:[3] the connexion is clinched I think by Scott's motto from Don Q., in the original too[4] — whether confined to the *Tales of my Landlord* series I am not sure. . . .

Yours ever,
F. P.

BEVERLY FARMS, September 8, 1925

Dear Pollock:

. . . I have finished the *Odyssey* and am glad, though I have had pleasure. Most reading that is worth while bores me at the moment. Great thoughts need time for adjustment.

[2] See *Leet Jurisdiction of the City of Norwich*, (*Selden Society*, 1892), p. 52; cited in Pollock, *Contracts* (9th ed., 1921), p. 426.

[3] In the summer of 1925 Holmes read *Don Quixote.*

[4] See *The Heart of Midlothian* and its motto, quoted from *Don Quixote*, Parte I, Cap. XXXII.

. . . Just for the moment I am blank. I think of a novel by Hardy — a gent. whom I have left alone since I was young. I suppose I ought to know something of him. Can you recite on Doughty (I think the name is) author of travels in Arabia called, in *These Eventful Years*, the greatest book of travels and the author pronounced the greatest living English poet? I found in the work I quote that I did not know even the names of the most illustrious authors and artists now going. I think of rereading *L'Éducation Sentimentale* which you read [?] within a year or two — but like other great books (as I presume it to be) I fear it is pretty dull.

I must go forth to drive. The next term sheds an approaching shadow. It will spare me the effort of choice! My love to the Lady.

Yours ever,
O. W. H.

LONDON, October 22, 1925[1]

My dear Holmes:

At Venice we picked up a Tauchnitz edition of Emerson's *English Traits*, which I have possessed at home many years in the two vols. of his works published in London half a century ago, but somehow had never read. It seems to me some of his best stuff, and of double importance:

(1) as proof that Emerson was no dreamer but had lots of Yankee common sense and was a keen and shrewd observer. Not to mention the toughness of his constitution: a man whom Harriet Martineau failed to bore to death.

(2) as a capital historical document on the state of English Society about 1850 — which is now almost ancient history.

The picture is of course not infallible, both light and shade inevitably exaggerated, and a certain number of mistakes are now obvious to any tolerably informed student of history, but most of them were current in England at the time. The chief

[1] In a postal card, dated Sept. 14, 1925, which is omitted, Pollock stated that he and Lady Pollock were going to leave for Venice two days later and would return to England at the end of October.

real defect is ignorance of the rest of Europe and especially of medieval history, hence some want of proportion, and setting down as specially English, various things which were common to Christendom in the Middle Ages and later, such as the policy of exploiting colonies for the trade of the mother country. Then E. did not know enough of France to discover that French habits of thought are or then were even more insular than ours. There are some extraordinary good summary judgments on India, and our administration of foreign law. . . .

Yours ever,
F. P.

WASHINGTON, October 31, 1925

My dear Pollock:

Welcome back. It is many many years since I read Emerson's *English Traits* or indeed anything of his except his *Essay on Montaigne* (when I was reading the latter) which struck me as surprisingly good. I think I must have read the *English Traits* however as there comes back to me from time to time a charming passage about how at first he was near laughing as Wordsworth recited his poetry in his garden but then he thought here was an old bard whom he had come three thousand miles to see, chanting his poems to him, "and I saw that he was right and I was wrong." I wonder if I did retain the substance correctly after fifty years?

I know nothing of Harriet Martineau at first hand, but I thought Morley regarded her as his Virgin Mary; also I have a family tale. She stayed here with my wife's grandfather [1] — a great mathematician — translator of La Place and author of a still used Bowditch's *Navigator*. In those days the privy was a structure at a little distance from the house. The first morning they met, and Bowditch, a shy man, I believe, changed his hour; a second time they met. The third day they met again, whereat she smiled at him and said, "one goeth and another cometh," which I have always set down to her credit. As to

[1] Nathaniel Bowditch (1773–1838).

insularity of thought, I have yet to discover a place that is not Little Pedlington. I was pleased to note once that Montesquieu said it of the Parisians in his *Lettres Persanes*, and when I used to see the Souls I was struck with the fact that with them as with the rest the dominant interests were those of contiguity....

I have been working about as hard as one should, from the time I got here to the day before yesterday. Then I wound up by sending round two opinions that I thought pretty good, and hope to dig up some culture roots in the next two weeks of adjournment — but leisure is always the day after tomorrow.

My old friend Rice[2] head of the print department in the Library died last year to my grief, but I mean to go there to look for what they have of Adam Elsheimer and his predecessor Philipp Uffenbach who was precursor of Rembrandt and I guess gave Blake a hint. When I was a little boy at the rooms of one of the early China Merchants, then an old man, among other marvels I was deeply moved by an engraving by Count Goudt — a mysterious firelight that I used to dream about. He got it I imagine from Elsheimer, of whom I fain would know more.

While I have played solitaire in my resting time after 9 P.M. my wife has read to me from *The Grammar of Michael Neo Palaeologos*, a whimsical book with passages that made me roar, and a suggestion of more thought than I could pick up during my game. If the leisure comes I think I shall look into it more seriously.

My love to the dear lady.

Yours ever,
O. W. H.

London, November 16, 1925

My dear Holmes:

A few notes and a query are set down on another leaf. The detached house of office you mention was common in English farmhouses and cottages in my younger days and I suppose is still to be found. I have heard of it in a good French country

[2] Richard Austin Rice (1846–1925).

house and met with it in Canada. Before the recent improvements of sanitary engineers there was really a good deal to be said for it.

My doctor gives me to understand that I am not likely to recover the full bending of the left knee, so I must be content to walk more or less hobbling and go on wheels much more than I like. But I am to be dispensed from a valet next month, which will be no small relief to both person and purse, and from my protective machine in the new year. It will go as an *ex voto* to the Orthopaedic Hospital when the time comes and I hope serve others there. We had a dull bleak Armistice Day, but the sun came out for a few minutes just at the solemn hour of eleven: an excellent omen for the peace of the world if the days of omens were not past.

My wife has got up a little festival party for my 80th birthday[1] — family, . . . and one or two distinguished friends: Arthur Balfour is coming. Meanwhile I have found by trial that a fencing lesson with immovable feet is possible, and even an assault with a charitable adversary who does not mind suppressing half the game by a special convention. So I need not abandon the Fencing Club yet.

Did I tell you of a recent judgment in the Judicial Committee that a Hindu family idol is a kind of corporation sole and must have counsel assigned to it in a suit about the custody of the idol?[2] — really, of course, in the interest of the family as a whole to secure the cult being properly kept up. One would think the notion of a charitable trust more appropriate, but it does not seem to be known in Hindu law. *Vide, si libet*, an article in October number of *L. Q. R.*[3]

I am now free, by the way, of my emergency editorship.[4]

Yours ever,
F. P.

Good for H. M. in her actual converse: in writing she was a consummate prig. Also did not know where the things she did

[1] December 10, 1925.
[2] Pramatha Nath Mullick v. Pradyumna Kumar Mullick, L. R. 52 I. A. 245 (1925).
[3] By S. G. Vesey-FitzGerald, entitled, *Idolon Fori*, 41 *L. Q. Rev.* 419 (1925).
[4] Arthur L. Goodhart became editor of the *Law Quarterly Review* in January 1926.

not know began — said in a letter *c.* 1860 that the Indian Penal Code was a failure (I suppose because she hated Macaulay as a typical Whig).

Then she quarrelled with her brother James the philosopher, whom I knew, a dear old man; a sister capable of quarrelling with him must have been extra cantankerous.

Emerson and Wordsworth: The incident, quite correctly remembered, belongs to the first visit to England (1833).

What is *Neo-Palaeologus*? I never heard of it.

WASHINGTON, December 1, 1925

My dear Pollock:

Welcome to old age — which begins at 80. So you are a child again in a new zone. I wish I were to be or to have been at your birthday party. If you had given the date I should have cabled unless the time has gone by. No doubt those present appreciated the story of your fruitful and gallant life. I hope we may keep on together for a good time yet. If I pass the line of 85 in March I shall set 90 as a goal. When I turned 80 my wife sprung a dinner party with nearly all my old secretaries on me. I didn't know anything about it until I entered the dining room.

Your tail piece bothered me for a moment — as to "H. M." I said to myself I didn't know that Her Majesty wrote books, unless he means Queen Victoria and I didn't think he would write about her quite in that tone. At last the glimmering light came to me from the context and I remembered that I had written of Harriet Martineau.

The book I mentioned is:

Michael-Neo Palaeologos
His Grammar
By his father Stephen N.
Palaeologos.
London and Toronto — J. M. Dent & Sons Ltd.

I couldn't be sure whether you would be tickled by the whimsicalities and funny illustrations (I don't mean the pictures) as

I was, or whether you would be repelled by the humorously intended but rather over-worked fantastic terminology. I think on the whole that the book is quite amusing and acute. In its criticisms of other writing I think it loses sight of its own insistence that everything depends on the context and finds obscurity when from that point of view there is none. Also you may think that he says things that are old to philosophers. But I recur to the opinion that I haven't had such a peck of oats for some time.

I am very hard at work again as we are sitting, but in good shape and enjoying it, preparing small diamonds for people of limited intellectual means.

My love and felicitations to you both.

Yours ever,
O. W. Holmes

London, December 14, 1925

My dear Holmes:

What my wife calls a little dinner was the largest in number we have yet got into our dining room: still it was domestic. The only drawback to my felicity has been the crowd of messages from good friends that had to be answered. . . .

It is related of Confucius that one day as he walked with his disciples an old man sitting by the roadside saluted him. But the Master said: "In youth — not obedient to parents; in mature age — doing nothing worthy to be remembered; in old age — living on and not dying; this it is to be a pest." Therewith he hit him on the shank with his staff. You and I have escaped that malediction, I trust.

Yours ever,
F. P.

LONDON, January 21, 1926

My dear Holmes:

. . . As to Whitehead [1] he is in the very front rank of mathematicians — he wrote a great book with Bertrand Russell some years before the war [2] — and can speak with Einstein in the gate. Moreover he can explain things to you and me: there is an admirable little introduction of his to mathematical methods in the Home University series of handbooks.[3] Four or five years ago I read his *Concept of Nature* — not very elementary, and stiff in places. I don't know what his philosophy is like (here I have filled my pen with a new and ingenious device which can't ink one's fingers) when it gets loose from mathematics, or just what work he does nowadays at Harvard.[4] I know him in person by means of the Cambridge Society called the Apostles, having met him sundry times at our annual dinner. It is a body to which I owe much [5] — friendship with Maine and Fitzjames Stephen and an earlier discovery of Maitland than I should have made otherwise — as my father owed not less to it before me.

Birkenhead has produced a volume on *Fourteen English Judges*: the only actual notice of it was mine in the *Morning Post* last week: it is not exactly bad but ought to have been much better. I can't forgive him for mentioning that Eldon loved port and omitting the dialogue with his brother —

Lord Stowell. Brother John, this port is good.

Lord Eldon. Brother William, all port is good, but some port is better than other.

The style is so unequal that one suspects a secretary's unrevised devilling in places. If it comes in your way it is just worth looking at, but will tell you nothing new.

Yours ever,
F. P.

[1] It appears in Holmes's Journal that at the end of 1925 he read Alfred North Whitehead's *Science and the Modern World* (1925). The letter in which he appears to have mentioned the book is missing.

[2] *Principia Mathematica* (3 vols., 1910).

[3] *An Introduction to Mathematics* (1911).

[4] Whitehead had become Professor of Philosophy at Harvard University in 1924.

[5] See Pollock, *For My Grandson* (1933), pp. 30–38.

WASHINGTON, February 6, 1926

My dear Pollock:

Your letter finds me at the end of a week of seclusion with a cold, now coming right but ending with fits of coughing at night. Luckily the Court adjourned on Monday and as all of my work is done, there was no inconvenience, except that of being lolopping about and dozing instead of reading some noble work in philosophy that I shouldn't believe, or a classic that would bore me, or perhaps going to the dentist and having him look me over. Apropos of Eldon, Stowell and port, is there not a tale of someone saying to Stowell that he supposed they drank a good deal of port — a bottle? "More." "Two bottles?" "More." "Three?" "Don't ask any more questions." I don't know if I get it right. 'Tis sixty years since.

My grandfather [1] had some letters or notes from L. Stowell which I lent to Jim Putnam [2] and after much labor got but one little one back. I remember a family story that when my grandfather was sitting on the bench with him and he was delivering a judgment my grandpa was abashed to hear him declare that, "I say this with the more confidence that I am assured by a learned American gentleman, that that is the law in his country," or words to that effect; and one day I was looking at a volume of his decisions in the Suffolk Law Library and I came on a passage to that effect, and some unknown hand had written "Judge Jackson" in the margin, so evidently the family yarn is true.

I have just written a decision that won't be delivered for a month in which I have to discuss a matter connected with war risk insurance by the Government. I have said that the relation of the government to the soldiers if not strictly paternal was at least avuncular (having in mind of course Uncle Sam).[3] I have hopes that the censors who prune my exuberance will let that pass (the most severe are gone — McKenna & Day).

[1] Charles Jackson.

[2] Dr. James Jackson Putnam (1846–1918), Boston neurologist and cousin of Holmes. In Dr. Putnam's *Memoir of Dr. James Jackson* (1905), pp. 111–112 there is a brief account of Justice Jackson's connection with Lord Stowell and a reprint of one of Stowell's notes to Justice Jackson.

[3] White v. United States, 270 U. S. 175, 180 (decided March 1, 1926).

Yesterday I read Chateaubriand's *René* — rather thin stuff — *hein*?, also Vauvenargues's *Maxims*. He says some good things, but it is a misfortune for him to be printed in the same volume with Rochefoucauld. The chaps that think a man will be damned, or will fail to escape damnation, because he doesn't believe this or that, approach in a rudimentary way to the truth that heaven is more a matter of intelligence than of virtue, but like early cases of contract the doctrine is hidden in the concrete. It strikes nine and I must go downstairs to solitaire and stories. My love to your honored Lady.

A month from next Monday I shall be 85 if I last till then. Well — it's still good sport.

Yours ever,
O. W. H.

London, March 1, 1926

My dear Holmes:

This is a rather summary epistle: I have a consultation today on a case from a Berlin firm of lawyers about expropriation of Hungarians in Transylvania for a merely illusory compensation, contrary, *sicut dicunt*, both to the common justice of nations and to the Peace Treaty (Trianon) articles in such case made and provided. I don't believe there is much sense of either legal or natural justice beyond the Danube, and one's sympathy for aggrieved parties is tempered by the reflexion that they would do — or have done — just the same things, being a majority instead of a minority.

My brother Walter,[1] whom perhaps you never saw, possibly never heard of, died a week ago after living many years as it were next door to Jane Austen's house at Chawton, ever since he was evicted from editing the *Saturday Review* by the sale of the paper. His literary production was distinguished in quality but curiously desultory and scattered: some of it ought to live if only in anthologies.

I read Vauvenargues some time ago: an interesting human

[1] Walter Herries Pollock (1850–1926).

figure to my mind, on paper less brilliant than the more celebrated masters of aphorism, but I found one good motto in him.

Dr. Johnson, whose letters I have been reading in a neat new pocket selection (Oxford Univ. Press, quite cheap) was troubled about his soul apparently as regards works, not faith. The Hellenistic Alexandrian Hebrew was wiser: *Iustorum animae in manu Dei sunt.* Not that one can be even tolerably just without a certain modicum of intelligence, so the ancient Socratic problem εἰ διδακτὸν ἡ ἀρετή has many sides.

Glory be — there is a fine spring sun, and I hope you have the like. . . .

Yours ever,
F. P.

WASHINGTON, April 2, 1926

My dear Pollock:

It is a month from the date of your last letter and must be two or three weeks since I sent a bulletin.[1]

I was overwhelmed with letters, telegrams, and papers on and after my birthday, and they with my work drove me to the limit of my powers. I was surprised and no little pleased at some of the articles. But that is over now and for the rest of this and next week I am as near the feeling of leisure as I am likely to get. I need it and mean to be as idle as I can. The only book I read, at odd minutes, is Horace Walpole's Correspondence — just the thing for such moments. He once in a while is surprisingly ahead of his beef-eating contemporaries, and his style is so pleasant that one can read on indefinitely without fatigue. For all round, I think you might put him at the head of English letter writers; of course Charles Lamb is more pungent and has more genius, and very possibly Byron whom I don't remember so well, but take the world he tells you about and the way he tells it, I think one could read him longer with undiminished pleasure. But, oh, my dear Pollock, I began talking about leisure and since I began this letter three

[1] No letter from Holmes between that of Feb. 6, 1926 and this one has been found.

opinions have come in that I must read carefully, and a man has called to jaw with me about writing something to be engrossed on parchment and put under a corner stone! (a decent chap though) and one of my brethren is coming later, and I have a polite letter from Belgium with a signature that I can't read but concerning which I must consult the Belgian Embassy. I may say with Betsy Prig — leisure, I don't believe there's no sich a person. Even when I am ready to be idle I say to myself what duty am I neglecting? I turn to your last letter. I think I met your brother in former days but I knew only his name. You speak for the need of a certain modicum of intelligence for justice. It seems to me that the whole scheme of salvation depends on having a required modicum of intelligence. People are born fools and damned for not being wiser. I often say over to myself the verse "O God, be merciful to me a fool," the fallacy of which to my mind (you won't agree with me) is in the "me," that it looks on man as a little God over against the universe, instead of as a cosmic ganglion, a momentary intersection of what humanly speaking we call streams of energy, such as gives white light at one point and the power of making syllogisms at another, but always an inseverable part of the unimaginable, in which we live and move and have our being, no more needing its mercy than my little toe needs mine. It would be well if the intelligent classes could forget the word sin and think less of being good. We learn how to behave as lawyers, soldiers, merchants, or what not by being them. Life, not the parson, teaches conduct. But I seem to be drooling moralities and will shut up and go up to the Belgian Embassy as I said. My love to Lady Pollock.

Yours ever,
O. W. H.

BURFORD BRIDGE HOTEL
BOXHILL, SURREY
April 11, 1926

My dear Holmes:

Go to, who told you I was disposed to think of man as a little god over against the universe? That is the damnable heresy of dualism which I do *ex animo* renounce, repudiate, reject, explode, exsibilate and consign to thirty thousand cart-loads of doubting and self-tormenting devils. It is the old serpent with infinite heads, the cradle of illusions, the weaver of a sevenfold veil of darkness, the builder of Doubting Castle, the begetter of the pedants and formalists let loose from their proper hell (which is *in podice Sathanae*) to torment tender consciences, the framer of the old law which (as holy Paul saith) is the strength of sin, in brief the enemy of light in this our secular warfare. Great prophets have in all times lifted up their voices mightily against it; in the East from Lao-Tze and the Buddha to the Súfi poets and Kabir (who said "I laugh at the fish in the water who says he is thirsty") and at this day Rabindranath Tagore; in the West from Plato through the Neo-Platonists (linking the East and the West in ways not yet fully explored) to Eckhart and Jacob Böhme and William Blake: they have spoken in divers tongues and many tones, often darkly, and yet their witness agrees. Ten years ago I tried a very liberal parson with Blake's *Marriage of Heaven and Hell*: it was too strong meat for him: the devils are not dead yet, and your wish that people would leave off prating about sin is not like to be fulfilled in our time.

Yes, Horace Walpole is the senior English letter-writer if one must make a senior. Lamb is unique — but are his letters really letters? one may doubt. Byron is good, rather in flashes I think. I am not sure that Johnson is not the right second to Walpole. FitzGerald is delightful but somehow stands in a world of his own. And did I tell you to get hold of Walter Raleigh's letters? I won't say a word about them till you have seen them.

The Selden Society is embarking on a new diversion, editing as an extra volume a ms. (acquired by Lincoln's Inn, 1909) of Selden's *Table Talk* which was unknown to the only critical editor, no longer living, Reynolds (Oxford 1892, a thoroughly good piece of work). This Ms. gives improved readings and by certain signs looks nearer to the original than anything yet known and used.

The job falls to me as Literary Director, and, the *Table Talk* having been a cherished book of mine for half a century, I think I shall enjoy it. By the time you get this I hope a capable copyist will be started on writing out the ms. There will be little occasion for a commentary, Reynolds having done that very well, beyond critical notes on the text, and anything that occurs to me to say will go into the introduction. Meanwhile the Society's regular work will not be interfered with in any way. It seems to me the text may be made ready this summer. I may get my editorial matter done by the end of the long vacation, and the book — which will not be in the rather cumbrous form of our Year Book and other medieval texts — may come out in the autumn. For me it is amusing to have found something to do different from touching up old work and writing (mostly for love) reviews and occasional papers I am asked for: I have written . . . a notice of Ilbert for the British Academy.[1] . . .

Mackail's *Classical Studies* (Murray) is a book I recommend, especially to you who have lately read the *Odyssey*. He discusses Penelope very prettily. . . .

Yours ever,
F. P.

WASHINGTON, April 30, 1926

My dear Pollock:

You give me pleasure by your repudiation of the belief that man is a little God over against the Universe even while I misgive that it lives to the extent of thinking him an independent centre. But this is not to be a letter. I am too hard driven for a week longer at least, to write at length, so I send two photographs of the phase of our spring that has just passed — the Japanese single flowering cherry trees, framing the Lincoln and Washington Monuments. The double flowering ones are now just at their height and are even more splendid. And near the Lincoln monument there was an alleyway of magnolias, known to comparatively few, I think, that I wish you could have seen. I look forward to your edition of Selden's *Table Talk*

[1] Pollock's memoir of Sir Courtney Peregrine Ilbert (1841–1924) was published in 11 *Proceedings of the British Academy* 441 (1924–25).

and shall expect to receive from the British Academy[1] your notice of Ilbert of whom I am curious to know more than I do. At rare odd half hours I read Murray's *History of Political Science from Plato to the Present* with high satisfaction. In spite of a (very) faint flavor of the parson, I find it most readable and instructive, in spite also of all that one had read before and its brevity, 400 pp., 8 vo. But until I take off my harness I shall do little to keep civilized. Yesterday P.M. I had a call from Cardozo, (N. Y. Court of Appeals) who has a beautiful face I thought, and Learned Hand (U. S. C. C. A. if you know what that means). I should like to see both of them on our bench. My love to Lady Pollock.

Yours ever,
O. W. H.

I must add a word about Borglum the sculptor, recently dispossessed from working out his mighty design for a memorial to the Southern leaders and soldiers on the face of a mountain. He said to me that when he began he felt like a fly on an elephant — at the end he felt as if the mountain were a handful of clay in his hand.

LONDON, April [May?] 16, 1926

My dear Holmes:

Many thanks for the photographs of Japanese cherry blossom. We do what we can here with horse chestnut and white and red may blossoms.

Who talked of man being an independent centre? one of William James's young men? I don't remember any such phrase in his own books. For what I think of it — apart from any possible excusing context — see the enclosed slip.

We are through our nine days' attempted general strike, and if the result is to discredit the extremist trade union bosses for another generation it may be worth the price. Baldwin comes out well, Simon has improved his position beyond expectation;[1]

[1] Holmes had been a Corresponding Member of the British Academy since 1907.

[1] Stanley Baldwin was Prime Minister at the time of the General Strike. On May 6 and 11 Sir John Simon in the House of Commons made important speeches condemning

as for the so-called leaders of the Labour party doubtless God could have made a more contemptible worm than Ramsay MacDonald, but doubtless he never did.

The Seamen & Firemen's Union stood out valiantly under Havelock Wilson, who used to be thought a revolutionary, and got an injunction against the strike bosses or some of them against interfering with its branches.[2] I *may* be able to get the judgment into the June issue of the *Law Reports* — will send you a spare proof anyhow when it is in shape. . . .

Yours ever,
F. P.

[*Enclosure*]

Learner. Some of my companions tell me I can do as I please. Others the contrary. Which shall I believe?

Master. Not that you can do as you *darn* please. Yet a man may do as he pleases if he will make God's pleasure his own; or (you may say to those who have a superstitious objection to that venerable symbolic name) if he will fit himself into the universal order. Freedom comes only by service.

L. Methinks that is no easy way.

M. It is not easy; therefore fools run after the short cut of self-will, not regarding the commandment of our teachers.

L. Which commandment, Sir?

M. Thou shalt cut off the head of Self.

L. May their folly be called doing the Devil's pleasure?

M. Yes, for there is no other Devil.

L. Then there is one who says he is an independent centre.

M. You may e'en tell him to go and make himself independent of his own guts, and come back with or without them to continue the argument.

London, June 12, 1926[1]

My dear Holmes:

Ramsay MacDonald is rational in the sense of being neither a fool nor as ignorant as Lloyd George, but he is a feeble and futile opportunist — no principle beyond watching the jumping cat, and then often wrong, as in the war, when he was a flabby

---

the General Strike as illegal. His argument was reiterated in a speech at Cleckheaton a week later. See his *Three Speeches on the General Strike* (1926).

[2] National Sailors' and Firemen's Union v. Reed, [1926] 1 Ch. 536.

---

[1] The letter from Holmes, to which this is apparently responsive, is missing.

pacifist; as a leader hopelessly incapable of either leading his party or keeping the extreme wing in any sort of order, as appeared during the strike. So much for him.

Of O.'s book [2] I know nothing.

In Geo. Fox's diary (extracted in Q's admirable *Oxford Book of English Prose* [3]) is a dream of two voices — one supposed diabolical; All things come by nature; There is a living God who made all things, answered a supposed heavenly one. Pity there was not a wiser angel to tell him both were true.

Surely the Civil War is not forgotten by historians at any rate. One Sandburg has just produced a new life of Lincoln said to be good. I wonder how much the generation of my granddaughter will know about the world war: anyhow they will have a new map of Europe to learn. (She was born in 1913.) . . .

In due time I will send you my note for the *L. Q. R.* (now in ms.) on a sort of leading case [4] — tho' the law was elementary — in which the officials of a branch union were restrained from calling a strike against the will of their superior executive and disregarding their own rules of procedure: unluckily it came before the one weak judge of our Chancery Division [5] and I had to edit his offhand judgment considerably to make a decent show of it for the *Law Reports* ("first" and "secondly" all of a tangle).

Our August holiday is to be a cruise in a liner up the Norway Coast, the best thing for people who can't walk, perhaps a little motor tour in our own country later.

Yours ever,
F. P.

P. S. Now I know about the *Forensic Fables*, having seen them at Lady Mathew's. The author is her son, my learned friend and fellow bencher Theobald Mathew: why "O." *non liquet.* We missed hearing of the book, I think because the press

[2] *Forensic Fables* by "O" (undated), reviewed by Pollock, 42 *L. Q. Rev.* 423 (1926).

[3] *The Oxford Book of English Prose* (1925) was edited by Sir Arthur Quiller-Couch.

[4] See note on National Sailors' and Firemen's Union v. Reed, [1926] 1 Ch. 536, in 42 *L. Q. Rev.* 289 (1926).

[5] Sir John Meir Astbury (1860–1939), Judge of the High Court of Justice, Chancery Division, 1913–29.

notices came out just when we went to Paris. It is that rare thing a really good book of professional jokes; the cuts I think, on a hasty view, even funnier than the text. I expect to meet the author, both of us being on duty to dine at Lincoln's Inn to-night, and will tell him you appreciate it.

Yours,
F. P.

BEVERLY FARMS, June 27, 1926

My dear Pollock:

Your letter and postscript were welcome as usual. I am glad to know your view of Ramsay MacDonald and to hear about the author of the *Forensic Fables*. Also I note for future acquisition the *Oxford Book of English Prose*. I have just ordered down here the *Home Book of Verse* published here by Henry Holt & Co. and I rather think American, which I believe *ex relatione* and from partial inspection, to be the best, *i.e.* most complete collection, in one rather too fat volume. Everything just now conduces to a serenity not very natural to my temperament. I have made my annual tax and probate returns, have made a valuation of my property, and have had my last term's decisions bound and have indexed them, so that no duties are imminent. I have read some stories and a good book by a Harvard professor on the Recent Industrial Revolution in the U. S.[1] He says the revolution is that Labor is becoming Capitalist — witness increased deposits, purchases of stock, labor banks — and despises as I do the talk about a class war. Now, impelled by Laski, I am reading, slowly and at odd minutes, Declareuil, *Histoire Générale du Droit Française, Des Origines à 1789*. I should gather, a good Catholic and certainly keen to negate German claims to the sources of law. When I used to read Sohm I ventured to have considerable reserves, and it makes me chuckle to see Declareuil pronounce the notion that the Salic law established a general ascendancy to be pure imagination. Certainly I thought Sohm's glorification of it as a

[1] T. N. Carver, *Present Economic Revolution in the United States* (1925).

rival to the Roman was all my eye. His vogue led me to realize that there was fashion in ideas as well as in bonnets. Meantime I drive about as usual; the automobile brings me within reach of the whole of Cape Ann. Yesterday I had two calls, unusual here, one in the P.M. from Sir Esme Howard [2] whom we have known from the time when he was an attaché, and whom I always find very pleasant, the other from two little boys 10 & 13 who seemingly just came in to see the old man and whom I found delightful. Have you noticed that the baroque has begun to look up? Spengler, *Untergang des Abendlandes* over whom I sweated last summer, if I remember rightly, cracked up M. Angelo for it, treating it as a step in the giving way of sculpture to painting as human experience, *en route* for music which ends, and with it the west, in Parsifal! . . . You see that I am revolving no mighty thoughts, but am having a good time. It has been rather cold and the season is backward, *per quod*, we have seen things that usually we are too late for. The lilacs were still going when we arrived, our roses are mainly still in bud. My love to Lady Pollock.

Yours ever,
O. W. H.

LONDON, July 12, 1926

My dear Holmes:

. . . The Selden Society has discovered by luck, in the remoter parts of Lancashire, a 15th–16th century ms. of Year Books of H. VI and Ed. IV — mss. of that date being apparently very few. This one is now deposited at the Record Office: I rather hope the Society of Lincoln's Inn may be moved to acquire it, having been the property of a Serjeant who was a Reader of the Inn — possibly written in part by his own hand, If *Manu* followed by name or initials (so the book is inscribed, Bolland [1] tells me) doesn't mean "written by the hand of" I am d — d if I know what it does mean, as John Williams, J.,

[2] Lord Howard of Penrith, British Ambassador to the United States, 1924–1930.

[1] William Craddock Bolland, editor of the Selden Society's edition of the Year Books, 1909–27.

said. By the way I think Spengler must be of the class defined by that learned judge as damned (in contradistinction to natural) fools. . . .

It never occurred to me to think of the Salic Law as more than a typical frankish custumal which for some reason came to be regarded as a model of its kind (an odd kind at that). My impression is (or was, for it is long since I have looked at the texts) that Lombard custumals have more affinity with our Anglo-Saxon documents. If I ever read Sohm on the matter I have clean forgotten what he says. Now a learned Frenchman appears (*ex relat.*) to maintain that the Germanic seisin or *gewere* is a real *dominium* [a] — quite contrary to what I have always collected from English sources, *viz.* that our ancestors simply couldn't understand owning anything one does not actually possess ("Give me the handle of the church door," says the grantee or an advowson), and I seem to remember that *possidere* and *potestas* are conspicuous in Continental documents. Some learned Germans, however, did, I suppose, persuade themselves that there was a Germanic virtue in being too thick-headed (if their ancestors really were) to learn any Roman law. Fustel de Coulanges *contra* was much more readable but not more reasonable.

Our Selden *Table Talk* Ms. is interesting: the editing proves more niggling work than I expected by reason of many small variations which must be noticed though they don't really matter. But it is a job I am well pleased to have. . . .

Yours ever,
F. P.

BEVERLY FARMS, July 28, 1926

My dear Pollock:

A good one from you came two or three days ago. I didn't answer at the drop of the hat as I usually do, because I was hasting to be through with Declareuil's 1061 pages on the *His-*

[a] Presumably Joüon des Longrais, *La Conception Anglaise de la saisine du xiie au xive siècle* (1925).

toire Générale du droit Française, 70 to 100 pp. on the development of French law, and the bearing of Roman law, Frankish law, etc., extremely good. The rest, details that I no longer care to study; and altogether it was a chore. I don't remember any remarks of his as to *Gewere* (that you mention), but in general if a learned German has maintained a proposition it is pretty safe to contradict it, with a very smug and unpolemical air. Also the clerk of our court sent me 20 applications for *certiorari* (to let me consider them at leisure and avoid the rush at the beginning of the term). My man is just this minute doing them up for return, so I now am free and looking for trouble, or novels, or some volumes of Everyman's Library. . . . I don't think that Spengler properly can be described as a d — d fool except in the undiscriminating sense that one doesn't believe his conclusions. He is very ingenious and I think one might say original, only most of his postulates, processes and results, left me unmoved, but stimulated by suggestions which enrich even if untrue. Oh how blessed it is to have nothing on hand more serious than a letter. I reread Pepys's *Diary* (unfortunately expurgated in a cheap edition in the house). What a disgust it gives one for Charles II. If you have it and don't remember the passage, let me recommend to you the page of a long entry July 29, 1667 telling of the duel between Sir H. Bellasis and Tom Porter, and a few words August 7 or 8 — a striking, tragic little tale. I spoke of Everyman's. I just now have got two volumes of Dryden's *Dramatic Essays*, as they are called, and Dorothy Osborne's *Letters to Sir Wm. Temple*, which Macaulay long ago made me want to read. I don't remember ever to have read any of Dryden's prose and one has heard so much about it that it is time one did. I am not sure that it is not even necessary for the Day of Judgment, although I thought my preparation for that was finished. . . .

Yours ever,
O. W. H.

LONDON, July 29, 1926

My dear Holmes:

Recent distinguished visitors to London: President Lowell, whom *Gentlemen Prefer Blondes* did not amuse; Ruth Draper, whom it did.

But Mr. Hooley's [*sic*] deprecation of Col. House's excessive modesty[1] (sent me by the Selden Society's correspondent in Boston,[2] so you see there may be little perquisites in being a Literary Director) did amuse the President of Harvard.

The ms. of Selden's *Table Talk* I am collating is written with a spelling one would call Elizabethan at first sight tho' in fact hardly earlier than 1685. Printers had already adopted a practically modern spelling, see *e. g.* Hobbes' *Leviathan. Inde quaere.*

Boy waits for letter.

Yours,
F. P.

BEVERLY FARMS, August 9, 1926

My dear Pollock:

Good man to realize that one may as well send a note across the Atlantic as to the next door. The same man who sent you Dooley on House read it to me. I have not read House but this was enough. And the book that has made me laugh, and which I don't send only because I fear it would be too local to hit you, is *Nize Baby*, the goings on and talk on the different floors of a New York apartment house. A book I am reading with pleasure Höffding, *History of Modern Philosophy*. Is your *quaere* about Selden whether to keep the spelling of the ms.? I believe in exact transcripts. As I have told you the only edition of Shakespeare seems to me that which reproduces the folio first and notes the variations. All goes well here.

My love to Lady Pollock.

Yours ever,
O. W. H.

[1] Finley Peter Dunne, "Mr. Dooley Reviews a Book," *Liberty*, May 8, 1926. The volumes reviewed were *The Intimate Papers of Colonel House* (2 vols., 1926).

[2] Richard W. Hale.

WASHINGTON, October 1, 1926

My dear Pollock:

. . . We arrived here yesterday and of course I am up to my ears in things to do, but on the whole have got the upper hand of the giant. I have seen nobody except my brother Stone who called this afternoon, and Hough of the New York C.C.A. whom I was very glad to see. He says spicy things in his opinions, and has also chaffed me in the public prints . . . and has made criticisms that I think I easily could smash, but he has said kind things also. He has seemed to have me on his mind. We jabbered away like old acquaintances in two minutes.

No more reading I fear for the present. In the vacation and since getting here I have examined fifty applications for *certiorari* and there is a huge pile of others waiting to be considered. I am in good shape as to health and spirits. But although I might make one small philosophic reflection, the residuum after reading Höffding's *History of Modern Philosophy*, it is not the moment for expatiation.

My love to Lady Pollock.

Yours ever,
O. W. H.

I always chuckle to remember one thing that probably you have forgotten.

When Sir A. Lyall was at your dinner and after some talk of Jowett said there were no *personages* now — and the grey-beards wagged — I said, "Possibly you gentlemen don't remember that you have grown a little older. If you should ask the young men they might perhaps find some without leaving this table," — which I think was true.

OCTOBER 18, 1926

My dear Holmes:

This is but a scrap. We are settled down after a rather idle end of our Indian Summer in Surrey, and I go on nibbling at the Selden ms.

If the vexed *renvoi* question in Conflict of Laws interests you, look at a note at the beginning of the October *Law Quarterly* on a recent case[1] of Russell, J's. The sting is in an extra-judicial tail which he would not have mentioned in the head-note.

Exit Asquith from his command of what was our Liberal party:[2] an accomplished scholar, eloquent advocate, and straight politician and excellent House of Commons man — and peradventure a statesman if only he had not wholly lacked imagination and initiative.

Don't remember that saying of A. Lyall. Anyhow he was himself a personage.

Yours ever,
F. P.

WASHINGTON, October 31, 1926

My dear Pollock:

The swain responsive sends line for line. We adjourn for three weeks on Monday and I heave a sigh of relief, for I have been hard at work for the month. About 200 applications for *certiorari* (when the case does not come up as of right) besides sitting in court and writing three opinions. The last is hung up for a dissent that may put me in a minority.[1] It is a question of the time for computing the value of the mark in a suit here to apply property in the hands of the Alien Property Custodian to the debt of a German bank to an American depositor there. I have paid little attention to the decisions in other jurisdictions but have gone on what seems to me unanswerable reasoning, but the dissentients twit me with my remark in my *Common Law* that the life of the law has not been logic but experience and I suppose will quote cases English and others as

[1] *In re* Annesley, [1926] 1 Ch. 692; noted by Pollock in 42 *L. Q. Rev.* 435 (1926).

[2] In October Lord Oxford and Asquith, largely for reasons of health, was compelled to resign the leadership of the Liberal Party.

[1] Deutsche Bank Filiale Nurnberg v. Humphrey, 272 U. S. 517 (submitted Oct. 12, '26; decided Nov. 23, '26); majority opinion by Holmes; Sutherland, McReynolds, Butler, and Sanford, JJ., dissenting.

leading to a different conclusion. I don't go into it now as it is *sub judice*, but I am much interested. No case that I have seen seems to me to go to the bottom of the question. I shall try to look at the note you mention on Monday.

It is a rainy day and so dark that I hardly can see the letters as I write them, which is somewhat depressing coming on top of a departing cold, but I am cheerful in the consciousness of a prospect of some leisure, of one or two matters of business satisfactorily ended — my most feared tax bill paid, and my court work done up to date. I have one case just assigned to me that I think will be a short and easy matter; so I expect soon to turn to Graham Wallas: *Art of Thought* which lies on my table, sent to me by a friend the other day.

In a few days Brandeis who is next to me in age among the judges will be seventy. That is one lifetime and makes a complete package, with a chance if you are lucky to begin a new one. I think he has done great work and I believe with high motives. To me it is queer to see the wide-spread prejudice against the Jews. I never think of the nationality and might even get thick with a man before noticing that he was a Hebrew. You know the poem: "How odd — Of God — To choose — The Jews."

I also have on my table, as yet unopened, a typewritten chapter of Beveridge's *Life of Lincoln*;[2] he likes to have me among others read and criticise what he writes. He has taken enormous trouble and I think is likely to do the job definitively. He writes with accuracy of detail and with the power to tell a story, although his writing of English leaves something to be desired. Other news have I none. My love to Lady Pollock.

Yours ever,
O. W. H.

LONDON, November 15, 1926

My dear Holmes:

We are glad to have a good account of you. The question of the date for fixing the conversion of a sum due in foreign

[2] Two volumes, published posthumously in 1928.

currency has been giving some trouble in our Courts of late, but I don't give references because

1. they would be too late to be of use to you
2. presumably the cases have been cited already
3. I don't know that they would really be in point.

The best reason I know for Jews being unpopular is the answer given by a Tavistock man to the question why all the rest of Devon made a laughing-stock of Tavistock: "They'm jealous."

Then there is the general feeling of suspicion against people who hang together with peculiar customs of their own and don't marry outside — with the special religious aversion at the back of it but not extinct. (Whereas by the paramount custom of Asia every group of men is entitled to its own customs so long as they are not actively offensive to others — exceptions of fanatical despots like Aurangzib excepted.)

Enclosed a rather good sample of the improvements I find in our ms. of Selden's *Table Talk*. . . .

Yours ever,
F. P.

[*Enclosure*]

A specimen of the improved readings in the Lincoln Inn ms. of Selden's Table Talk: —

Title: *Measure of Things*

"We measure from ourselves. . . . Bring a pear to the table that is rotten, we cry it down, 'tis naught; but bring a medlar that is rotten, and 'tis a fine thing."

So all other copies. But our ms. reads: "bring a medlar, O! 'tis a fine thing."

Plainly the vulgate is the gloss of a dull copyist who thought the true text too abrupt, or did not know that a medlar brought to table is always rotten.

London, December 13, 1926

My dear Holmes:

Thanks for the judgments in *Deutsche Bank, etc.* v. *Humphrey*.[1] I agree with yours: There could be no question of any

[1] See *supra*, pp. 190–91. If Holmes wrote to Pollock when he sent him the opinions, the letter is missing.

sum payable in dollars until there was an effective demand made in your jurisdiction. The contrary view that the claim is to be treated as a claim in detinue for chattels, *viz*: German marks, appears to me fallacious tho' ingenious. *Quaere*, if German law allowed unliquidated damages to be recovered for the detention of a debt; it seems to be assumed that like ours it does not. In that case it might be said that the damages sued for could be calculated only in the currency of the jurisdiction.

Our Court of Appeal has a rather pretty question of personal capacity under foreign law.[2] *A*, of Guatemalan nation and domicil, assigns to *Z* by an instrument sufficient in English law, *A*'s current balance at a London bank. *Z* is a Guatemalan minor and by the law of G. (admitted to be his personal law) a minor cannot *accept* a gift without the consent of his guardian witnessed by a notary: which here is wanting.

Is this a matter of local form, of which the Court here takes no notice, or of personal incapacity whereby the gift has no effect anywhere? The Court of Appeal will hold the latter, so Lawrence, L. J., tells me, but all for different reasons. It seems to me the notary might be mere formality, but not to be able to do a thing without one's guardian is a matter of personal condition.

But I think the bank (which in fact has paid into Court) might well have acted on the transfer *as against the transferor*, and so does (privily) Lawrence, L. J. . . .

All good wishes for New Year.

Yours ever,
F. P.

London, February 28, 1927 [1]

My dear Holmes:

This is but a scrap, news being scant for the moment. We have had foul and dark weather, specially dark, for several days

[2] Republica de Guatemala v. Nuñez, [1927] 1 K. B. 669; noted by Pollock 43 *L. Q. Rev.* 296 (1927).

[1] A letter from Pollock, dated December 28, 1926, is omitted.

and have never had a really good sight of the once-in-a-blue-moon show of Flemish pictures at the Academy. After having the copy for the whole book in hand about a month, the printers have begun to send me proofs of the Selden Society edition of the *Table Talk* and produced a dummy specimen volume. It should make a sightly book (a smaller quarto than the Society's regular publications), with two pretty good *gimages*.[2]

Tomorrow the Bench of Lincoln's Inn will decide, I hope, to buy an unusually well written Year Book manuscript offered by the Quaritch Co. (There is no live Quaritch now; by the way, E. FitzGerald's Letters to Q. were hardly worth publishing.) As our Inn has a notable collection already, and in fact most of the Selden Society's work on the 14th century Year Books has been done in our library, or with photographs of our mss., clearly we ought to add this. But my fellow-Benchers want exhortation, for most of them have the vaguest notion (if any) what a Year Book is.

Reading of Whitehead's *Science and the Modern World* still awaits me, but I have bought his shorter book of lectures on religion,[3] which seems to me the straightest sincere attempt to get to the bottom of things I have seen for a long time — not easy reading, though short and not technical. His definition is wide enough to contain materialism as a religion though a bad one. When did people begin to chatter about a "personal" God? I know no ecclesiastical authority whatever for such an adjective (Person of the Trinity being of course quite different), nor literary before the 19th century.

A misguided judge of Annapolis wrote to me with an inquiry t'other day and sent a U. S. stamp under the mistaken but not uncommon belief that it would frank my answer — it may as well not be wasted, so it recrosses the ocean enclosed.

Yours ever,
F. P.

[2] Concerning the word "*gimages*," see 42 *L. Q. Rev.* 423 (1926).

[3] *Religion in the Making* (1926).

LONDON, March 17, 1927

My dear Holmes:

. . . We have lost my cousin Dighton,[1] most loved if not most learned among all his fellows at the Chancery Bar. You and I pay for long life by having to say more and more with Victor Hugo's sea rover:

En partant du golfe d'Otrante
Nous étions trente,
Mais en revenant à Cadiz
Nous étions dix . . .

Now I am tackling Whitehead's *Science & the Modern World* — a great book I think, though not bulky, which will need much dilution and comment before the world assimilates it. I like his thesis that the Middle Ages were dominated by reason and the eighteenth century by faith. The medieval doctors did not reason amiss — being amply guarded by cumbrous but accurate logic — but reverence for classical antiquity prevented them from criticizing their premisses: whereas the 18th-19th century scientists committed themselves to a gigantic act of faith in the mechanical uniformity of nature. And now we are in a rationalist revolution: the results will I suppose be somehow cast in an elementary form for our grandchildren. . . .

We get lurid reports . . . about the demoralizing effects of Prohibition in the Middle Western States. New England, I trust, has less of that trouble. Bolshevism is not the only alarming product of half-educated sentimentalism.

Yours ever,
F. P.

WASHINGTON, March 27, 1927

My dear Pollock:

It is a month within one day from the date of your last letter (enclosing a stamp that shall be used to forward this).

[1] Dighton Nicholas Pollock (1864–March 8, 1927).

I may have written in the interval[1] as we don't confine ourselves to an accurate reciprocity, but I have been having a busy time. The work has been hard and my birthday required a good deal of extra activity. The papers all made more talk than I expected on an anniversary not a multiple of 5.[2] As I wrote to the President in answer to a polite letter from him, an old fellow excites something of the interest that my father expressed after the visit of a well known traveler, you think of the chances that the next time he will be eaten by savages. This reminds me to say a word about a notice of me you spoke of reading, by Miss Sergeant.[3] You remarked on the gravy being laid on rather thick. I hope you understood that I was in no way responsible for that, as I was not responsible for one of the stories at least that she had picked up, I suppose from some friend. Such things however kindly meant make one squirm a little and if anyone asks an interview that I suspect to have that end in view I decline it. Miss Sergeant now has published a book in which I appear in rather queer company.[4] I suggested to her that some of her stories blunted the edge a little and could be made more exact by some slight changes, which she made, although they still perhaps are a little flatter than they need be. These corrections for the book are my only conscious share. I think I once sent you a book about my uncle John Holmes in which the flattening process was marked.

Now a blissful moment has come when the work is done and we don't sit for two weeks. I dare say I may get a case to write in the last week and there is some little business that I want to attend to, but I am as near to leisure as I ever get in term time and hope to read a book or two and certainly to get some drives. The cherry blossoms have been out, around the Poto-

[1] No letter from Holmes in this interval has been found.

[2] Holmes was eighty-six on March 8, 1927.

[3] Elizabeth Shepley Sergeant, "Oliver Wendell Holmes," 49 *New Republic* 59 (Dec. 8, 1926). Pollock in his letter of December 28, 1926, which is omitted, had written that he had read in the *New Republic* "a panegyric on O. W. H. — quite nicely and intelligently done, but in your place I might be disposed to say with the classical Carpenter: The butter's spread too thick. However, as another person in the same epic observes elsewhere, it was the best butter."

[4] *Fire under the Andes* (1927). The other studies in the volume were of Amy Lowell, Robert Edmond Jones, William Alanson White, William Allen White, Eugene O'Neill, Elinor Wylie, Charles Townsend Copeland, Pauline Lord, Paul Robeson, Alice Hamilton, H. L. Mencken, Willa Cather, and Robert Frost.

mac basin — a wonderful sight, worth a long journey to see — and magnolias almost as wonderful. I trembled lest a frost should spoil them coming so prematurely and I still tremble for the fruit tree blossoms. I believe it is or just has been snowing in New York, but bad spells often seem to go round us and to leave us untouched.

I had a call yesterday P. M. from Graham Wallas who is teaching, next door, for a space. He seems a very pleasant as well as gifted man, but I have to pay for talking just now by fits of coughing at night and therefore don't seek it more than is inevitable. My wife is reading *Pickwick* to me, omitting the stories — and I find it mighty pleasant, but the atmosphere has changed so much that the young I believe don't read it, or indeed Dickens, much. It is a pity as there has been no such genius since, writing English at least.

Yesterday I received a leaflet written by the treasurer of the American Federation of Labor in favor of a five day week that contained a sentence that gave me real pleasure: "Labor and Capital are now talking the same language — that of the informed economist." A remark like that seems to indicate a great advance from the rhetorical period.

I will stop my rambling. Please give my love to the Lady. I await the advent of John Selden. I infer that you have found it interesting to edit.

Yours ever,
O. W. H.

I read Whitehead's *Science and the Modern World* some time ago, but got only a very blurry impression if any. It needed more study than I could give it at the time. . . .

LONDON, April 11, 1927

My dear Holmes:

Your last epistle was almost on the heels of the last but one. Thanks from both of us. I agree that Bryce was in some danger of lacking *crust*: the Alpine Club saved him. His addresses to the Club, of which specimens were given in my article on him in *Quarterly Review*, 1922, were perhaps the most alive of his writings. Moreover he was wholly free from pedantry. If he had not been so when he was presiding in the Schools at Oxford as Regius Professor, there would have been a pretty kettle of fish when on a certain occasion a too hasty colleague began tearing up papers not yet looked over. Holland [1] and I gathered up the fragments, reconstructed the contents conjecturally and gave them the most favourable construction in case of doubt, and Bryce, who was at the moment in London, approved, and nobody else heard of it. . . .

Selden's *Table Talk*, with Edward Fry's biography, is all in print now and awaits only the index, which I am finishing. (No hack work index-makers for me.) It has been very interesting job — partly because none of my predecessors have been really critical. They never realized how bad the vulgate text was nor tried to make out how it was corrupted. . . .

If you want to read a man free from *crumb* (too much for this world) get hold of Lawrence, *The Revolt in the Desert* (there ought to be a better map with it). As to *crumby* men, Asquith is perhaps our chief: never had an idea of his own, or decided anything. Scholarship is his saving virtue, if any. R. Macdonald is visiting your shores. I wish you joy o' the worm (but apologize to the worm, for I never heard that the common earthworm goes in fear of his own tail).

Yours ever,
F. P.

London, May 11, 1927

My dear Holmes:

Since I last wrote the learned Victor Morawetz has sent me his essay on the elements of a Contract; it is not a treatise on substantive law, but a memorandum prepared for the American Law Institute (whatever that is) with a view to a "scientific restatement" intended to "clarify the law."

So far as I can see on a cursory view (life being too short for more) he is a sound lawyer enough but a poor draftsman. It is odd how learned persons fail to see that new terms and defini-

[1] Sir Thomas Erskine Holland (1835–1926); Professor of International Law and Diplomacy at Oxford, 1874–1910.

tions are apt to mean new doubts and litigation. Now my old friend Mackenzie Chalmers (Bills of Exchange, Sale of Goods) and I (Partnership) have drafted codifying Acts without inventing a single new term, and they have worked for a full generation with a minimum of friction. It is true that, when the law is pretty well settled, adventurous definitions do less harm than might be expected (Indian Contract Act — and the N. Y. draft Civil Code in your Western jurisdictions which foolishly adopted it). All which adds to the *aduncity* of our lady the Common Law's nose.

Yours ever,
F. P.

LONDON, May 19, 1927

My dear Holmes:

. . . *Re Wait* [1927] 1 Ch. 606,[1] forthcoming in June, the Master of the Rolls[2] and Atkin, L. J. — Sargant, L. J. rightly, as I think, dissenting — hold that a sale of 500 tons out of an ascertained cargo of 1,000 tons (by the buyer of the whole cargo, which is at sea) confers only a claim sounding in damage, and, the vendor being bankrupt when the cargo arrives, the buyer of the 500 tons (who has paid for them) has no remedy *but* to prove in the bankruptcy. This seems to me — as to Sargant — to upset the whole doctrine of equitable assignment. Such questions don't often come your way, I suppose. The old notion that equity is a roguish thing and not to be encouraged appears to die hard.

Yours ever,
F. P.

WASHINGTON, May 30, 1927

My dear Pollock:

. . . With regard to the case *Re Wait* I am reminded of an article on Grain Elevators that I wrote in the form of a note to a case, in 6 *Am. Law Rev.* 450, April 1872, in which I believe I

[1] Noted by Pollock, 43 *L. Q. Rev.* 293 (1927).
[2] Sir Ernest Murray Pollock, 1st Viscount Hanworth, 1861–1936.

developed the desirableness of recognizing the property interest in purchasers *ex* a mass. 55 years ago is a good while. Of course I don't know the details of this transaction. My prejudices are with you.

Morawetz has had a great practical success in life, but I do not see on a casual examination that he had justified his return to theory. You always have regarded my notion of contract as a pardonable eccentricity (that when you commit a tort you incur a liability to damages *simpliciter*. When you commit a contract you incur a liability to damages *nisi*, illustrated by the fact that in most contracts if not in all you have only a limited, and it may be no, power over the event). It is a particular case of my general definition of a right as the hypostasis of a prophecy — like gravitation. I should be glad if we could get rid of the whole moral phraseology which I think has tended to distort the law. In fact even in the domain of morals I think that it would be a gain, at least for the educated, to get rid of the word and notion Sin. But on these themes I fear we are not at one. I have seen Graham Wallas several times and have found him a very pleasant man and yesterday p.m. I had a long call from our philosopher Morris Cohen, a man of great learning and great gifts, and since I wrote the last word today I have been out at Arlington (Memorial Day) with some, not quite all the old emotion. And since my return Wallas has been in to say good bye — so that's that. . . .

I think I have had quite an interesting lot of cases this term, and have felt rather pleased with the output. One is always on the alert for signs of weakening. How I should like to have a month in London! My love to Lady Pollock.

Yours ever,
O. W. H.

London, June 13, 1927

My dear Holmes:

Yesterday morning (Sunday) I found your letter half buried in a heap of (very) second-class matter on our return from spending a week in Paris with great content. . . .

If you mean by the notion of Sin the habit of condemning actions not because they tend to destroy the actor's self-respect or cause unjustifiable harm to others, but because they are deemed to contravene a prohibition laid down by an external power (gods, or lawgivers claiming to be infallible) which will resent and punish disobedience, I quite agree that such a habit is irrelevant in law and mischievous in ethics (the juridical analogue is Hobbism, the denial that "just" and "unjust" mean anything but what the sovereign allows and forbids). But I don't think any competent schoolman would admit that *peccatum* or any vernacular equivalent really involves this. Anyhow, it is orthodox doctrine that if your conscience is wrongly informed, so that you think it right to do that which is in fact (or "materially") wrong, it is a less sin to follow an erroneous conscience than to do the materially right thing believing it to be wrong.

If the promise in a contract were held to be in the alternative — perform *or* pay damages — then (1) there could be no decrees for specific performance: (2) there would be no reason for allowing any implied exception of frustration or the like: (3) (and chiefly) it would not answer reasonable expectations of promisees. Those are my reasons: I don't see where moral phraseology comes in. No doubt it might be the law in some other planet.

Yours ever,
F. P.

LONDON, July 11, 1927

My dear Holmes:

This to assure you under my own hand that I am doing as well as possible, and now let out of bed into a chair.[1] The only moral I can see is that the guts of *homo sapiens* have never properly learnt biped habits. . . .

I wish some ingenious young fellow would work out, after the manner of non-Euclidean geometry, the consequences of

[1] In a letter of the same date John Pollock wrote to Holmes telling him that on the preceding Friday his father had undergone an operation for a strangulated hernia.

your contract theory if it had prevailed. I forget in what reported case somewhere about 1600 it was argued that equity should not meddle with the promisor's election to perform or pay damages.[2]

I have fallen back on Dumas *père* with interludes of modern scraps.

F. P.

DRUMMOND ARMS INN
ALBURY, SURREY
August 11, 1927[1]

My dear Holmes:

This morning I see you are dragged into the Sacco-Vanzetti tangle.[2] I should have thought there was no possible question of Federal jurisdiction, but the whole thing is bewildering. I knew that many States had made a most ungodly jumble of criminal procedure by piling an elaborate system of appeals on the top of unreformed common law technicality, but I assumed (without cause I fear) that it was better ordered in Massachusetts.

According to our practice the sentence would have been commuted long ago, pending consideration whether there was a case for pardon. Our Home Secretary consults as many discreet persons as he likes — but privately. Meanwhile I deeply sympathize. . . .

Time for our midday post to catch tonight's mail.

Yours ever,
F. P.

[2] Probably Bromage v. Genning, 1 Roll. Rep. 368, described by Holmes in his speech "The Path of the Law," 10 *Harv. L.Rev.* 457, 462 (1897); *C. L. P.* p. 167, at p. 175.

[1] All letters from Holmes which he may have written to Pollock during the summer months of 1927 are missing.

[2] On August 10, 1927, a petition for a writ of *habeas corpus* was presented to Holmes by Arthur D. Hill, counsel for Nicola Sacco and Bartolomeo Vanzetti who stood condemned to execution during the week of August 10. The petition was denied. Holmes's opinion denying the petition may be found in 5 *Record of the Sacco-Vanzetti Case* 5532 (1929).

THE DRUMMOND ARMS
ALBURY, SURREY
August 21, 1927

My dear Holmes:

You are I think the kind of reader B.d.S. desired.[1] He says expressly that it is not a wise man's part to want to found a school to be called after his name: and there is nothing to show that he regarded his own work as final or even finished. His letters show that to the last he was turning over and reconsidering the fundamentals in physics at any rate, and quite open to intelligent criticism. In the 17th century a philosopher was expected to make a system. In the 20th, so far as I have observed, it is the wiser fashion to expound one's thoughts in the form of critical studies. Still less does the recent and quite active study of Spinoza (some very good stuff produced here) start from any notion of agreeing with him at all points. As for necessity, B.d.S. is quite clear that when you look on the universe as a whole there is no other necessity than the fact that it is what it is and not otherwise, and does hold together. . . .

Sterne[2] needs a larger dose than most great writers of the charity pointed out in a pretty figure by some Lines of Callimachus — the great river must needs carry down rubbish. I forget the context, but I think Callimachus is consoling himself and other minor poets with the reflection that their work, though lesser than the Great masters, may be less faulty. On a re-reading of *Tristram Shandy* or the *Sentimental Journey* it is easy to discount the dross. By the way do you know that the curse of Ernulphus is quite genuine? Sterne lifted it from the *Textus Roffensis*, then lately published: it is a late 10th or early 11th century formula — *quaere* whether meant for practical use.

But — of things medieval — there is a perfectly charming book by one Helen Waddell, *The Wandering Scholars*. . . . Saintsbury, to whom she makes acknowledgment for assistance, is rhapsodical about her: . . . She is a Pantagruelist as

[1] In Holmes's Journal it appears that in the summer of 1927 he read Spinoza's *Ethics* in the Everyman's Edition.

[2] Holmes's Journal shows that he had recently read *A Sentimental Journey* and *Tristram Shandy*.

well as an excellent scholar, has worked in Paris, and is not above mentioning Gilbert & Sullivan. . . .

Yours ever,
F. P.

AUGUST 29, 1927

My dear Holmes:

President Lowell has sent me the report of the committee of which he was a member in the Sacco & Vanzetti case,[1] from which I collect that the grounds of appeal must have been not only weak but mostly frivolous. Monstrous that you should have to listen to a perfectly idle argument for more than the whole time allowed in the Court itself (you set a two hours' limit if I remember right).[2] But I still think a commutation of the sentence at an early stage would have been the thing most unpleasant to the Moscow gang who I suppose were the real paymasters of the defence, and therefore the more politic course. As it is, S. and V. will go into the Communist *Acta Sanctorum* against all the evidence. I am just through with the proof of a thin volume of collected diversions [3] which some of my friends, and I hope you in part at least, will like, and suspect very few people will buy.

Yours ever,
F. P.

[1] The Report of the Governor's Advisory Committee, made up of Robert Grant, A. Lawrence Lowell, and S. W. Stratton, dated July 27, 1927, was made public by Governor Fuller on August 7. It is reprinted in 5 *Record of the Sacco-Vanzetti Case* 5378 i (1929).

[2] On August 20, 1927, counsel for Sacco and Vanzetti presented and argued to Holmes petitions praying for an extension of time for applying to the Supreme Court of the United States for writs of *certiorari* and for a stay of proceedings pending the applications. Holmes denied the petitions. His opinion is printed in 5 *Record of the Sacco-Vanzetti Case* 5516 (1929).

[3] *Outside the Law* (1927).

BEVERLY FARMS, September 18, 1927[1]
Antietam was 65 years
ago yesterday.

My dear Pollock:

A week from tomorrow, or Monday the 26th, we expect to leave here for Boston and to go on to Washington on the night of the 28th, Wednesday, arriving Thursday morning. I shall go with riches in my pocket for I have done well over a hundred applications for *certiorari* which are the great burden at the beginning of our term. Everything smiles, so far. What with the *certioraris* and the Sacco & Vanzetti business it has not been entire leisure, but enough so to enable me to get constant pleasure and to read without too much anxiety for improvement. My last book, Ludwig, *Wilhelm Hohenzollern*, kept me acutely interested all through, which is rare for me. I generally read more or less by the sweat of my brow. Walter Lippmann's *Men of Destiny* did the same for me, as he is a born writer. His criticisms of Sinclair Lewis & Mencken I thought A-1. Perhaps you don't know those names — they are more than well known here.

So leisure comes to an end and I shall miss it sadly, but I shall enjoy the work in a different way. It is very pleasant with the present Chief. . . .

My love to Lady Pollock.

Yours ever,
O. W. H.

LONDON, October 27, 1927

My dear Holmes:

. . . Did I tell you I came home from Rye with the seeds of a violent cold which broke out about three days later? I believe I know where I got them — evening Church at Rye our last Sunday, the reputation of a formerly celebrated preacher tempting us: the preacher had preserved a good delivery but had nothing to say: there were four mortal hymns one

[1] A postal card from Pollock, dated September 15, 1927, is omitted.

flatter than the other, congregation shouting, what is called *hearty* singing — doubtless filling the air with millions of germs, many noxious — and for a final damper we stepped out into a shower of rain at the end. Nevertheless my wife did not catch cold.

Talking of parsons we have a most unedifying fortnight or so of clerical controversy[1] — most like you don't hear of it. Think of a professor of theology never having learnt that the Papist has a complete answer to any argument from the senses against transubstantiation. "You poor heretic, of course your senses perceive nothing — the *accidents* are the same as before, preserved by an auxiliary miracle."

The real objection (which nobody mentions) is that nobody knows what the scholastic *substance* is: it is a speculative figment, whether genuine Aristotle or not is more than I know.

My little book should be in your hands by this time and I hope you may like some of it. . . .

There was a gleam of Indian summer at the end of September — but fleeting — and the barometer is as capricious a jade as Fortune. . . .

Yours ever,
F. P.

LONDON, November 17, 1927[1]

My dear Holmes:

. . . Giving credit to the great mystics,[2] as I do since the 1890's, before which time I knew nothing of them, involves a

[1] Early in 1927 the Bishops of the Church of England had produced a new Prayer Book which was approved in February by the Church Assembly. It then became necessary to secure Parliamentary approval for the Prayer Book. The principal issues concerned changes in the Holy Communion and the Reservation of the Sacrament, the alterations being such as to lead many persons to feel that the new forms approached too closely the ritual of the Roman Catholic Church. On December 12 the Archbishop of Canterbury laid the new Prayer Book before the House of Lords for its approval, which, after three days of heated dispute, was given. On December 15, the House of Commons debated the question and by a majority of 33 votes the new Prayer Book was rejected. In June 1928 the bill was once more offered and again rejected by the Commons.

[1] A brief note from Pollock, dated November 14, 1927, is omitted.

[2] The first essay in *Outside the Law* was entitled "The Relation of Mystic Experience to Philosophy." It was a paper read before the Oxford Philosophical Society.

definite turning down of dogmatic formulas, not mere scepticism (including the tribe of pseudo-scientific formulas like A. Comte's); as indicated in the first pages of *Outside the Law.*

Yours ever,
F. P.

LONDON, November 24, 1927

My dear Holmes:

. . . Selden's intimate view of the nature of things is not clear to me.[1] He shows himself as accepting historical revelation — *quantum suff.* — as the only way of getting any rule of conduct for keeping society in order. Practically he was a Whig publicist before Locke, as I have noted. . . .

Yours ever,
F. P.

I told you, I think, I don't believe Sacco and Vanzetti's defence was honestly conducted in their interest — tho' I see no reason to think the jury was in fact prejudiced.

WASHINGTON, December 7, 1927[1]

My dear Pollock:

. . . I am interested in your credit to the mystics. The book that I remember as marking my transit from boy to young man, before I went to college, is *Hours with the Mystics.*[2] At a later date I used to say every wise man is a mystic, at bottom, and I should say so now with explanations: that I don't believe any men have private conversation with God or illumination of any sort different from that furnished by the ordinary human faculties. No doubt I have said before that I think a real sceptic (who hasn't reserved a little Godhood for

[1] Holmes, it appears from his Journal, had recently read Pollock's edition of Selden's *Table Talk.*

[1] A letter from Pollock, dated December 1, 1927, is omitted.

[2] See *supra*, Vol. I, p. 274.

himself) may come nearer to what I should call religion than most if not than all of those who go to church.

Tomorrow is an anniversary — twenty-five years since I took my seat on the bench down here — forty-five years of judging. Now if I can live a few months longer I must begin again. I think Taney [3] when he died was 9 or 10 months older than I am now, but without any examination I think that although still Chief Justice he had ceased to deliver opinions before he had reached my age; whether he took any part in the deliberations of the court I don't know. He died in 1864 and I believe tried to obstruct Lincoln by issuing a writ of *habeas corpus* during the war [4] — but that would have been his single act. I doubt if any judge has been actively at work on this bench at very near to my age. I don't care for such things except in a very superficial way and as an amusement. If my work is not as good as ever I don't care to prolong it. So I try to keep a sharp eye on myself in that way.

The Massachusetts Historical Society has just published the letters of John Gray and John Ropes written during the war.[5] I should think that they were a very touching and intimate picture of the time but I haven't read them. I don't know, although I am a member of the Society, whether it is possible to get the volume for non-members but I should suppose so, and if you would care to see it I should be glad to try at least. I have just finished a fairly interesting case in which a time charterer of a vessel tries to get damages from a dry dock company, for negligent delay in repairs *per quod* the charterer lost a fortnight of valuable time.[6] I have no doubt that he can't recover but I have not yet heard from my brethren. Perhaps I should explain that there was no demise of the ship, that the owner remained in possession and put the vessel into dry dock without reference to the charter, having a right to do so by the terms of the instrument. A little book of pamphlets published by the Oxford University Press [7] gives me pleasure at odd

[3] Roger Brooke Taney (1777–1864); Chief Justice of the United States, 1836–1864.

[4] *Ex parte* Merryman, Fed. Cas. No. 9487 (1861).

[5] *War Letters, 1862–1865, of John Chipman Gray and John Codman Ropes* (1927).

[6] Robins Dry Dock and Repair Co. v. Flint, 275 U. S. 303 (argued Dec. 1; decided Dec. 12, 1927); opinion, for a unanimous Court, by Holmes.

[7] *A Miscellany of Tracts and Pamphlets* (1927).

moments, but naturally I can't read much. Love to Lady Pollock and the children.

Yours ever,
O. W. H.

LONDON, December 15, 1927

My dear Holmes:

. . . My learned friend Goodhart[1] tells me you have written the judgement of the Court in an important case of contributory negligence,[2] which I hope you will let me see. (*N.B.*, a new edition of Pollock on Torts is called for.)

Recent and current controversies here convince me that the ignorance of clergymen in both history and theology exceeds any assignable quantity — even with all reasonable allowance for deliberate falsehood and suppression.

Yours ever,
F. P.

LONDON, December 22, 1927

My dear Holmes:

. . . Your judicial record beats my grandfather's;[1] he was of my present age or nearly so, 82–83, when he resigned in 1866 — having been on the bench 22 years, and Attorney General before.

Of course there is no watertight mystical faculty (*disposition* in the French sense would be a better word) any more than mathematical or — a nearer analogy — musical. The notion of separate "faculties" is I believe thoroughly discredited. Vaughan's *Hours with the Mystics* is not a bad book but would

[1] Arthur L. Goodhart, editor of the *Law Quarterly Review*, 1926 to date.

[2] Probably Baltimore and Ohio Rd. Co. v. Goodman, 275 U. S. 66 (1927). In an opinion by Holmes the unanimous Court held that if the driver of a car, about to cross a railroad track, "cannot be sure otherwise whether a train is dangerousl near he must stop and get out of his vehicle . . . if he relies upon not hearing the train or any signal and takes no further precaution he does so at his own risk." *Id.* at p. 70.

[1] Sir Jonathan Frederick Pollock (1783–1870); Attorney General, 1834–1844; Lord Chief Baron of the Exchequer, 1844–1866.

have been better if the author had not been afraid of being thought to countenance popish superstition. William James (*Varieties of Religious Experience*) was free from that prejudice but might have enriched his examples considerably if he had been anything of a medievalist.

Our Prayer-book revision controversy has taken an odd turn, the Revisionists breaking down unexpectedly in the House of Commons. It amuses me as a pretty detached layman to have three parliamentary cousins on the winning side: in H. L. the Bishop of Norwich and the Master of the Rolls,[2] in H. C. Malcolm Macnaghten, who is on the father's side a cousin of my wife's also. Nobody pointed out that the Episcopal Church on your side has long had a ritual very like the proposed alternative book, and has not been devoured by popery. The case for the revised book was bungled in other ways too, which would not interest you. In the craft of which I am a Grand Officer we have a pretty elaborate ritual and do without any authorized book at all. But very few clerics have a working sense of compromise.

Yours ever,
F. P.

WASHINGTON, January 7, 1928

My dear F. P.:

. . . I am just back from our Saturday's jaw over the week's work and my prophetic soul tells me what case will be assigned to me to write — an easy one. They all have been pretty easy this week. So "all quiet along the Potomac to-night," as went a line in a poem of my war days. But very few minutes for reading. I am running through a little book on the *Disregard of the Corporate Fiction* [1] because it is dedicated to me and the writer seems to think that I am a hellerverfeller which one should encourage. I'm rather up in the world for those, as this is the second dedication within a month or two

[2] Right Reverend Bertram Pollock and Sir Ernest Murray Pollock, Lord Hanworth.

[1] I. Maurice Wormser, *The Disregard of the Corporate Fiction and Allied Corporate Problems* (1927).

and the December *Harvard Law Review* has an article on me in connection with the Constitution [2] which has led to other somewhat flattering discourses. But as long as one continues to write, the question is always of tomorrow and not of yesterday, and tomorrow one may show what a fool one is. So one's head does not swell beyond the dimensions of one's hat.

As one who doesn't read the paper and who doesn't profess to know the things that are necessary for the outfit of an intelligent man of the day I know nothing of the row over the prayer book. It is so remote from anything that seems to me credible that I accept my darkness happily. Those gentlemen with aprons are largely responsible, I suppose, for men taking themselves so seriously — rightly enough no doubt if they take a grain of sand seriously. Otherwise I see no ground for it. But this comes near to twisting the tail of the cosmos — that one who has gone through a conference had better not attempt. So fare thee well.

Yours ever,
O. W. H.

LONDON, January 12, 1928

My dear Holmes:

Thanks for the judgment.[1] It seems to me plain that, in the language of some one in the House of Lords getting on for fifty years ago, the man ran into the train at least as much as the train ran into the man. We have long ceased here to hold the verdict of juries in civil cases in any superstitious reverence.

Rylands' book [2] is unknown to me. Other able writers (J. M. Robertson in England, quite lately Couchoud in France) have doubted the existence in fact of Jesus Christ. To me it is like denying that there was such a man as Charles the Great because there are incredible legends of Charlemagne. How much of the current orthodox "synoptic" story can be accepted is

[2] Felix Frankfurter, "Mr. Justice Holmes and the Constitution," 41 *Harv. L. Rev.* 121 (1927).

[1] Presumably Baltimore and Ohio Rd. Co. v. Goodman, *supra*, p. 209.

[2] In the summer of 1927 Holmes had read L. G. Rylands, *The Evolution of Christianity* (1927).

another matter. The very learned and ingenious Salomon Reinach has doubts about the Crucifixion which I share (I believe there were two conflicting legends and that we have traces of the suppressed one). . . .

Wind and rain still prevail in this latitude.

Yours ever,
F. P.

Thomas Hardy is dead:[3] our greatest recent English writer I think, on the level of Turgenev, besides being no mean poet.

WASHINGTON, January 19, 1928

My dear Pollock:

. . . As to hypostasis[1] — I don't remember ever using it but once; at first as an intentionally magniloquent and pedagogical answer to Pound's question: What is a right? And then in an article, as a real reduction of a right to its rudiments.[2] It starts from my definition of law (in the sense in which it is used by the modern lawyer), as a statement of the circumstances in which the public force will be brought to bear upon men through the courts: that is the prophecy in general terms. Of course the prophecy becomes more specific to define a right. So we prophesy that the earth and sun will act towards each other in a certain way. Then as we pretend to account for that mode of action by the hypothetical cause, the force of gravitation, which is merely the hypostasis of the prophesied fact and an empty phrase. So we get up the empty substratum, a *right*, to pretend to account for the fact that the courts will act in a certain way. We have got accustomed to

[3] Hardy died on January 11, 1928.

[1] In a letter from Pollock, dated January 6, 1928, which is omitted he had written: "I am puzzling to think in what sense you use *hypostasis*, known to me only as a theological term of art which the Latins unhappily rendered by *Person*. But that may keep." See *supra*, pp. 64, 200.

[2] "Natural Law," 32 *Harv. L. Rev.* 40, 42 (1918); *C.L.P.*, p. 313. "But for legal purposes a right is only the hypostasis of a prophecy — the imagination of a substance supporting the fact that the public force will be brought to bear upon those who do things said to contravene it — just as we talk of the force of gravitation accounting for the conduct of bodies in space."

our phraseology and might find it hard for a time to do without it; but in that as in other cases I think our morally tinted words have caused a great deal of confused thinking. I should like to write a first book of the law keeping to hard fact and using no images.

So much, in haste.

Yours ever,
O. W. H.

LONDON, January 26, 1928

My dear Holmes:

. . . It is pleasing to see that the learned Felix Frankfurter has written in your praise in the *Harvard Law Review* warmly but without being fulsome or tedious. He cites more than one opinion that I wish I had seen at the time.

Other learned persons I see have gone crazy in the pursuit of new verbal formulas. When I read of such a result as confounding an offer with a conditional promise there seems to me to be something wrong with the method.[1]

There is a book by J. S. Haldane of physical-speculative essays entitled *Possible Worlds* which I think would interest you. . . .

Yours ever,
F. P.

By the way, our grotesque Prayer Book controversy is to some extent constitutional, therefore not void of legal interest.

LONDON, February 6, 1928

My dear Holmes:

I am glad to know that your *hypostasis* was a way of talking with schoolmen according to their scholasticism. In that

[1] In Section 24 of the American Law Institute's Tentative Draft of the Restatement of the Law of Contracts (1925) an offer was defined as "a promise which is in terms conditional upon an act, forbearance or counterpromise being given in exchange for the promise or its performance. . . ." Professor George W. Goble criticized the proposed section in 22 *Ill. L. Rev.* 567 (Jan., 1928).

special sense I suppose the moon's visible position tonight is the hypostasis of the same as predicted by lunar theory and printed in the Nautical Almanack — three years ago, I think.

As to the juridical notion of right I quite agree with you. The word is still ambiguous, meaning an expectation *either, in genere* (*jus*), that the Court will assist you, if duly required, in case of interference with certain of your lawful liberties *or, in specie* (*actio*), that here and now you can call on the Court for redress in some form.

Such adjectives as *antecedent* and *remedial* are correct but rather clumsy.

It may be said that English-speaking lawyers usually know which category they are talking about and understand one another. But the Common Law (through the Anglo-Indian Codes founded on it and otherwise) is more and more being worked by people not born to its language, and then confusion is very possible. . . .

Piquet and Lamb's *Essays* alternate of evenings. C. L.'s taste was never *bad* but at times odd: he seems to have rather preferred Smollett to Fielding.

Yours ever,
F. P.

WASHINGTON, February 17, 1928

My dear Pollock:

. . . We come in again on Monday and the last days of recess have been crowded, more or less, with work. Thirty odd applications for *certiorari* meant that so many cases must be examined sufficiently to make up my mind whether they should be allowed to come up. Then there have been two cases on which I have got excited — one that hasn't been passed on and that will be discussed tomorrow. It is a time-honored practice for the U. S. judges when a case between citizens of different states is tried before them and the question is one that depends, according to the common phrase, on "the general law," to say that the parties are entitled to their independent opinion, and, if so minded, to decline to follow the

Supreme Court of the State. I say that this is a pure usurpation founded on a subtle fallacy.[1] They say the question is a question of the common law and that they must decide what the common law is. I hit at this once in a dissent by saying that the common law is not a brooding omnipresence in the sky.[2] The question of what is the law of Massachusetts or of Louisiana is a matter that Mass. or La. has a right to determine for itself, and that being so, the voice of the state should be obeyed as well when it speaks through its Supreme Court as it would be if it spoke through its Legislature. It all comes from Story in *Swift* v. *Tyson* [3] who declined to follow New York law upon a commercial question, I forget whether it directly or indirectly concerned negotiable instruments. The decision was unjustifiable in theory but did no great harm when confined to what Story dealt with, but under the influence of Bradley, Harlan, *et al.* it now has assumed the form that upon questions of the general law the U. S. courts must decide for themselves — of course expressing a desire to follow the state courts if they can. I doubt if I can carry a majority, for the tradition is old, and some ex-circuit judges will not have forgotten the arrogant assumption to which they have been accustomed. This of course strictly between ourselves. The other question is whether states can tax patents,[4] a dictum of Marshall treating patents as standing like U. S. banks and other instrumentalities of government has led to a general opinion that patents can't be taxed — a notion that I shall try to smash. Brandeis is with me on these points and we are so apt to agree that I am glad that he dissents from the only opinion I have to deliver.[5] It will indicate that there is no preestablished harmony between us.

[1] Black & White Taxicab Co. v. Brown and Yellow Taxicab Co., 276 U. S. 518 (1928). Holmes wrote a dissenting opinion in which Stone and Brandeis, JJ., concurred. *Id.* at p. 532.

[2] Dissenting in Southern Pacific Company v. Jensen, 244 U. S. 205, 222 (1917). "The common law is not a brooding omnipresence in the sky but the articulate voice of some sovereign or quasi-sovereign that can be identified. . . ."

[3] 16 Pet. 1 (1842).

[4] Long v. Rockwood, 277 U. S. 142 (1928). Holmes wrote a dissenting opinion in which Brandeis, Sutherland, and Stone, JJ., concurred. *Id.* at p. 148.

[5] Casey v. United States, 276 U. S. 413 (1928). The majority of the Court, in an opinion by Holmes, held that the petitioner's conviction under a statute forbidding the purchase of morphine from an unstamped package should be sustained. The majority

The result of all this is that I haven't read much. I have nearly finished Greville's *Diary*, unexpurgated but edited in a way that I dislike — gathering passages of widely different dates on particular subjects instead of letting the diary go its quiet chronological way, and with sensational headings to the chapters. But the book is entertaining and instructive — on themes of which I know too little. Also for my sins I have been let to take up Demogue, *Notions Fondamentales du Droit Privé* — a very intelligent writer but so far telling me nothing that is new to my mind. Having begun it I don't like to back out but I wish he was at the Devil.

This morning among others comes a letter from a minister asking my views, *pour encourager les autres*, as to immortality. I think I had better treat it as not received. . . .

Yours ever,
O. W. H.

LONDON, March 1, 1928

My dear Holmes:

Your problem — which I grasp only in outline, never having had occasion to consider the relations between Federal and State jurisdiction — is interesting. On principle it would seem that the "proper law" of the case (where doubt is possible) has to be ascertained in the same manner as in all cases where a conflict of laws is in question. (I suppose Federal Courts take judicial notice of State law, for the contrary practice would be too absurd.) The proper law need not of course be the law of any State at all: the parties may by express terms or by conduct have agreed to be judged by some other law (*e.g.*, contract to be performed outside the U. S.). If it is the law of a State, I conceive the authorities received in that State should be followed except (besides fraud) in a case of manifest error or *incuria*, as we do with foreign laws here. Can a Federal Court

denied that the prosecution should fail because of the alleged action of the Government in inducing the defendant to commit the crime. Brandeis, J., wrote a dissenting opinion in which he urged that the Government's agents had instigated the defendant to commit the crime. Butler and McReynolds, JJ., also wrote dissenting opinions.

disregard the refusal of the New York courts to receive the rule in *Fletcher* v. *Rylands* because that rule is generally received (if so it is) in the Courts of other States? Similarly as to certain peculiar doctrines about the formation of contracts in Massachusetts. On the other hand it *may* be possible in some Western States for rules to be laid down clearly contrary to natural justice, and in such an extreme case the Federal Court might disregard them.

Why condemn yourself to read textbooks written (judging from the title) as manuals for rising French Bachelors in the Faculty of Law? From such a book there is nothing new to be expected. I too have committed a book on Jurisprudence, but took care to save it by making nearly half of it an exposition of the sources of the methods of the Common Law in particular — giving some information hardly to be found within two covers elsewhere. . . .

The talk of arbitration and security among the nations leaves you untouched I guess. What I think is that publicists expect more assurance than any man of sense expects in his own affairs. We all take remote risks (such as our bankers' insolvency) and don't even try to insure against them. An efficient Court and standing machinery for conciliation are far more important than stopping every possible earth. And if the Fathers of your Constitution had attempted to provide for everything!

Yours ever,
F. P.

WASHINGTON, April 4, 1928 [1]

My dear Pollock:

Your most sound advice, why read a book for rising French Bachelors in the Faculty of Law, came to deaf ears. I had begun the thing and had to finish it. Morris Cohen, a philosopher of whom I think very highly, had cracked it up in an essay.[2] I have written to him and cursed him for my loss of time.

[1] A note from Pollock, dated April 2, 1928, is omitted.
[2] "Property and Sovereignty," 13 *Cornell L. Q.* 8, 18 (Dec., 1927).

I have been working pretty hard and with very little break. Just when you think you see leisure in plump 30 new applications for *certiorari*. On Monday next we sit again, I shall have an opinion [3] and three dissents [4] to pass off — two opinions held up, one for McReynolds to make up his mind about, the other for him to write a dissent. He takes his time, which I must confess gets on my nerves. I always myself consider that the opinions of other judges have the right of way, and that I can't keep them waiting while I turn to other work — but this between ourselves. The spring is coming on apace, Magnolias everywhere, bloodroot in the woods and on the hillsides, and in a few days the Japanese Cherry — a world show of which no doubt I have spoken often.

My 87th birthday brought me a lot of letters and telegrams to be answered. If I live seven months longer I shall be the oldest ever and shall have beaten Taney. . . .

I am well enough but rather tired. There seems to be no intermission.

Yours ever,
O. W. H.

London, May 7, 1928 [1]

My dear Holmes:

The judgment you sent me, or rather the majority opinion, upset all my notions.[2] I thought the court of last resort in every State was the final interpreter for its own jurisdiction (subject to Constitutions of U.S. and State, and saving such an extreme case as flagrant denial of justice or wilful disregard

[3] Casey v. United States, see *supra*, p. 215. On the same day, April 9, Holmes also delivered a brief opinion for the Court in Chesapeake and Ohio Ry. Co. v. Leitch, 276 U. S. 429 (1928).

[4] On April 9, Holmes delivered only two dissents: Untermeyer v. Anderson, 276 U. S. 440, 446; Black & White Taxi Co. v. Brown and Yellow Taxicab Co., *supra*, p. 215. In the Untermeyer case a majority of the Court held that the gift tax statute of June 2, 1924, was not constitutionally applicable to a gift made on May 23, 1924. Brandeis and Stone, JJ., concurred in Holmes's dissent, and Brandeis wrote a separate dissenting opinion.

[1] Two letters from Pollock, dated April 15 and April 26, 1928, are omitted.

[2] Black & White Taxicab Co. v. Brown and Yellow Taxicab Co., *supra*, p. 215.

of elementary principle) in all questions of domestic law. Does the decision mean that your Court may be called on to lay down that the rule in *Rylands* v. *Fletcher e.g.*, now received in some States and not in others, is or is not good "general law," and require all Federal Courts to act on that ruling? Or does the doctrine apply only to matter of public policy? And if so limited, why? But I don't believe any English lawyer can put himself at the centre of these questions.

The Kentucky judgment is in English eyes, antediluvian, but that does not matter.[3] . . .

Next Saturday we start on our cruise:[4] no address till end of the month.

Yours ever,
F. P.

WASHINGTON, May 17, 1928 [1]

My dear Pollock:

Your surprise at the majority judgment that I sent to you does not surprise me, but the decision follows a notion started by Story as to the general doctrines of commercial law, negotiable paper, etc., which as I intimate in my opinion was quite indefensible but did not much harm when confined to what he was thinking of. But the judges since that time not without some arrogance as I think have made a general principle as you saw, and no doubt what you ask as to *Rylands* v. *Fletcher* might happen. By the same mail as this I send you three other dissents two of which I think will secure your assent.[2] That as

[3] In McConnell v. Pedigo, 92 Ky. 465; 18 S. W. 15 (1892), the Kentucky court had held that a contract between a railroad company and a taxicab company by which the latter was granted the exclusive privilege of entering the railroad's station and surrounding premises for the purpose of soliciting trade, was invalid and unenforceable. The majority of the Supreme Court of the United States in the *Black & White Taxicab case* held that the decision of the Kentucky court was not controlling on the Federal court in Kentucky in a diversity of citizenship case. Holmes in his dissenting opinion maintained that the state decision on a matter of common law should be followed by the Federal court.

[4] To the Mediterranean.

[1] A postal card from Pollock, dated May 10, 1928, is omitted.

[2] On May 14 Holmes wrote dissenting opinions in Long v. Rockwood, 277 U. S. 142, 148, Springer v. Philippine Islands, *id.* 189, 209, and Panhandle Oil Co. v. Knox,

to the Philippines [3] may be more doubtful, but I took the chance to say something that I thought needed saying.

I hope your cruise is under way and that all will be pleasant and prosperous.

Yours ever,
O. W. H.

My love to the dear Lady.

LONDON, June 7, 1928

My dear Holmes:

Last Friday we came back from a most successful cruise — fine weather all the time from a seaman's point of view, and from a landsman's all but one wet day at Algiers. . . . We had a delightful coast drive at Naples: at Malta I revisited the notable armoury of the Knights of St. John, now rather encumbered with bulky German trophies including a torpedo

id. 218, 222. In Long v. Rockwood, the majority of the Court held the Massachusetts income tax to be constitutionally inapplicable to royalties received by a Massachusetts resident from a patent issued to him by the United States. Concerning Holmes's dissent, see *supra*, p. 215. In the Panhandle Oil case the majority held that a state could not constitutionally impose a sales tax on gasoline sold by a dealer to the United States for use by Coast Guard vessels and by a Veterans' Hospital. In his dissent Holmes said that in the time of Chief Justice Marshall "it was not recognized as it is today that most of the distinctions of the law are distinctions of degree. If the states had any power it was assumed that they had all the power, and that the necessary alternative was to deny it altogether. But this court which has so often defeated the attempt to tax in certain ways can defeat an attempt to discriminate or otherwise go too far without wholly abolishing the power to tax. The power to tax is not the power to destroy while this Court sits." 277 U. S. at p. 223.

[3] Springer v. Philippine Islands, *supra*. In an opinion by Sutherland, J., the Court held that the provisions concerning the separation of powers in the Organic Act of the Philippines were violated by statutes transferring from the Governor-General to legislative officers the power to vote shares of stock of government-owned proprietary corporations. The voting power was found to be an executive and not a legislative function, and the statutes were, accordingly, invalidated. In his dissenting opinion, concurred in by Brandeis, J., Holmes said: "The great ordinances of the Constitution do not establish and divide fields of black and white. Even the more specific of them are found to terminate in a penumbra shading gradually from one extreme to another. . . . When we come to the fundamental distinctions it is still more obvious that they must be received with a certain latitude or our government could not go on. . . . It does not seem to need argument to show that however we may disguise it by veiling words we do not and cannot carry out the distinction between legislative and executive action with mathematical precision and divide the branches into watertight compartments, were it ever so desirable to do so, which I am far from believing that it is, or that the Constitution requires." *Id.* p. 209, 211.

that broke its head against the rocks without exploding. Going through the Straits of Messina we steamed right over Charybdis — not a proper whirlpool at all, but a rather large tract of broken water in the nature of whirlpool rapids, and no hindrance to modern navigation though a small boat would not be happy in it. I guess the learned Victor Bérard [1] was right when he put down this and other monsters of the *Odyssey* to the terrifying yarns told by Phoenician sailors to Greek traders whom they wanted to keep off their preserves in the Western Mediterranean. As for Scylla there is nothing at all to account for her: the now so called rock of Scylla is outside the Straits. I am sure the poet of the *Odyssey* knew nothing of Sicily but the name Trinacria. Samuel Butler's location of *her* (as he says) there is too absurd.

This week I am busy settling details of the dinner of the Cambridge Apostles (officially Cambridge Conversazione Society) at which I am to preside next week for the second time after forty odd years interval: I was elected a member in 1865, so I shall talk patriarchally about the past. Also I am off to Cambridge for the week-end. Thus I have barely glanced at the judgments you have sent me, nor do I think myself competent to form any clear judgment on such delicate points as one or two of them involve. I wonder on which side you were in the case of evidence obtained by tapping telephones which (as being connected with Prohibition) the lay press mentions in a huddled manner as usual.[2] . . .

The Prayer Book strife still rages, and to my great indignation my cousin Macnaghten on whom I counted for the Apostles dinner is engulfed in it in the House of Commons next Tuesday.

Yours ever,
F. P.

[1] Victor Bérard, author of *Les Phéniciens et l'Odyssée* (1902–1903).

[2] Olmstead v. United States, 277 U. S. 438 (1928). The petitioners had been convicted in a Federal court of a conspiracy to violate the Prohibition Act. At the trial, evidence of private telephone conversations between the defendants had been admitted, though it had been obtained by means of wire-tapping by Government officials. The defendants contended that the admission of this evidence violated the constitutional provisions against unreasonable searches and seizures and compelling a person in a criminal case to be a witness against himself. The majority of the Court, in an opinion by Taft, C. J., held that the evidence was constitutionally admissible. Holmes, Brandeis, Butler, and Stone, JJ., wrote dissenting opinions.

BEVERLY FARMS, June 20, 1928

My dear young Frederick:

It is good to see your handwriting again and to welcome you back from your youthful larks — my time for them has gone by. The fatigue of Washington to Boston and Boston to Washington is enough for me, and I walk very little. I am interested by what you tell of Charybdis and the truant Scylla. I dissented in the case of tapping telephone wires. The C. J. who wrote the prevailing opinion, perhaps as a rhetorical device to obscure the difficulty, perhaps merely because he did not note the difference, which perhaps I should have emphasized more, spoke of the objection to the evidence as based on its being obtained by "unethical" means (horrid phrase), although he adds & by a misdemeanor under the laws of Washington.[1] I said that the State of Washington had made it a crime and that the Government could not put itself in the position of offering to pay for a crime in order to get evidence of another crime. Brandeis wrote much more elaborately, but I didn't agree with all that he said.[2] I should not have printed what I wrote, however, if he had not asked me to. I am reading an able book: Parrington, *Main Currents in American Thought*, which gives a very interesting picture, or rather analysis, of the elements at work from the beginning. But I shall not easily believe the thesis running through it and started by earlier works of Beard (*An Economic Interpretation of the Constitution*, etc.) to the effect that the Constitution primarily represents the triumph of the money power over democratic agrarianism & individualism. Beard I thought years ago when I read him went into rather ignoble though most painstaking investigation of the investments of the leaders, with an innuendo even if disclaimed. I shall believe until compelled to think otherwise

[1] Olmstead v. U. S., 277 U. S. at p. 466.

[2] In his dissenting opinion Justice Brandeis stated that the tapping of telephone wires and the use of evidence so obtained violated the constitutional provisions against unreasonable searches and seizures (4th Amendment), and against compelling a person in a criminal case to become a witness against himself (5th Amendment). Holmes in his dissent said: "While I do not deny it, I am not prepared to say that the penumbra of the 4th and 5th amendments covers the defendant, although I fully agree that Courts are apt to err by sticking too closely to the words of a law where those words import a policy that goes beyond them." *Id.* at 469.

that they wanted to make a nation and invested (bet) on the belief that they would make one, not that they wanted a powerful government because they had invested. Belittling arguments always have a force of their own, but you and I believe that high-mindedness is not impossible to man. The result is that I am not taking unmixed pleasure in one of the ablest and most instructive books that I have read for a long time. I have brought with me Bertrand Russell's *Philosophy*, but that must wait till I have finished Parrington's second volume. I have let in a little sweetness and light by reading *en passant*, *But Gentlemen Marry Brunettes*, a sequel to *Gentlemen Prefer Blondes*, with which perhaps you improved your mind. But sexual talk or innuendo is displeasing from a woman, I think. Perhaps because we know, though the older literary tradition is the other way, that they take less interest in the business than we do. We have been here a week and a half and are settling into our routine, the main event a motor drive of two hours, which is about my limit. (I interrupted myself here to write to the Clerk to send you the opinion and dissents in the above mentioned case if he still has copies.) Please give my love to Lady Pollock. I rarely see anyone but am happy in solitude. Most of the places here now to me are sockets from which the occupants that I knew have been extracted by the final dentist.

Yours ever,
O. W. H.

. . . The Prayer Book is a mystery that I do not touch.

LONDON, July 2, 1928

My dear Holmes:

The early date of your Court rising and your migration to Beverly Farms always takes me by surprise, though it ought not. . . .

Parrington is not known to me, nor Beard, but I have heard of economic interpretations of politics. Brooks Adams worked that line to death, about 30 years ago was it? Some one did say, more reasonably, a few years ago, that a time of commercial prosperity was a material help to the success of the Constitution.

Bertrand Russell is a mighty clever philosopher, too clever I think. His theodicy so far as I make out consists in being angry with the gods for not existing, because if they did he would like to break their windows.

I have just done touching up the chapter of my *Torts* on Wrongs of Fraud, Bad Faith, & Oppression, covering what one may call for short the Ground of *Vegelahn* v. *Guntner* [1] (you know that dissenting judgment of yours is now treated, here at any rate, as good authority): touching up I say, for unluckily the latest talk all round it in the House of Lords (*Sorrell* v. *Smith* [1925] A. C. 700) has settled nothing and only given us more conflicting *obiter dicta*. . . .

The sequel to *Gentlemen Prefer Blondes* appeared to us to follow the general law of sequels in not coming off (the clearest exception I know is Samuel Butler's *Erewhon Revisited*). A. P. Herbert's *The Trials of Topsy*, which has just now run through *Punch*, is to me more amusing.

N. B. I have my own private history of your Constitution, which tells how George Washington was called upon at short notice to forge the Declaration of Independence, and Benjamin Franklin crushed his conscientious objections by exclaiming "Then what *is* the good of not being able to tell a lie?" . . .

Yours ever,
F. P.

P. S. *Olmstead* v. *U. S.*

I agree generally with the dissenting opinions. The point of substance, apart from any question of construction, is whether tapping telephone messages is mere eavesdropping, or on the same footing as intercepting and reading a closed letter. Common sense appears to favour the latter view.

Was it ever doubted that a telegram follows the analogy of a letter in this respect? (The message itself is alike incorporeal in either case — writing is only a memorandum in telegraphic

[1] See *supra*, Vol. I, p. 81.

communication — a message in Morse can be received as well as sent without any writing at all.)

All communication between human beings is by symbols needing interpretation, and to dwell on the diversities of methods for producing visible or audible symbols is to stick in the bark.

As to the Fourth Amendment, it seems that even if you are bound to the letter, *effects* [2] is a word of large import and may well be held to cover interests not falling within any recognized denomination of property.

To confine *search* to seeking for corporeal chattels is a poor mean and narrow conception, as the Rev. Tobias Swinfen [*sic*] (*On the Nature and Place of Hell*) [3] said of Drexelius's opinion that the interior of the Earth is large enough to hold all the damned.

The supposed parallel of assuming disguise to get at criminals' plans is fallacious. There no offence is committed, nor necessarily anything contrary to good morals. I never heard of any real authority for any such proposition as that one owes full disclosure of the truth to all men at all times.

F. P.

BEVERLY FARMS, July 12, 1928

My dear Pollock:

A delightful letter from you just arrived. Your summary of Bertrand Russell delighted me especially. . . .

I haven't much to tell, applications for *certiorari* have begun to arrive (by my direction in anticipation of next term) and I have done twenty odd of them. I am reading at odd minutes Morison's *Oxford History of the United States* — well written, sensible, and clear. As usual now, giving more standing to the economic causes than formerly but not of course supposing that the leading men took their positions because of their investments, which would be idiotic. You know that G. Washington

[2] "The right of the people to be secure in their persons, houses, papers and effects, against unreasonable searches and seizures, shall not be violated. . . ."

[3] Tobias Swinden, *An Enquiry into the Nature and Place of Hell* (1714), p. 75.

cannot tell a lie business was a fiction in a popular life of him by an itinerant parson. The best form of it is in a song which I imperfectly recall. (In some form of words, "Father I cannot tell a lie," the noble boy replied),

"It was not I who cut
Your a—a—apple tree
But Little Ben Franklin."

My wife has read to me a good piece of Hugh Walpole, *Wintersmoon* (if that is the name), some good characteristic English talk but a lot of people who don't interest me at all, and whose modernity (so far as I see in those who profess to be modern) consists in taking their own very ordinary foibles seriously and as entitled to respect. They have to think they are free about sex, but I don't see much evidence so far as I have got. Owen Wister has sent me *The Sun Also Rises* by Ernest Hemingway, which he seemed to think of great promise when the writer got away from garbage. I haven't read it yet, but it sounds brisker than Walpole.

I hope before vacation ends to improve my mind with books and slumber but haven't got far yet. My love to Lady Pollock.

Yours ever,
O. W. H.

August 14, 1928

Postal Card, Lady Pollock and Pollock to Holmes

My dear Holmes:

Yesterday our grandson arrived in Paris — all well.[1] We are going in there tomorrow (this is a rustic little town,[2] the President's country seat with a charming country hotel, and we don't know what are the American mail days — distance from Paris about 30 m., Versailles about half way between). And nothing else seems to matter much at present.

[1] George Frederick Pollock, the son of John Pollock and his second wife, Madame Alix l'Estom Soubiran, was born on August 13, 1928.

[2] The postal card was mailed from Rambouillet.

We may be moving about before you write — please address London as usual.

G. H. P.
F. P.

BEVERLY FARMS, August 30, 1928[1]

My dear Pollocks:

Rejoicing over your grandson — I hope that all has continued well; and I appreciate and sympathize with your joy. I suppose that this will find you both in London again, looking out of those delightful back windows at a load of hay going off or the children playing there — the privileged few. But the children I watched have grown up now and it may be their children that you see. I have no great show to make for my vacation. Latterly mostly short stories in the way of reading: some of Chekov's, (I believe that is not quite the right spelling) — a clever pen, but on rather squalid themes. It did not give me pleasure. Thinking of him and of an American living in Paris, Hemingway, author of *Men Without Women* & *The Sun also Rises,* I wonder at the illusion that one is more real if one evokes sordid situations and bad smells, than if one invites one's readers to fresh air and agreeable and even noble people. Also I was induced by a very dull interesting book, Dill, *Roman Society from Nero to M. Aurelius* to read Petronius. The fun of course is dead and stupid (for us), but generically of all time for those who are coarse enough to like it. But how many admirable and quotable things can be picked out of it. It really repaid one for the few hours that it cost. I was talking yesterday with Morris Cohen, a most learned and able philosopher, and he said he went back and reread the classics, being apt to feel his time wasted on modern books. I told him that I on the other hand always had scruples lest I was wasting time when I read the classics. I am thinking now of rereading *Moby Dick* which for several reasons would come nearer to me than to you and which seemed to me great when I half read it. I am trying to feel unscrupulous and to read it for amusement but it comes very hard.

[1] A postal card from Pollock, dated August 14, 1928, is omitted.

My secretary comes on Saturday Sept. 1, and it will seem as if work were approaching but there is still nearly a month. I don't leave here till the last week of September.

Bless you both my children. Frederick really is growing up. At 90 a man is old.

Yours ever,
O. W. HOLMES

HOTEL DU GRAND CERF
SENLIS
September 9, 1928

My dear Holmes:

Thanks for your letter forwarded from London. We are still some way from being at home — the christening of master Geo. Frederick awaits us in Paris ten days hence, and we are (most irregularly) to be the godparents — but we are more available than any other relatives and the good English *padre*, rather a friend of Jack's, seems not to mind. I find indeed in a manual of French etiquette belonging to Jack (about as absurd as all such books are) that among R. C.'s in France it was formerly a custom for a paternal grandfather and maternal grandmother (not two of the same side) to be godparents; but now it is disallowed on the ground — sensible enough — that in modern times grandparents are generally too old.

Meanwhile we have lighted — rather by happy accident than our own diligence — on excellent quarters in a most interesting provincial and yet not rustic little town, which is quite at the heart of French history. Hugh Capet was elected here. In 1914 this was the nearest town to Paris actually occupied by the Germans in their first advance; the cathedral (rather small as French cathedrals go but very attractive, with a specially charming *flèche*) escaped with superficial damage from shell fire, but the modern main road, happily only skirting the town, was destroyed as reprisal for pretended firing on troops by civilians, the usual story: as I know it was false in Belgium I believe it was equally so here: and the Mayor and other citizens were shot on the same pretence. Which makes me indignant with armchair pacifists who preach to the French that they are to forget all about it. The town has its old crooked streets intact, and though small is possible to lose one's bearings in without a plan — the cathedral, a landmark in the country, being masked near at hand by buildings — and you can stroll under shady trees (material in this wonderful sunny September) along the ramparts and look down over a charming little river.

Then it is a capital centre for excursions. We have been to Pierrefonds — a great medieval castle of the dukes of Orleans restored by Viollet-le-Duc, — Compiègne — Chantilly, only half a dozen miles to the west. . . .

So altogether we are in clover. Chekhov — according to the Committee of the British Academy which reported on Slavonic transliteration in 1917, but some scholars write plain *h* for the Russian x (the Greek x, our *h*, is unknown to the Cyrillic alphabet and is arbitrarily represented by G when Western names occur in Russian writings). Frenchmen write Tchékhov (or—of). Germans Tschekhov (or — ow). Spell him as you may, present Russians think his world rather fusty and out of date.

Petronius — I read Trimalchio's dinner party a year or two ago in an Oxford scholar's edition and there is a good deal of permanent human nature in that grotesque *nouveau riche*.

We are travelling light, so I have few and small books: Dante's *Paradiso* in Dent's pocket edition for one: having lately read some recent Italian books I understand better how archaic the language is to a modern Italian. Latinists have a pull there, and the flashes of quite modern thinking among the scholastic divinity strike one with more admiration every time. When we go home I shall turn again to Benvenuto da Imola's Latin commentary — good because so like medieval Latin with no classical affectations, and mighty good sense. I should feel like a pottering old idler if I had not left my new edition of *Torts* (with few but not trifling postings up of controversial points) ready for the printer.

This afternoon we are back in the trail of a thunderstorm (no warning of barometer) from Ermenonville, where the Marquis de Girardin invited J-J. Rousseau to spend his last days — having already laid out a 'Desert' according to his principles (we saw it from the road and can assure you it is real sand), as

John Morley and other esteemed authors shall fructify unto you. Being Sunday, there were crowds of excursion vehicles at the gates, and we left the merry Parisians taking cover in their charabancs. (The landscape gardening of the Desert was only making paths and putting up some stones with sentimental inscriptions in a piece of sandy heath land: the novelty was in the revulsion of taste.) Talking of sentimentality, I have had a circular from a Universal Negro Improvement Society (with an office in London).

Yours ever,
F. P.

Beverly Farms, September 20, 1928

My dears:[1]

A joint and several letters from you came this afternoon and brought much pleasure. Your function as godparents interests me. Years ago an ex-secretary of mine telegraphed to me from California asking me to be godfather by proxy to his daughter. I answered, "Yes — I do not know what it is," — and I never have found out, beyond sending a silver mug or something, I forget what. I envy you your temporary abode, changed I presume before this, and I agree with your condemnation of armchair pacifists on the general ground that until the world has got farther along war not only is not absurd but is inevitable and rational — though of course I would make great sacrifices to avoid one. But I don't pass moral judgments, least of all on nations. I see the inevitable everywhere. Also I do not forget that before we were in the last war a German wrote to me of similar killings on the part of the French. I receive all stories with doubt and, if I believe them, I feel much as I should if the same deaths had occurred by shipwreck or earthquake. The South still has stories about Sherman's march to the sea that I believe to be fictions.

I am glad to hear that Chekov, however spelt, is out of fashion. His stories gave me little pleasure. As to Petronius, F.'s comment is the same that I made, but I add that there is a

[1] This letter was addressed to Sir Frederick and Lady Pollock. Lady Pollock had added a postscript (here omitted) to Pollock's letter of September 9.

large number of quotable passages when P. speaks *in propria persona*. To be sure one can find quotable passages almost anywhere where the stenographer is unknown — where he is used the sentences grow verbose and flabby. I bet you could pick a good one from a column of advertisements. How suggestive are jute and gunny bags, or one that my father used to like for fireworks, "gerbs mutating with rayonant sunfires," or to take poetry that I read on a street car:

"Tell me not in mournful numbers
That things are not as of yore
We can give you for two dollars
A better hat than Caesar wore."

Not to speak of Mark Twain's variation on an original that I have seen:

"The conductor when he takes a fare
Will punch in the presence of the passengare
A pink trip slip for a ten cent fare
A green " " " " five cent fare."

I forget the rest.

I congratulate you on the new edition of *Torts*. I have nothing to show since I polished off 125 applications for *certiorari* that will come up at our first conference. I believe I shall find 100 more awaiting me in Washington — but now I am idle until next Monday, 24th, when we go to town, and on Wed., 26th, to Washington.

Oh dear, I willingly could idle longer.

Yours ever,
O. W. Holmes

London, October 15, 1928

My dear Holmes:

Enlarged snapshot of our grandson within. We think it shows intelligence. The other person is the French nurse.

. . . Mark Twain's lines as I remember them are:

"Conductor, when you receive a fare
Punch in the presence of the passenjare:

a blue trip slip for a two cent fare,
a brown t. s. for a three cent fare,
a pink t. s. for a five cent fare:

(Chorus) Punch, brothers, punch with care,
Punch in the presence of the passenjare!"

There was some prose patter to the effect that you had better not read the lines because they would haunt you for the rest of your life — which was quite true.

As to shorthand notes I deeply sympathize. Almost every month I have to restore one or more sentences in unwritten judgments to grammar or sense or both. The old reporters edited their own abbreviated long hand notes freely and made good English of them: their less courageous (and more hustled) successors have lost the art — all but one or two of the best.

Judicial obituary today: Sir E. Ridley, good scholar, Fellow of All Souls, successful, *sicut dicunt*, as an official Referee, and by general opinion of the Bar the worst High Court judge of our time, ill tempered and grossly unfair: which is rather a mystery.

Our Old Hall of Lincoln's Inn is most successfully restored, the old brick delivered from stucco defacement and the fine timber roof from a sham stucco ceiling. The King (as an honorary Bencher of the Inn) and Queen will come to the opening next month. . . .

Yours ever,
F. P.

LONDON, November 29, 1928 [1]

My dear Holmes:

The "economic" view of your Constitution always seemed to me a kind of specialist pedantry and I am glad to hear it is discredited.[2]

[1] A letter from Pollock, dated November 8, 1928, is omitted.

[2] It appears from Holmes's Journal that at approximately this date he had read Charles Warren's *The Making of the Constitution* (1928), a volume which contained critical discussion of the economic interpretation of the Constitution. Although no letter from Holmes referring to the volume has been found it seems probable that he had mentioned it to Pollock.

Sentimentalism embodied in some form of crankiness is the badge of almost all the Russell tribe.[3] Odo R. was, and his son Lord Ampthill whom I know middling well, is an exception.

I have not seen the later versions of the re-stated law of Contract,[4] but doubt whether the promoters have an adequate draftsman among them. Crabbed and obscure definitions are of no use beyond a narrow circle of students, of whom probably every one has a pet one of his own. As to your conception I don't know exactly how much I differ, never having seen a clear-cut statement of it. Provisionally I don't see as an equity lawyer how you make room for specific performance, or, on the common law side, how you escape censuring the common form of declaration in assumpsit. Don't you want an averment of *neither* performance *nor* tender of damages. For my part I stick to the promisee's reasonable expectation, which is, in the first line, performance. But I suspend any positive opinion.

Last week we re-opened our Old Hall:[5] (see card and take it for an ante-dated Xmas card; observe the roof now visible after being hidden by a sham plaster ceiling for a century).

Yours ever,
F. P.

WASHINGTON, December 11, 1928

My dear F. P.:

Thanks for the impressive picture of the Old Hall. With regard to contracts I will bore you no more except to say that your suggestion that I ought to criticize the declaration in assumpsit for not denying tender of damages, shows the persistence of the impression that I say that a man *promises* either X or *to pay damages*. I don't think a man promises to pay damages in contract any more than in tort. He commits an act that makes him liable for them if a certain event does not come to pass, just as his act in tort makes him liable *simpliciter*. But

[3] Holmes had recently read Bertrand Russell's *Sceptical Essays* (1928).

[4] Tentative drafts of the American Law Institute's *Restatement of the Law of Contracts* had been published in March 1924 and September 1928.

[5] Of Lincoln's Inn.

while I could expatiate I will not, and let you have peace; but I will add that I don't expect the most respectable and excellent workers on the *Restatements* to inflame either the Potomac or the Thames. A cove yesterday wanted me to say that I would review some little forthcoming book dealing, I understand, with covenants running with the land.[1] It was intimated that the author ran counter to some of my views. It gave me a spell of the dry grins to remember and to write that very nearly half a century had gone by since that was a burning question for me. An adjournment has begun and as all my work is done I hope for some leisure. It never comes. But I shall try to read something outside the law, and if the weather should be as fine as it has been today, to get some drives. But as life draws near the end (one never quite believes it) I think rather more than ever that man has respected himself too much and the universe too little. He has thought himself a god and has despised "brute matter," instead of thinking his importance to be all of a piece with the rest. But the carnal man still is strong within me and I take a good deal of interest in the job — the job of life. My love to Lady Pollock.

Yours ever,
O. W. H.

LONDON, December 24, 1928

My dear Holmes:

Thanks for your correction: I did suppose, not alone it seems, that you conceived a contractual promise as being in ultimate analysis for performance *or* damages: I must have misunderstood what you said long ago in *The Common Law* (now out of my reach till after vacation), and remain in doubt what your real thesis is to lead to. I don't see the way to any neat contrast-parallel between contract ++ tort liability. There is no act I have committed beyond being born to make me liable for my own trespasses when I trespass: whereas I am not in a position to be liable for my cattle trespassing unless

[1] Presumably Charles E. Clark, *Real Covenants and Other Interests which 'Run with Land'* (1929).

I choose to keep cattle, which in fact I don't. But the language and pleading of our law make no distinction until it comes to assuming a position which makes me answerable to some certain person or sort of persons *e.g.* invitees in my place of business — the original *super se assumpsit* inducing a declaration in Tort is typical of this. Not that pleading can be taken as a test, for the forms of action, notably Debt, ignore the fundamental difference between duties imposed by law and duties created by the will of the parties. But our lady the Common Law seems to interpose, with a tolerant slightly bored smile, "My dear little sons fussing with your systems, why try to be logical when the facts are so often in a mess with people not stopping to think what they mean or not having the wit to make it plain? I don't mean O. W. H. who knows better."

The barometer has been making a chart of sharp zigzags for some weeks, giving us a mixed lot of weather and temperatures and about one fine day in a week — and I am struggling with a rather violent cold. After the New Year we go to Paris for a week to see our young people. The grandson has been putting on weight like a good boy.

We are happier about the King,[1] and hope the Prince of Wales will begin to think seriously of his future duties, not so easy for him as the job of running round the world and being pleasant to everybody.

Yours ever,
F. P.

Last week we entertained to supper in our repaired Old Hall the staff employed on the work from the architect to the leading workmen in every craft — of our Bench, only actual office-bearers and Treasurers during the work were present: I was the junior and said grace before meat in Latin as a tribute to the age of the building. It was a unique occasion. . . .

[1] In the latter part of November King George V was seriously ill. The Prince of Wales was called home from Africa and a Council of State was formed to carry on the Government.

LONDON, January 21, 1929

My dear Holmes:

Imprimis I am fully with you[1] in thinking talk about "primary" and "sanctioning" rights unprofitable: I have never used those terms myself and wish we could get rid of the ambiguous "Right," meaning according to the context:

(a) *Potential Claim*: a liberty or title which the law recognizes and will at need protect, (something more than mere material freedom to do whatever one is not hindered from doing — as it were an energy of position), or,

(b) *Actual Claim*: a present cause for calling on the court to enforce someone's duty (*quasi* an energy of motion).

But usage, the usage moreover of classical and highly respectable writers, is I fear too inveterate. See further ch. 3 of my *First Book of Jurisprudence*, written not so much to expound my own views as to help intelligent students to a rational reading of their books. So I don't think we really differ in principle.

Item: I have seen an instructive paper on your dissenting judgments in *Scribner* by a writer otherwise unknown to me — very properly pointing out how some of them have prevailed later: and therewith a portrait which seems to me to show you in an exaggerated mood of dissent.[2]

Item: the new edition of *Torts* is on its way to you and I hope you will approve the last paragraph of the preface.[3]

We have read an interesting book by Arthur Weigall (his trade is Egyptology), *The Paganism in our Christianity*. Reviewers have seemingly fought shy of it. My only quarrel with him is that he is not free from the old rationalist fallacy of picking out from a narrative incredible as a whole the parts you think least improbable and reconstructing a story of your own

[1] The letter referred to is missing.

[2] Joseph Percival Pollard, "Justice Holmes's Dissents," 85 *Scribner's* 22 (January 1929), accompanied by a reproduction of a drawing of Holmes by S. J. Woolf, dated February 23, 1926.

[3] 13th edition, 1929, p. vii-viii: "As I write these lines I hear that a very learned committee of the American Bar is engaged on a restatement of the law of torts. Nothing but good can come of this if it is borne in mind that the object of any such statement is not to effect a verbal reconciliation of all the authorities, but to frame such a rule as a well-informed Court of last resort might lay down; and that, if in any case the result is a proposition which cannot be made intelligible to a jury, there is like to be something wrong either with the drafting (which should not happen to a committee including expert draftsmen) or with some of the less authoritative decisions."

with them (even Loisy has done this). Then the only certain result is that, whatever really happened, your plausible story did not. However, it is a good book in the main, and it would take a bold man to carry it into Tennessee.

Another fascinating book, ending in heroic tragedy, is Younghusband's on the Mt. Everest expedition [4] — attractive it seems, by the number of reprints, to the large public as well as to mountaineers. Y. says the Tibetan rulers are now loth to give any more permits for transit, thinking that the mountain gods are angry, and not satisfied that even mad Englishmen would take all that trouble merely to climb the highest known mountain. So the attempt may not be renewed in our day. There is now no doubt that it is possible, indeed it may be that the two lost climbers actually reached the summit in 1924.

I have seen the *L. Q. R.*'s copy of the three-volume profusely illustrated *Panorama of the Legal Systems of the World*, directed and (as to the letterpress) wholly executed by our very learned friend Wigmore. He should have associated a few expert subeditors with himself: as it is there is inevitable disproportion (Scotland gets about half a page and the very interesting South Slavonic customs nothing, while there is a lot of little better than padding about the wholly unimportant paper codes of Czarist Russia). Illustrations again a jumble of really useful facsimiles and photographs, with worthless reproductions of so-called historical 19th century pictures. Also some odd little mistakes, probably slips due to haste. Still there is a lot of information, especially for the multitude of fairly intelligent readers who can't read any language but English with ease. Nobody will buy it here but a limited number of public libraries.

A Scottish court lately held by a majority, in a trespassing infant's case, that knowledge on the defendant's part of habitual trespasses by both children and adults, coupled with more or less frequent but on the whole ineffectual warnings off, nothing being done to make access to the dangerous thing physically difficult, was equivalent to tacit license: [5] wrong, I think. The danger was obvious to persons capable of discretion. . . .

Yours ever,
F. P.

[4] Sir Francis Younghusband, *The Epic of Mount Everest* (1927).
[5] Robert Addie and Sons v. Dumbreck, [1928] S. C. 547.

WASHINGTON, February 5, 1929

My dear Pollock:

Imprimis, forgive me for writing on this lousy paper but the comfort of a block is so great that so far as I dare to I sacrifice elegance and politeness to my own ease. 2do, I did not scrutinize the article in *Scribner's*, but I thought the portrait bad. 3°, I am pleased to see that you note what I often have thought of sardonically: "The picking out from a narration incredible as a whole the part you think, etc." The imbecility of rationalizing the miracles in this way seems to me great, apropos of which — did you ever hear of and if so what about him — Montague Summers? He published a translation of the *Malleus Maleficarum*, which is before me, lent to me by a curious friend; and to it prefixed an introduction dated *In Festo Expectationis B. M. V. 1927* that I could not have believed possible had I not read it. He believes the whole business of witchcraft from the beginning and thinks that the old women who were burned were the tools of a great conspiracy against religion and society that has emerged later in the Bolsheviks, etc. He thinks the world would be much better today "had the most excellent tribunal (the Inquisition) continued to employ its full prerogatives and the full exercise of its salutary powers" (p. xviii). He seems to believe that you or some bad people can cause death or grievous bodily harm by melting or sticking pins into an image of an enemy. His criterion of truth seems to have no relation to experience but to be solely whether it is sanctioned by a papal bull. It makes me gasp — and yet they had or still have a trial going on in Pennsylvania where it seems that the whole local population believes in witches and that the murder involved was in some way connected with this belief.[1] I did not read about it and so am fuzzy in my account.

Redlich[2] (whom probably you know) now in Cambridge, Mass., has published a biography of the Emperor of Austria, Francis Joseph, which although off my beat I read with interest. The Emperor not only did not entertain, he did not surmise

[1] In January, 1929, John H. Blymyer, John Curry, and Wilbert G. Gess were found guilty of murdering Nelson D. Rehmeyer whom they accused of having "hexed," or bewitched them.

[2] Josef Redlich (1869–1936); Professor of Comparative Law, Harvard Law School.

the ideas that make life worth living to me; what he did believe I loathe, yet he was a gentleman and a hero. He is a perfect illustration of my old saying that no gentleman can be a philosopher and no philosopher a gentleman: To the philosopher everything is fluid — even himself. The gentleman is a little God over against the Cosmos.

I have seen only the advertisement of Wigmore's book. He has been a benefactor to the problems in many ways, but this sounds to me rather *ad captandum*.

I think your Scotch decision as to the trespassing infant wrong, unless there were elements that I have missed. I wrote a decision the other way: *United Zinc & Chemical Co.* v. *Britt*, 258 U. S. 268.

I like your "Caution & Valour"[3] though Valour seems to me a little strained though I remember your use in connection with Willes in your dedication of *Torts*.[4] I am cut off by my messenger. My love to the Lady.

Yours ever,
O. W. H.

LONDON, February 18, 1929

My dear Holmes:

Why can't your stationers sell blocks of good paper? This leaf is from a block — and one can get better if desired. Nothing is easier than to believe in witches, Jews' ritual murders & circumcisions of Christian children. St. Thomas of Canterbury's miracle attested by the mayor and notables of Bedford, the dragons seen in the Alps in the 16th century as deposed by credible witnesses (see the affidavits and the portraits made after them in Scheuchzer's *Itinera Alpina*), and the whole bag of tricks of modern spiritualism — if only you

[3] On March 6, 1929, Pollock lectured at King's College, University of London, on the topic "Judicial Caution and Valour." He had enclosed in his letter of January 21, 1929, a syllabus of the lecture.

[4] The 13th edition, like earlier editions of Pollock's *Torts*, was dedicated "To the memory of the Right Honourable Sir James Shaw Willes, Knt. sometime a Justice of the Common Bench, a man Courteous and Accomplished, a Judge Wise and Valiant; and to my Friend Oliver Wendell Holmes, an Associate Justice of the Supreme Court of the United States."

start by assuming that the ordinary rules of historical evidence will hold in an atmosphere of credulity. When such an atmosphere is set up in a crowd (it need not be a large crowd) they won't — not even the supposed cardinal one that self-accusation is the strongest kind of testimony. Many witches were convicted on their own voluntary confessions which they themselves believed (though also confessions that were not voluntary are said to have been officially so called). Compare the story of Holt, C. J.[1] and the old woman whom he asked whether she could fly. When she said, "Yes," he answered: "Why then, so you may. I know of no law against flying." Hale[2] would have felt bound to take her seriously.

So the 20th century introduction to the *Malleus Maleficarum* (a book I have never seen, and I forget if I ever knew the reputed author's name), does not surprise me much. It seems harder to believe, on no evidence at all, that we are the lost Ten Tribes, but there is a British-Israel Federation numerous enough to run a journal (I found one just now among a week's heap of circulars). Why a week's heap? Because we stole a week to go and see our youngsters in Paris. Last Friday the grandson was photographed sitting in my lap — by an accomplished lady who is also a musician: she plays the harp and her husband the organ, so they are fine children of Jubal. Paris was main cold, but our rooms in a generally excellent hotel overheated. As to witchcraft embodying pagan and prehistoric superstitions, I find in the *Encyclopedia Britannica* that in Italy it is called *la vecchia religione*, and an ingenious lady (name Murray I think) developed the thesis at large a few years ago.[3] But the notion of an organized conspiracy seems as fantastic as the similar one about the French Revolution put forth by Mrs. Webster[4] (who dragged in Freemasonry: now 18th century masonry was quite as innocent in France as in England). Your Catholic introducer to *Mall: Malefic:* would I suppose not

[1] Sir John Holt (1642–1710); Chief Justice of England, 1689–1710. Many witchcraft cases were prosecuted before him; none successfully.

[2] Sir Matthew Hale (1609–1676); Judge of the Court of Common Pleas, 1654–1658; Chief Baron of the Exchequer, 1660–1671; Chief Justice of England, 1671–1676. The only discreditable aspect of Hale's career was his belief in witchcraft and the resulting convictions.

[3] Probably Margaret Alice Murray, *Witch-Cult in Western Europe* (1921).

[4] Nesta H. Webster, *The French Revolution — A Study in Democracy* (2nd ed., 1919).

be consoled for the Inquisition by the witch-huntings of heretical Puritans, which I rather think were more systematic though packed into a shorter time. . . .

A year or two after the War I met Redlich here: we consider him a very sound author on English institutions, and I conceive he must be trustworthy about Franz Josef — who surely was not a hero but only a conscientious 18th century Habsburg tho' born I think some time after the Congress of Vienna. That no gentleman can be a philosopher I flatly deny. Which of the two characters can you refuse to Arthur Balfour, William James, Boutroux, Count Keyserling? and I will add Count Dunin-Borkowski, S. J. who wrote an excellent book on Spinoza in or about 1910, though I have only corresponded with him. Not to mention Bacon, Pascal, Descartes or Berkeley before our time.

You will find the *United Zinc Co.'s case* cited and relied on in P. on *Torts*. I have no doubt that Scottish decision is wrong.

The word valiant is Willes, J.'s own; see the close of his great judgment in *Fernandez' case*, 10 C. B. N. S. 1,[5] suggested (I think he told me himself) by Geo. Herbert's praise of "a sad wise valour" in *The Church Porch*.

Concerning human testimony, did I ever tell you what G. S. Venables,[6] an accomplished scholar and very shrewd man, once said to me? — Historians have never made sufficient allowance for the deliberate lying of witnesses incapable of deception. Froude built up some fine picturesque fiction on his real or pretended faith that the preamble of an Act of Parliament must be true.

Yours ever,
F. P.

[5] The question presented for decision in this case was whether a judge of assize had power to commit a witness for contempt of court. In sustaining the Judge's power Willes, J. said: "We have been urged to be careful of being misled by our own way of thinking, in the decision of this case, because, as it was suggested, our privileges are involved in the question. As that course had been adopted, I take leave to say that I am not conscious of the vulgar desire to elevate myself or the court of which I may be a member, by grasping after a pre-eminence which does not belong to me; and that I will endeavor to be even [*sic*] valiant in preserving and handing down those powers to do justice and to maintain truth, which, for the common good, the law has intrusted to the judges." 10 C. B. (N. S.) 56–57.

[6] George Stovin Venables (1810–1888); barrister and man of letters.

LONDON, February 28, 1929

My dear Holmes:

P. S. The Scottish case we thought wrong is now reversed in the House of Lords.[1] The report should be interesting when it comes, as Lord Hailsham L.C. (Douglas Hogg) gave a pretty full exposition. He tells me the *United Zinc Co.'s case* was not cited: which was rather stupid of counsel, seeing that it is exactly in point.

Yours ever,
F. P.

LONDON, May 2, 1929[1]

My dear Holmes:

John Dewey's *Experience and Nature*[2] is in my hands, and I find life (at my age) too short to appreciate a long serious book which has no summary of the results, no proper table of contents (only bare chapter-headings), and a strangely elusive index — where you see Berkeley, turn to the page indicated and don't find Berkeley's name at all: as who should say, "Look at that page, and if you know your Berkeley already you will see that I was thinking of him."

So I really don't know whether the book has a beginning middle and end or is a collection of detached studies. I have formed a sort of notion that Dewey holds reason not to be something outside the order of nature, but the order itself: to which I need no persuasion to agree. But if (as is likely enough) that guess is wrong, I don't see what he drives at.

The most intelligible sentences I have lighted on are those of yours which he adopts near the end (not saying, to my annoyance, exactly where they are to be found).

The sun has come out today after the blackest and foggiest May-day within my memory.

[1] Robert Addie and Sons v. Dumbreck, [1929] A. C. 358. Noted by Pollock, 45 *L. Q. Rev.* 280 (1929).

[1] Two letters from Pollock, dated March 18 and April 22, 1929, are omitted.

[2] From Holmes's Journal it appears that he had read this book, published in 1925, in 1926, in 1927, and again in 1929.

Sir Dunbar Barton has brought out a diverting and profitable book called *Links between Shakespeare & the Law*, with a "foreword" by James M. Beck, on *int. al.* Mark Twain's conversion to the Baconian heresy.

Yours ever,
F. P.

WASHINGTON, May 24, 1929

True thanks dear friends for your kind and affectionate words.[1] Of course I knew I could rely upon your sympathy. I am reconciled by the certainty that a continuance of life would have meant only a continuance of pain and suffering of which my wife had had too much before the final accident. (She fell and broke her hip bone.) We have had our share. For sixty years she made life poetry for me and at 88 one must be ready for the end. I shall keep at work and interested while it lasts — though not caring very much for how long.

Your affectionate,
O. W. HOLMES

[1] Mrs. Holmes died April 30, 1929. The letter referred to is missing.

IX

1929-1932

LONDON, July 17, 1929

My dear Holmes:

We are glad to have a pretty good account of you.[1] The only effect of *Anno Domini* that I have to complain of is that somehow everything takes a little longer to do when the time can be computed (as in shaving), therefore probably also when

[1] The letter apparently referred to is missing.

it cannot. One result is that I find it harder to read a serious new book, but I must get a sight of Sumner one day.[2]

Talking of "folk" legends some one has dug up in Egypt an ancient story — seemingly popular — of a magician who divided the waters of a lake, made them "stand on an heap," so that he might recover the ring a princess had dropped. But the relation of this, in date, to the Passage of the Red Sea does not seem clearly made out. Nor will one case show that this was a common item in Egyptian magic. Also there is mention of some one with a name very like Moses who is a great man and interferes to restrain oppressive officials.

I should not expect Smuts to be very much of a philosopher[3] either by learning or by nature (in the latter case he may or may not have produced, like F. Younghusband, an interesting autobiographical document).

But just now I have got a quite short lecture *Science & the Unseen World* by Prof. Eddington of Cambridge which is really to the purpose even if you don't agree with it (which mainly I do). He is in the first rank of living mathematicians — a rank that as I roughly guess might about make the front of an infantry section (¼ of what used to be a company and is now a platoon), and is also a Quaker. So the spiritual half of him, being indifferent to dogmatic definitions, is in an excellent position for discussing the nature of things with the exact science half, and not being tempted to take refuge in putting itself in a water-tight compartment, or one might say better behind a *purda* of tradition and formalism.

N. B. I believe the Society of Friends are nearer to the really primitive, *i.e.* pre-Pauline-Church than any other denomination: not that they live as St. Paul did in expectation of the world coming to an end very shortly, but I know of nobody who does.

An English merchant at Alexandria said that the Lord in his wrath created Greeks and in his wrath created Jews, but in his infinite mercy never created a Greek Jew. But in his

[2] It appears from Holmes's Journal that he had recently read W. G. Sumner's *Folkways* (1st ed., 1907).

[3] Holmes had recently read portions of General Jan Smuts's *Holism and Evolution* (1926).

wrath he did create Armenian Jews, or their names belie them: a pair of solicitors who have been claiming to dictate to the *Law Reports* exactly how their trumpery case should be reported. But the Lord in his wisdom has also made blue pencils. After they had written me two or three pompous epistles I turned them over to the Council of Law Reporting as my superior officers: from whom I don't expect they will take much.

I wonder why unwritten judgments in the Court of Appeal — there chiefly if not only — run to bad journalese jargon: *such* as a mere demonstrative, *prior to* as an indiscriminate substitute for *before*, *as to whether*, hardly ever required and seldom tolerable, and the like. With you, of course, it cannot happen. . . .

Yours ever
F. P.

LONDON, July 22, 1929

My dear Holmes:

. . . The London Library has Sumner's posthumous *Folkways*, 1925 (I seem to have seen a notice of a recent English reprint or reissue) — a puzzling book even when one remembers that it was never finally revised.

He was as you say an acute and independent critic of vulgar platitudes and catchwords: even so not always discerning. Such an aphorism as "He who holds the sea will hold the land" — backed up by the solid history of sea power — should not be lumped in with the slang of politicians: the proper criticism on it is that Bacon's "To be master of the sea is the abridgment of a Monarchy" is both more impressive and more accurate. The Ciceronian *Qui mari potitur eum rerum potiri*, quoted by Bacon,[1] is even better.

However, one would expect Sumner, having laid down his thesis, to justify it by working out carefully selected examples in sufficient (but not more) detail to illustrate and support it. Instead of which he throws at your head a vast mass of roughly

[1] Francis Bacon, "Essay of the True Greatness of Kingdoms."

classified material with very little discrimination of origins (cannibalism of necessity, for want of other food, and magical or ritual cannibalism, evidently belong to different orders of facts: S. does next to nothing to explain the difference) and no ordered argument to show how and why his view accounts for the facts best.

It looks like the workshop of a man so much overweighted by book-learning that his selective judgment was dulled and his critical faculty blunted and he forgot how to keep his own eyes open. Not a very human man unless (as many do) he lived in water-tight compartments and hung up the live man outside the study door.

Strange, for one little thing, that an American anthropologist should, when collecting examples of odd currencies, have overlooked a Johns Hopkins University tract now some 40 years old on the customs developed in a boys' school in these parts, whereby it appears that the more thrifty boys made savings from their butter rations a medium of exchange till the butter ration became a money of account. "*Also eine Butter-Währung*," said a German economist when I told him of this, the first time I was in Berlin. Sumner should have welcomed modern instances (be they more or less relevant to his argument).

About Hindu custom S. is weak, relying on Monier Williams, a second-rate Sanskrit scholar at best, knowing nothing of Indian life at first-hand, and ignoring Alfred Lyall, one of the few Europeans who have ever learned to think like Asiatics. However, too many anthropologists are like the kind of real property lawyer who has never seen an original medieval charter and could not read a word of it if he did.

Still more strangely, Frazer's *Golden Bough*, first published 1890 (tho' much revised and enlarged since) is not even mentioned. Any episode of Frazer's, say *Psyche's Task* (1906, I think, now embodied in the great work), is more enlightening than S.'s whole mountain of samples. Montesquieu knew in a general way as well as we do that custom and convention are extremely various and often "pretty odd" (per Holt, C. J., on Acts of Parliament),[2] though his information was fragmentary

[2] City of London v. Wood, 12 Mod. 678, 687 (1701).

and not always trustworthy. And S. is now and then as uncritical as Montesquieu in mixing up examples from widely remote forms and stages of society.

Sir James Frazer is an excellent Hellenist. Sumner certainly was not, or he would not have vouched an encyclopaedic German for the familiar fact that in the Greek republican period tyrannicide was popular and admired. Did he not know (which it does not even need Greek to know — Campbell's (the poet) version must be in anthologies tho' his poems at large are little read nowadays) the Harmodius and Aristogiton song?[3] Then S. might have noted that there are quite respectable medieval justifications of tyrannicide — but Lord Acton, whom he might have found profitable on that and sundry other things, is not among his authorities.

S. says, truly enough, the Latin-Mediterranean people of the Roman Empire had an ugly vein of cruelty. He might have paused to note that the Greeks had not. Persian tortures and mutilations were as disgusting to Aeschylus (and presumably his audience) as to us: see Apollo's scolding of the Furies, *Eumenides*, 177 [186], where he tells them their place is not in his temple but with barbaric devilries:

> ἀλλ' οὗ καρανιστῆρες ὀφθαλμώρυχοι
> δίκαι σφαγαί τε . . .[4]

One can hardly censure him for ignoring the Eastern churches when he talks of Christian ethics, that being a common fault of historians in Western lands: but in fact the Eastern discipline is the more rational, to a layman's thinking, in several points (married clergy, divorce, autocephalous churches). He is not free from the temptation, common in anthropology, to go digging in savage muck-heaps and not look at what is happening

[3] May it be that Pollock was mistaken in ascribing the poem to Thomas Campbell? It seems likely that the reference was to a translation by Lord Chief Justice Denman (1779–1854) of the lines on Harmodius and Aristogeiton by Callistratus. Lord Denman was a contemporary and friend of Thomas Campbell and was succeeded as Lord Chief Justice by John Campbell, first Baron Campbell (1779–1861). Of Lord Denman's two versions of the Harmodius and Aristogeiton song, one was praised by Byron and both have been reprinted. See Sir Joseph Arnould, *Life of Thomas, First Lord Denman* (London, 1873), I, 16–17; II, 365–366.

[4] "No, your place is where there are sentences to beheading, gouging out of eyes, and cutting of throats. . . ." (Lines 186–7, H. W. Smythe, tr.)

under one's nose. You shall find learned discourse of newfangled metal spoiling (or being a counter-charm to) the magic and ritual of the Stone age, with never a word of a metal knife being forbidden in Hebrew (*quaere*, also Moslem) circumcision to this day. Fashion in costume, with more attention to the history we really know and more skill in arrangement, would have made him an excellent and persuasive section: imitation of civilian fashions in armour down to minute detail, revulsion from quite rational dress *c.* 1650 to the extravagances of *temp.* Louis XIV, reckless disregard of convenience in military dress, our queer survival of buttons at the back of a coat supporting the ghost of a sword-belt, and, specially to his purpose, the known impotence of tailors and dressmakers to impose fashions. But the material is all scattered and jumbled.

My father had a taste for the history of costume (men's) and might have done something good with it, only he lacked the temper and patience for minute inquiry.

When all is said, Sumner's work does notably revive and confirm one's impression of the immense change in the educated world's points of view in about half a century — and a quick one as such things go. When we were young controversy went on between quite serious, even learned disputants of whom one set regarded the dogmas and conventions of their commonwealth or persuasion as sent down from heaven (not considering how they knew their heaven to be the right one) and another (the rebels or heretics) as being imposed by a malignant power labelled usually "priestcraft" (not asking how there came to be priests), *e.g.* Bradlaugh as a coarse and John Morley as a refined type. Whereas now we conceive the dogmas and conventions as sucked up from an ocean of tribal magic, tabus, ritual, fashions, pseudo-scientific guesses, and the Lord knows what, and returned as the case may be in dews, showers, thunderstorms or waterspouts — with the ideas of prophets, philosophers and discoverers, not accounted for by any system, clearing the air at intervals. Of inventing new words I say nothing. "Societal" is vile, but other writers have made worse ones.

Friday last we had a little group of American students from divers colleges: two young men, two young women, an elder (youngish don) lady in charge, to lunch on the suggestion of a Welcome Committee — also a good sort of history professor from Ann Arbor and his wife, already met, and another friend or two: and mighty pleasant and intelligent they were, no priggery whatever. . . . In the universities lies, I think, the main hope of producing an educated public in North America (the Province of Quebec excepted, which is a kind of "peculiar"); but whether there is leaven enough for the very big lump is, I suppose, on the knees of the gods. Anyhow nobody here is competent to guess. . . .

Yours ever,
F. P.

GRAND HOTEL, CABOURG
August 16, 1929

My dear Holmes:

It appears to me from your frequent mention of *certiorari* that you and your companions are burdened with much work of the routine kind that in England is done by the Masters of the Court, subject to appeal when any real question of principle or practice occurs. Such cases, I suppose, are not a large proportion.

On greater matters I believe in the supremacy of reason because your *can't help* postulates it. The fundamental *can't help* is the law of contradictories: and there is nothing but reason to vouch for it. In a world of unreason (if there could be one) nothing would prevent A = B [and] A = not B from both being true under identical conditions, and there would be no *can't help* at all. But I wholly agree, for your reasons and others, on the vanity of prophesying in terms of Greenwich time concerning a beginning or end of the stellar universe.[1] One ground of such prophecies has been nullified in our own time by the discovery of radio-activity, another by our space turning out to be finite (not spherical, nor, it seems, even of uniform curvature), and it is a fair guess that other still unknown factors in the problem — apart from philosophical ob-

[1] If Holmes had written of these matters in a recent letter, the letter is missing.

jections to the problem being a legitimate one — are no less important. You and I were brought up on indestructible atoms and infallible Euclidean parallels. I wonder what elements my grandson will have to learn. . . . The English of the opinions delivered in your Court — and eminently though not exclusively of yours — has always appeared to me excellent. As to *such*, this is the kind of attorney's clerk's slang I have to choke off: "The plaintiff was the tenant of a house in X Street. Such street was admitted to be a new street within, etc., etc." They think it looks more professional. And so it has crept even into judgments.

Yours ever,
F. P.

The sound foundation of Freud's (if his followers don't wrong him) crazy sky-scraper seems to have been discovered by you long ago. I have not read him at first hand.

BEVERLY FARMS, August 30, 1929 [1]

My dear Pollock:

To begin by answering two things in your letter. We have to consider the *certiorari* because it was only after effort that we got a bill passed that makes an appeal to our court dependent upon our discretion in many cases in which until lately it was matter of right. Let it ever be understood that the preliminary judgment was delegated, I should expect the law to be changed back again very quickly with the result that we should have to hear many cases that have no right to our time; as it is we barely keep up with the work. We used to be years behindhand. Now I think all the cases on our docket have been put there within a year.

2. I don't understand your seeming inclination to controvert my *can't helps*. I see nothing behind the force of reason except that *ich kann nicht anders* — and I don't know whether the cosmos can or not. I do not see what more there is in your law of contradiction, except to assert that the universe can't make

[1] A postal card from Pollock, dated August 28, 1929, is omitted.

nonsense sense. Even to that I should simply say I don't know. I can't imagine it — but I hardly think that a measure of the possible.

If there is anything that has been supposed to be compulsory upon us short of not affirming nonsense I should think it was that every phenomenon must have a cause. Yet I find scientific men suggesting nowadays (*e.g.* Eddington) [2] that there are phenomena for which no causes can be discovered and seemingly believing that they are outside the category of cause and effect. I am far from believing with them, but I am entirely ready to believe it on proof. Chauncey Wright [3] a nearly forgotten philosopher of real merit, taught me when young that I must not say *necessary* about the universe, that we don't know whether anything is necessary or not. So I describe myself as a *bet*tabilitarian. I believe that we can *bet* on the behavior of the universe in its contact with us. We bet we can know what it will be. That leaves a loophole for free will — in the miraculous sense — the creation of a new atom of force, although I don't in the least believe in it. I guess (strict sense) that you think man a more important manifestation than I do. I suppose that such differences depend a good deal on the ultimate make-up of different men and hardly can be argued about. Of course from the human point of view he is important; he hardly would live if he didn't think so. Also I hasten to admit that I don't dare pronounce any fact unimportant that the Cosmos has produced. I only mean that when one thinks coldly I see no reason for attributing to man a significance different in kind from that which belongs to a baboon or to a grain of sand. But the time approaches when I must go down stairs and play solitaire I fear. I have just finished *Political Thought in the Sixteenth Century* (J. W. Allen), a mighty good book. It is amusing to see what used to strike me with the abolitionists before our war, as an eternally recurring phenomenon. The abolitionists had a stock phrase that a man was either a knave or a fool who did not act as they (the aboli-

[2] During the summer of 1929 Holmes had read Eddington's *The Nature of the Physical World* (1928).

[3] University Lecturer on the principles of psychology, Harvard College, 1870–1871; Instructor in Physics, 1874–1875; author of philosophical essays.

tionists) *knew* to be right. So Calvin thought of the Catholics and the Catholics of Calvin. So I don't doubt do the more convinced prohibitionists think of their opponents today. When you know that you know persecution comes easy. It is as well that some of us don't know that we know anything. One month more here, and then back to work. I shall hold on until nature or man gives me a hint that the end has come. Meantime I get a quiet pleasure out of this day. My love to the Lady.

Yours ever,
O. W. H.

BEVERLY FARMS, September 27, 1929

My dear Pollock:

You open chasms between us that seem to reach the middle of the earth — but then I realize that they are only a foot wide at the mouth and I am comforted. I suppose that you will very likely have got home before this letter gets there. I meanwhile am spending my last days here. On Monday Boston, on Wednesday night off to Washington, due there Oct. 3, A.M.. I have done a good stroke of work, 226 ± *certiorari*, and I was looking for two weeks of idleness before I left, when there came a request from the Harvard Law School that I would stand for a full length portrait to hang as a counterpart to Marshall in their new Student Reading Room which I hear is very fine and 500 feet long. The compliment could not be refused, and so I have been passing my mornings between standing and sitting for Hopkinson to paint. As I see the result emerging I am very glad, for he not only has made an admirable likeness but a very vivid one, as it seems to me. But my idleness has gone. Tomorrow, Saturday, is the last day with me. He will finish the robe on some other man after I am gone.

The only thing I have had a chance to read in these later days is a part of Swift's *Journal to Stella*: it has a sort of Pepysian interest though not equal to Pepys, and perhaps a trifle squalid. I may have mentioned rereading *Anna Karenina* in the French translation. Novels don't give me the pleasure they used to, and after having read about Rasputin [1] I have come to think that perhaps the best thing that could have happened was to wipe out the society in which he flourished. So I was less sympathetic to what at least I used to think the greatest novel I ever read. I will not go into a review of my literary experience — but I may have confided to you, that bar Miss Bates, I was bored by *Emma*. I feel bound to test your friendship by this blasphemous admission.

28th. The last sitting is over, and just as it is finished I get news of the death of my sister-in-law.[2] . . . Dear me — everything that happens now is a reminder, and I feel time quietly taking down the building little by little. My love to the Lady.

Yours ever,
O. W. H.

VENICE, September 22, 1929

My dear Holmes:

Your letter of August 30 found me here yesterday, after lying certain days, it seems, in London. As to the betting element in all particular judgments and decisions we wholly agree, and are fortified by Bishop Butler who says, in effect, that even if the truth of Christianity is not demonstrable, you (the freethinker, sceptic, or Deist constantly lumped in with them by 18th Century apologists) risk very little by betting on it — and if it *is* true stand to gain immensely. I don't say that he actually uses any such word as wager, but that is one of his arguments.

That on which one bets is — obviously in most cases — the value of some material term in the data, an *x* which for aught one knows may be either *a* or *b*, but also, less obviously, the absence of any material but wholly unknown and not even suspected element: as, till the other day, radio-activity in physical speculation, which has made hay of divers plausible conclusions.

[1] René Fülop-Miller, *Rasputin, the Holy Devil* (1928).
[2] Mrs. Walter Scott Fitz, formerly Mrs. Edward Jackson Holmes.

As to *can't help*, I would amend ICH *kann nicht anders* into MAN *kann nicht anders*. A *can't help* not common to you and me would not be of much use to us as social animals: so the possibility of that community is fundamental. Which for me is another way of saying that the universe (or the only cosmos that can concern us) is reasonable.

On the vanity and mischief of dogmatizing we don't differ at all. As Flaubert said, *La bêtise consiste à vouloir conclure.*

I write now because I doubt the speed if not the certainty of post from Ragusa (now called Dubrovnik by Serbo-Croat patriotic pedantry). O' Friday I went ashore at a pleasing little Dalmatian town (Curzola, Italian, Korčula, Serbian) like a scene in a play, or still more like a walled town in a medieval miniature. An old peasant making wine presumably from the grapes of his own little vineyard (not bad neither, he gave his visitors a glass to taste) in a kind of shanty open to the public walk. No appearance of any wheeled traffic. I think I did see one mule-cart. Much too hilly for any motor.

Yours ever,
F. P.

Venice is looking its best. I had quite a good walk (for me as I now hobble) to the *Accademia* pictures this morning. The clerk of the weather suddenly remembered the equinox and gave us an autumnal night, but I think we shall have some warm days yet.

WASHINGTON, October 26, 1929

My dear Pollock:

Your last letter (Sept. 22) has remained unanswered partly because you were wandering and partly because the work at the beginning of the term checked the generous currents of the soul. The philosophical remarks I shall not deal with beyond saying that the "*I* can't help" is the ultimate. If we are sensible men and not crazy on-*ists* of any sort, we recognize that if we are in a minority of one we are likely to get locked up and then find a test or qualifications by reference to some kind of majority vote actual or imagined. Of course the fact that mankind or that part of it that we take into account are subject to most of the same can't helps as ourselves makes society possible, but what interests me is that we start with an arbitrary limit which I know no reason for believing is a limit to the cosmos of which I am only a small part. Most if not all our ultimates seem to me to bear the mark of the finite. Of course you may say *de non apparentibus et de non existentibus eadem est ratio.* I do not find in that a warrant for believing that this cosmos can go no farther than I can, little as I can imagine how.

I didn't see your Prime Minister[1] when he was here. He made an appointment to call but had to go to the White House instead. I did have some pleasant words with Lord Arnold[2] who came with the Ambassador[3] and afterwards sent me a charming little book by a New Zealander, Alan Mulgan's *Home*, and, better, I had a call from my former acquaintance and friend Nevinson (*Manchester Guardian*) in whom I delight. He sent me the 3d volume of *Last Changes and Chances* which is giving me much pleasure. There have been other incursions and alarums but in the main it has been work, with some drives into the country. Hardly any reading since I have been here, and the little not serious. Laski mentions with praise Kelsen, *Hauptprobleme der staatslehre*, but the book is many compact pages of raw German and I suspect from a glance labored problems that I should not labor on — perhaps quite unjustly, but I put off for better days, as I do Suarez and many other illustrious contributors to thought. This is all I can write now as a conference is impending today. My love to you both, and I hope you are now safe at home.

Yours ever,
O. W. H.

[1] Ramsay MacDonald made an official visit to Washington in October, staying with President Hoover.

[2] Sydney Arnold, Lord Arnold, accompanied the Prime Minister on his trip to the United States.

[3] Sir Esme Howard.

LONDON, October 24, 1929

My dear Holmes:

I have just learnt that the International Law Association is to meet at New York, beginning Sept. 2, next year, which holds out a good reason for crossing the Atlantic once more, and a possibility, by reason of special arrangements made by the Association, of doing so without being ruined by paying for luxuries one does not want. We — for my wife will be with me if it comes off — should put in an appearance at the Congress and then make for Beverly Farms or somewhere pretty near. Most of the papers read are like to be on matters of commercial law not in my line, or the fads of world-law menders, but anyhow the real object would be to see you face to face again. . . .

Was it prophetic that one day at Cabourg when I was changing a Travellers' Cheque the hotel clerk offered me French currency, by pure inadvertence, for so many *dollars* instead of pounds? (This is quite up to the average of prophetical interpretations.)

Yours ever,
F. P.

WASHINGTON, November 6, 1929

My dear Pollock:

Your letter speaking of a possible visit next year thrills me: the only drawback is the uncertainty whether I shall still be alive within half a year of ninety. But I hope I shall. . . . I hope the visit will come off. Please tell Lady Pollock so with my love.

This morning brings me news of the publication of a volume of my opinions [1] — I get the impression mainly dissenting ones — which I shall be curious to see. I can't conceive that it possibly can pay the publishers, but I await a chance to inspect it. I am hoping for time to read a little philosophy, but it has not been yet.

Yours ever,
O. W. H.

[1] *Dissenting Opinions of Mr. Justice Holmes* (Alfred Lief, ed., 1929).

February 3, 1930 [1]

My dear Holmes:

Court Hermann Keyserling's *America Set Free* will interest you if you have time to look into it. *Qu.* whether an aristocratic philosopher from the Baltic Provinces can see American things quite the right way though he tries his best: but I have not read far enough to see what kind of balance he strikes. *Qu.* also whether going about chiefly with the casual man in the street (K.'s avowed method) does not tend to a lopsided view even of that street. My own way has been the opposite (not by deliberation, but it has so happened): to converse with people of the best in their nations and callings. Not without its risk: I know very well that not all American scholars are like you and Goodwin [2] and Bill James (not meaning any particular likeness among you), nor all French like Renan, Italians like Balzani,[3] or Russians like Vinogradoff — still, after all discounts one thinks reasonable, the resulting impression must lean to the side of the angels. Well, and so it should if it must lean one way or another, as I believe all human judgment must. When people talk of Babbitt as typical I think of a dear half Quaker lady I knew at New Haven, who adored John Woolman, and others.

However, Keyserling makes one think, and if you and I think otherwise we shall be the wiser for knowing why. . . .

Very foul weather in the Thames Valley these last few days — just as Agricola reported of the climate to his son-in-law Tacitus: *caelum nubibus et crebris imbribus foedum.*

Yours ever,
F. P.

There is a peace problem for navies ahead, after the chance of *iustum bellum*, as the old publicists called it, between civilized States has been reduced to a negligible quantity. What is the naval strength required to protect mariners on their lawful

[1] Letters from Pollock, dated November 11, November 28, December 5, 1929, and January 2, January 23, and January 30, 1930, are omitted.

[2] William Watson Goodwin (1831–1912); Classicist; Eliot Professor of Greek Literature, Harvard College, 1860–1901.

[3] Count Ugo Balzani, 1847–1916.

occasions from pirates (still lively in the China seas) and filibusters? Perhaps the practical answer may be that anyhow it is less than the Powers will want to maintain for their own particular securities. Meanwhile we may possibly have to fight the Bolsheviks before we have done with wars.

LONDON, March 3, 1930

My dear Holmes:

This to confirm the telegram of congratulation that will overtake it before the week's end. Certainly 89[1] is a good honest number, a prime number, no multiple of anything mixed up with magic black or white, or with controversial dogmas, or with any manner of superstition or hocus pocus sacred or profane: though it might savour of rashness or be, as theologians say in one word, temerarious to deny positively that any heretic ever maintained the number of the gods to be eighty-nine, neither more nor less, though such a doctrine may be judged to be probably *pravitas hucusque nullibi gentium audita*. Latin is at my fingers' ends because I have had to relieve my feelings by a medieval cursing of Indian Law reporters — by all the sacred books of all their religions — concluding generally:

Illabatur super capita eorum liber divi Nasadae de legibus Brahmanicis quem diis immortalibus optulit et illi dixerunt quod iste liber propter prolixitatem suam mortalibus minime legendus erat.

I read very little more of Keyserling. My wife whisked him back to Mudie's library whence he came. But I was satisfied that for all his learning and curiosity and knowledge of European matters he was at sea in America, having for one thing no inkling of how many so-called Americanisms in speech and manners are just archaic English, and by no means always dead in England though not known in London. I have been at a reception of law society at Hull which, for the matter of

[1] Holmes was eighty-nine on March 8, 1930.

special formalities, might have been say at Cincinnati. And plenty of words not heard nowadays south of the Trent are still current in our north country.

It is said — I don't vouch for it — that when President Wilson *et ux.* were here Mrs. W. asked the Queen what she thought about the Freedom of the Seas, and the Queen answered that she had not quite made up her mind about mixed bathing.

Why do printers delight to sow commas broadcast? I must now turn to a complaint of too many of them in a case in the *Law Reports.*

Yours ever,
F. P.

LONDON, March 24, 1930

My dear Holmes:

The March number of *Harper's* has come to me by Laski's request. What he says about your judgments [1] is well written and quite true, but I wonder if it does not make you feel a little like one of the actors in that poem of many meanings "The Walrus & the Carpenter":

"The Carpenter said nothing but
'The butter's spread too thick.'"

On Saturday I was at the memorial service for Arthur Balfour:[2] a great function and I should think a unique congregation. . . .

Yours ever,
F. P.

WASHINGTON, April 6, 1930

My dear Pollock:

A swift but brief response to one from you. (1) Laski in *Harpers* — I was so touched and moved by the note of affection

[1] "Mr. Justice Holmes, for his Eighty-Ninth Birthday," 160 *Harper's Magazine* 415 (March 1930); reprinted in *Mr. Justice Holmes* (Frankfurter, ed., 1931), p. 138.

[2] Arthur James Balfour, first Earl of Balfour, died March 19, 1930.

and made so shy by the praise that I hardly like to speak about it and could not criticize. (2) Forthwith on reading what you said of *The Testament of Beauty* [1] I had my secretary telephone right and left until he found it and bid the Shopman send it forthwith. I have read a little of it — the Introduction — and stop in II, Selfhood, p. 48, to vent my despair. I greatly fear that I shall be against you, head on; I am not yet fully committed but I had to let out this slack to you. Also the rather faint rhythm and the forms of his speech do not charm my ear or my mind. Perhaps I don't get the hang and that on hearing him read properly I should succumb.

(3) Have you views on the varieties of modernist painting? They talk of wanting something new, being bored with the old — of balance of pattern — I know not what. I must say that the run of them if not mystifiers seem to me just yielding to vanity and lewd desire, as Bill Hunt[2] once put it, to do something damned smart right off, just as skirt dancing offers as a substitute for the training that makes a *danseuse*, the suggestion that you may see a little more at the next high kick.

I am afraid I am old, for I feel the same way about most of the modern experiments in literature that I have seen. I think I must be generous and give up to you some chaff of James Joyce that made me laugh consumedly.[3]

Yours ever,
O. W. H.

I should think the writer might get into trouble when his indecency was noticed. I should think it must have escaped the editors.

[1] In a letter, dated January 2, 1930, which is omitted, Pollock had written: "Robert Bridges, the poet laureate, . . . who was supposed not to be doing much, has been tackling the Cosmos, for sundry years I suppose, and has published *sub nom. The Testament of Beauty* the only great philosophical poem, so far as I know in the English language. . . ."

[2] Probably William Morris Hunt (1824–79).

[3] Enclosed with the letter was a cutting of "The Fable of the Three Limperary Cripples" by Edmund Wilson, 62 *New Republic* 100 (March 12, 1930).

LONDON, April 7, 1930

My dear Holmes:

If A. Maurois' book on Byron has not yet come your way I think it will interest you. The English version is better reading than the original because you get the extracts from letters and poems in English, and the translator has done his work so well that the author loses practically nothing. There are indeed one or two signs of fatigue towards the end: only so could a man of any sense write "Congreve *fuses*" which is nonsense. Even if he did not know that *fusée* is French for a rocket he might have looked in the *Dictionary of National Biography* to see what Congreve's invention was — but in the main 'tis mighty well. As to the Augusta Leigh affair I now wonder, reading the story as a whole for the first time, why there was ever any mystery. No one who had any interest in knowing seems to have doubted seriously at the time. True, the chief persons are (for very different reasons) not too credible witnesses: but taking conduct and communications, notably Lord B.'s letters to Lady Melbourne, together the sum of the evidence is irresistible: and the alternative of B. and his half-sister having conspired to plague Lady B. and mystify the public to their own prejudice is surely unarguable, tho' I could believe such a thing of *him*.

I quite forget what Mrs. Beecher Stowe professed to add to the known facts, if it was that illicit relations continued *after* B.'s marriage I don't believe it.

Yours ever,
F. P.

LONDON, April 17, 1930

My dear Holmes:

The correspondent for U.S. of the Selden Society Richard W. Hale of Boston has sent me the *Harvard Alumni Bulletin* with report of your portrait being presented to the Harvard Law School:[1] I suspect the reproduction does not quite do justice to the picture.

[1] 32 *Harvard Alumni Bulletin* 741 (March 27, 1930).

What was Learned Hand about to class your conception of law with Austin's;[2] and in fact did you ever take any notice of that clever but very narrow and grossly overrated dialectician? One reason of his success in English law schools may be that a cocksure dogmatic theory, however bad, is good stuff to examine, and cram for examinations, upon.

From the same *Bulletin* I learnt that President Lowell lost his wife about a month ago, for which I am very sorry. . . .

Yours ever,
F. P.

LONDON, May 5, 1930

My dear Holmes:

Just a week ago we came back from Paris, having found all well and our grandson running about and playing games of his own devising — and I am back to cursing most Indian law reporters and some Anglo-Indian judges.

It is a fortnight since R. Bridges died,[1] having lived to see his *opus magnum* received with fitting respect not only by discerning critics but by the multitude of readers. No doubt it is arguable that *The Testament of Beauty* is a splendid failure (much more splendid at worst than Blackmore's *Creation* or Cardinal Polignac's *Anti-Lucretius*), but I bet on the judgment of posterity that there is nothing like it till you get back to Lucretius himself, and R. B. scores greatly by

(1) an intimate knowledge and love of nature, such as Virgil would have had if he lived in English country

(2) the scientific training of a medical man combined with the humanity of a scholar.

Prosaic passages there must be in such a work, but again he scores there over Wordsworth.

[2] See Judge Hand's address, *id.*; reprinted, 43 *Harv. L. Rev.* 857 (1930), and in *Mr. Justice Holmes* (Frankfurter, ed., 1931) p. 127. In the course of his address Judge Hand had said: "Nor again do I suppose that I am asked to discuss . . . his [Holmes's] understanding of the meaning of the law, so strictly Austinian, so out of step with much that we hear lightly bandied about in these present times." 43 *Harv. L. Rev.* at p. 857–58.

[1] Robert Bridges, poet laureate, died April 21, 1930.

The pleasure of the score being also Eton and Oxford's may unconsciously warp me a little, but I have ears and am usually a rather fastidious reader.

I wonder what American spectators think of G. B. Shaw's *Apple Cart* — a marvellously impudent piece of fooling, clever but also tedious.

Yours ever,
F. P.

WASHINGTON, May 20, 1930

My dear Pollock:

You fire me by your bet on the judgment of posterity as to *The Testament of Beauty*. I read it very inadequately, with all manner of interruptions and distractions but even so I bet that posterity will let it calmly die. It seemed to me the Cosmos arranged to suit polite English taste. I would not deny passages of some beauty but I did not see the great lines in it (I mean the lines of greatness). You almost compel me to read it or in it again but I don't much want to. What do you think of other candidates for immortality like Browning's *The Ring and the Book*? I find it hard to believe that the world will take the trouble it demands. Other things that received superlatives when we were younger seem to me to have sagged a little like *In Memoriam*, and Ruskin and Carlyle. The only firebrand of my youth that burns to me as brightly as ever is Emerson, and I am bound to admit that for many years I have read but two or three pieces of his, coupled with *The Heart of Emerson's Journals* (I am not sure of the title) which impressed me a few years ago. Well, here is a battleground if we jaw together this Autumn. I speak cautiously of that because I don't venture to look far ahead although I now am rather hoping to reach my 90th birthday. It makes a difference as one gets near to that time. People are very kind to so old a man and make much of him. I suppose it makes their own horizon seem wider.

My work is pretty well done for the present. Opinions all delivered, etc. But during the summer hateful mailbags of petitions for *certiorari* will keep coming in. They are a great chore. Over 570 cases we have had to examine and more or less discuss this winter.

But this is just to knock the chip off your shoulder & I must shut up. My love to Lady Pollock.

Yours ever,
O. W. H.

LONDON, May 25, 1930

My dear Holmes:

A reference in *Times Literary Supplement* in a review of a book on Washington[1] has sent me to your introduction to Montesquieu and your remarks on his "fiction" of the balance of political powers.[2] It is true that the English Constitution does not lend itself to formulas. But as formulas go I don't think M. was far out in the middle of the 18th century. Not only in Blackstone's time but down to the end of the century (if not later) "the distribution of real political power between the Crown and the two Houses of Parliament was still undefined" as I say in a note at p. 84 of my little *History of the Science of Politics*. Pitt the younger was far from being the real head of the Executive: even when I was born the army was still directly under the Crown as distinct from the Cabinet, and linked with Parliament only through the Secretary *at* war — not a Cabinet Minister but a financial and administrative official. (You may see all about him in Kinglake's *History of the Crimean War*, which I suppose nobody reads now.) The Commons could indeed in the last resort paralyse the army or any public service by refusing supplies (a thing that has happened in our own time in matters of secondary importance not involving party issues). But no one thought of the King as a cogwheel: certainly not the fathers of the American Constitu-

[1] *Times Literary Supplement*, May 22, 1930, p. 422, reviewing John Corbin, *The Unknown Washington—Biographic Origins of the Republic* (1930).

[2] "His England — the England of the threefold division of power into legislative, executive and judicial — was a fiction invented by him, a fiction which misled Blackstone and Delolme." Critical and biographical introduction to a reprint of *The Spirit of the Laws* (1900); reprinted in *C.L.P.*, p. 250.

tion, who knew a good deal more than they read in Blackstone. Montesquieu's error was not in observation but in supposing that the balance of powers could be stable. Then Bagehot underrated the persuasive influence as distinct from the legal authority of the Crown. He would have written rather differently if he could have seen Queen Victoria's correspondence. No doubt the King must follow his Ministers' considered advice, but not till they have heard what he has to say. The old Queen had much to say, and often with effect: as in the reform of the government of India under the Crown, and the very ticklish affair of the *Trent* (which did no credit to the diplomacy of either side). And the King knows more than any other one man of the counsels of all parties. Moreover the importance of the Crown behind the scenes is much increased by the emancipation of the Dominions from the Colonial Office. In matters of offices and honours the King has more active discretion than you would learn from Bagehot.

The other day I found a little oasis in the wilderness of Indian law reports: a judge (by his name I guess a Parsee) of the Allahabad High Court quoted, not too relevantly, a Persian couplet, rather mangled in Roman letters by the reporter, which, helped by the obvious metre, I piously restored to its proper script. No reference was given and I thought it might be from some minor wisdom book, but it turned out to be conspicuous at the very opening of Sa'di's *Gulistan* — as if an English-reading Indian scholar should come across a verse from the *Book of Proverbs* and wonder whether it was somewhere in the *Apocrypha*.

"In time of need when no way out is left,
The hand grasps the sharp sword's hilt."

An aphorism that would have pleased Hobbes, and is pressing the Government of India at this moment.

By the way I knew Mrs. Sarojini Naidu,[3] the so-called Indian Joan of Arc, quite well in London before the war. She seemed quite rational then, and wrote very pretty English verse. But she is of the Southern Indian Brahmans (only by marriage: her father came from Bengal and was employed at

[3] 1879- ; poet; graduate of Girton College, Cambridge; active in Women's Movement in India; President of Indian National Congress, 1925.

the Nizam of Haidarabad's Court. My informant on this point, who also knew her, thinks her a bundle of nerves. She was spoilt at Girton College.) who living as a conquering clan in a foreign population ran to fanaticism like the Anglo-Scottish Protestants in Ulster. My dear learned friend Cornelia Sorabji is on the other hand more British if anything than the Anglo-Indian. She is now at a Women's Congress at Vienna and expects to be here by July. . . .

Yours ever,
F. P.

BEVERLY FARMS, June 9, 1930

My dear Pollock:

Here I am once more and was welcomed by your letter. You discourse with a learning that I do not attempt to emulate as to Montesquieu and the balance of political powers. The little I ever knew is, I am afraid, pretty well forgotten. So I accept your remarks in respectful silence. I read Kinglake's *Crimean War* when I was in the army, but that is some time ago. I met Kinglake, who said he had a question to ask — I knew what it would be. Did our men fight in line? I grinned and said I remembered his speaking of that as an Anglo-Saxon prerogative, and asked if he really believed it, to which he — yes, he certainly did. I said of course our men fought in line, and that I believed you could make baboons do it if you had the right sort of officers. That is my chief association with the author and the book nowadays. As to India also I am blank. You keep up with public affairs; I now avail myself of old age to excuse what in fact has been the neglect of a life-time. My adieu to the last Term was a dissent on the requirement in the 14th Amendment of due process of law from the States.[1] Of

[1] Baldwin v. Missouri, 281 U. S. 586, 595 (1930). The majority of the Court, in an opinion by McReynolds, J., held that the due process clause of the Fourteenth Amendment rendered invalid the attempt of Missouri tax officials to levy an inheritance tax on the transfer by will of bank deposits, United States bonds, and promissory notes, all physically situated in Missouri, the testatrix and the legatee being domiciled in Illinois. Brandeis and Stone, JJ., concurred in Holmes's dissenting opinion, and Holmes and Brandeis concurred in a dissenting opinion of Stone, J.

course it is too late to prevent the extension of the phrase to an artificial meaning but the Court has gone farther than I can possibly believe to be warranted on the question of the right of the States to tax, and in opinions by McReynolds has overruled decisions written by me and others, when I thought authority, logic and settled practice authorized the tax. I am on most friendly terms with all the judges, but I suspect that if I should be gathered to Abraham's bosom some of them would think it an advantage to the law, even if they missed a friend. I hardly have had time to get into focus here yet; not to speak of settling down to anything. I have one or two pretty solid books that I ought to read but I am not *quite* over the shaking up of the journey. I hope to improve my mind a little before the mail bags with *certioraris* begin to come in. While in Boston I ran out to the new and rather magnificent law school building to see my portrait which was not finished when I left and which pleased me mightily. It is hung as the pendant to one of Marshall, which of course was the handsomest compliment that they could pay. No more now from a cloudy and rather vacant mind. My love to Lady Pollock.

Yours ever,
O. W. H.

LONDON, June 19, 1930[1]

My dear Holmes:

So you are already at Beverly Farms, and perhaps have not there a spare copy of your dissenting judgment on the 14th Amendment, which I want to see and expect to agree with. I should have liked to hear your talk with Kinglake. The real English discovery (Sir John Moore the true inventor I think) was surely the *two deep* line — line formation of varying depth, which settled to three ranks in the latter part of the 18th century, was common long before the French Revolution — when once the bayonet had emancipated the musket from the shelter of pikes. The stroke of genius was in seeing that a rank of

[1] A letter from Pollock, dated June 1, 1930, is omitted.

mute muskets, or at best barking with very little bile, was not needed to support the two effective firing ranks.

How long the third rank lingered as a parade formation I don't know: not after the Peninsular War I think. Could you have taught baboons the required steadiness and confidence, not to speak of shooting? I doubt it.

Maida (a combat of no strategic significance which gave its name to Maida Vale, then suburban) is the classical leading case of British line repulsing a superior number (by something like fifty per cent) of French attacking in column. The silence of the line till the head of the column was near enough for a crushing volley had a great moral effect.

When we are in Boston we must remember to go and see your portrait in company with Marshall's. Indian imbecility (of reporters I mean) is now vexing my professional soul only within tolerable limits.

Yours ever,
F. P.

I don't know whether you ever look at English memoirs of the middle and late 19th century — some recent ones are pretty flat, so I will not name them.

The learned Frenchman Victor Bérard has been pointing out how like the *Odyssey* quite modern and genuine narratives of travel in unknown seas have been — it is a curious anthology.

Beverly Farms, June 28, 1930

My dear Pollock:

On receipt of your letter this morning I wrote at once to the Clerk to send you the opinion and dissent on the effect of the 14th Amendment upon the power of States to tax. You are right in your doubts about my reading English memoirs and biographies of the 19th century or any other. I don't read biographies at all except under some special pressure. Not that they don't interest me but that my time is limited and I have to choose, and other subjects interest me more. Under pressure I have begun Trotsky's *Autobiography* and expect to finish it: probably it's thrilling when I get beyond his youth, but I wish he was at the devil. Meantime the first installment — 51 applications for *certiorari* — has arrived, which is a fly in the ointment, but all is going well so far. More people than I could wish have come here in the last few days but that will not last. They are all pleasant but I get tired easily now. An hour and a half is about as much as I want for a steady jaw.

Talking of fighting in line reminds me of our misfortune at Antietam. Sumner[1] who was an old cavalry officer I believe shoved our second line (I am talking of *lines* not ranks), a *quasi* reserve, up so close to the front line that we could have touched them with our bayonets, and we got hit about as much as they did, but of course could do nothing, and when the enemy broke through on our left we were surrounded with the front. Whereas had we been a little further back they would have got a volley. When I was hit we were getting it all round and I remember chuckling to myself as I was leaving the field, to remember that *Harper's Weekly* was flamboyant on my first wound at Ball's Bluff — about Massachusetts hit in the breast, etc.[2] I thought to myself this time I am hit in the back, and bolting as fast as I can — and it's all right — but not so good for the newspapers. . . . I didn't quite understand your difficulty with the India reports. Do you have to put them all into shape? My love to Lady Pollock.

Yours ever,

O. W. H.

[1] General Edward Vose Sumner (1797–1863).

[2] In an editorial entitled, "New England Never Runs," The Lounger wrote in *Harper's Weekly* for November 9, 1861 (p. 706): "Through the tears with which friends and lovers read the story of Edwards's Ferry they can still smile upon the steadfast bravery of the Massachusetts boys. In the front of fearful fire, with no means of retreat, with every chance against them, those young men stood serene, each man a hero — each man showing the quality of which invincible armies are made. . . . Lieutenant Holmes, said the first brief despatch, 'wounded in the breast': not in the back; no, not in the back. In the breast is Massachusetts wounded, if she is struck. Forward she falls, if she falls dead."

LONDON, July 17, 1930[1]

My dear Holmes:

The Clerk of the Supreme Court has sent me the judgments in *Baldwin* v. *Missouri*. I should have thought there might be a pretty argument on the rather elusive topic of a thing in action's local habitation, quite apart from the Fourteenth Amendment: when that comes in I am sure your opinion is the reasonable one, whatever the authorities may say.

And so you were nearly killed at Antietam because your superior had never learnt the use of supports: even the old Roman disciplines of the wars as preached by Capt. Fluellen might have taught him better. Certainly a considerable interval was prescribed and observed in our infantry drill of the 1870's. A supporting battalion was normally, I think, in open column of companies ready to deploy as might be needful and if all went well finally to deploy to the front and reinforce the attacking line.

I suppose all the old minor tactics have gone to limbo in a cloud of ghostly black powder smoke. Never again will a battalion advance in line firing — a pretty movement in which I once took part as an Inns of Court Volunteer in manoeuvres; the moral effect on the enemy (a regular regiment) was that they got excited and began to fix bayonets — strictly forbidden in manoeuvres — and a mounted staff officer shouted to us to lie down and jumped clean over us to stop them. He must be λελασμένος ἱπποσυνάων even if he is alive.

I have discovered a perquisite of a Privy Councillor: this morning my wife, her maid and myself repaired in our proper persons to the American Consulate to get visas for our passports, and to my agreeable surprise (for the fee is fairly substantial) I learnt that by virtue of that office I was exempt from fees. Our Foreign Office would I suppose be as polite to you, but I fear that won't induce you to come next year and be invited by me as Treasurer[2] (as I may expect to be in the regular course) to dine at Grand Day — not even with the attraction of no speeches.

Yours ever,

F. P.

[1] A letter from Pollock, dated June 30, 1930, is omitted.

[2] Of Lincoln's Inn.

Beverly Farms, July 26, 1930

My dear Pollock:

Your very handsome new edition of Maine's *Ancient Law* has come and I send you my thanks. I expect to reread it after many years and to enjoy your learned notes. At the moment I am staggered by a mailbag with 74 new applications for *certiorari* — but one gets through such obstacles after a time. I am hoping always for news of your intentions when you come here. You know that my house and, so far as age permits, myself are at your and Lady Pollock's command. I don't press you because I don't want to be a bother. . . .

Just now I have finished reading Whitehead's *Process & Reality*, and got the general drift, I hope, but two thirds of it I failed to understand accurately because I don't know the meaning of the phrases. Whitehead talks and thinks like a mathematician and I am not in it. I like one thing — that he like Dewey begins his cosmos without any conscious ego, and lets that come in later as *quasi* an accident. I should think W.'s mode of approach as I certainly thought Dewey's an advance on Berkeley and Hume. But although Dewey doesn't talk mathematics, he is a bad writer and I found him very hard reading. Still his view of the universe came home to me closer than any other that I know. I have had some other *pièces de résistance* and a lot of *belles lettres*. One story of the western prairie, *My Antonia*, by Willa Cather, moved me unexpectedly and deeply. But I won't send you a catalogue. The very young authors and painters rarely hit me. I seem to see a good deal more conscious egotism than genius. As I write the sudden doubt strikes me whether by any chance you will have started earlier than I was expecting and this may miss you. It stops my pen — but I hope that I am destined to see you and Lady Pollock again.

Yours ever,
O. W. H.

BEVERLY FARMS, July 27, July 30

My dear Pollock:

This is a p. s. to yesterday's letter to acknowledge yours of July 17. What you say as to the local habitation of a chose in action has been much discussed and I have given my views as to where it should be domiciled if anywhere and my reasons for thinking it an unprofitable way of deciding the cases.[1]

Also, let me protect the reputation of my Superior at Antietam, our corps commander General Sumner, an experienced old soldier who I don't doubt knew as well as anyone the use of supports. That he was wrong in shoving us up onto the first line I can't doubt. Whether being an old cavalry man he thought he could slam right through the other line or what I don't know. It may have been hot-headedness, but it can't have been ignorance — except ignorance that I find it hard to believe that some of the higher powers weren't responsible for, *viz.* that Longstreet's corps was on the other side of a little hill, ready to walk into our rear as it did.

Yours ever,
O. W. H.

I infer that you may be starting for the U. S.

LONDON, July 20, 1930

My dear Holmes:

This is in the nature of a P. S. to answer your questions about my tribulations with Indian reporters. It is a full quarter of a century since the first edition of Pollock & Mulla on the Indian Contract Act appeared.[1] Mulla of Bombay (now Sir Dinshah, for a short time a judge of the High Court there and a thoroughly competent lawyer) undertook to work in the Indian cases, and has worked with me in succeeding editions down to the sixth, now in the press. But last year the Legislative Department annexed him for some big drafting work, including

[1] See, *e.g.*, his opinion in Blackstone v. Miller, 188 U. S. 189 (1903).

[1] The first edition was published in 1905.

a Sale of Goods Act, now passed, which supersedes a chapter of the Indian Contract Act. So I have to work on the Indian cases myself with only a list of references furnished from Bombay by an assistant . . . and the work is increased by the need of including this time — in order, I am told, to satisfy the demands of practitioners — the unauthorized serial reports as well as the authorized ones. The latter, not bad on the whole, fall short of our mark: the former are produced by reporters who don't know the elements of reporting, not even that a decision on a question of pure fact is not authority. So I find tedious disquisition on elementary settled law, argument hardly ever properly reported (often it is obvious that the reporter was not there), so that one can't see what points were really disputed, offhand judgments wholly ignoring the authorities, and many cases really deciding nothing. Moreover there are a half a dozen independent High Courts bound only by the judgments of the Judicial Committee of the Privy Council in last resort, and they seem to enjoy differing with one another. Result, as it may be, a short foot-note or the mere addition of the name to a string of cases already cited. However, I am through the worst of it. I hope my learned colleague Mulla won't think I have been too drastic. The judges are of various quality — I don't mean only those of Indian birth — and, except in the old High Courts of the Presidency towns, get scant assistance from the Bar. . . .

Yours ever,
F. P.

LONDON, September 29, 1930

My dear Holmes:

We are both delighted to have your note which awaited us on our return (landing at Plymouth) yesterday.[1] After a pretty

[1] Following their stay in New York City during the meeting of the International Law Association, at which time Pollock received the degree of LL.D., from Columbia, Sir Frederick and Lady Pollock went to Beverly Farms and stayed with Holmes for a week's visit. Thereafter they went to Chocorua, New Hampshire, to visit the William Jameses and to Cambridge, Massachusetts, to visit President Lowell of Harvard University. They sailed for England from New York on September 19. Letters from Pollock, dated August 14, August 30, and September 4, 1930, the last written from New York City, are omitted. The note from Holmes to which Pollock refers is missing.

dull voyage (empty ship, passengers a mighty dull lot, the captain happily conversable) with the compensation of a good stateroom apiece, we arose early and had a long wait at the docks after getting off by the tender, and then, being Sunday, a pretty long train journey. Shall you or I survive the plague of red-tape mania that has afflicted all nations since the war — the U. S. and G. B. as badly as any? I fear not, for there be clerks who thrive on it and the suffering public is an unorganized crowd.

We had an excellent time with President Lowell, and I saw the recent adornments of Harvard, including your portrait in Langdell Hall, which more than answers the expectation raised by the photographs. Also the new Houses — we should call them hostels in the slang of English universities. The President has no intention of letting them become autonomous and practically squeeze out the University as our Colleges did. *Sed qu.* what would happen if he had a weak successor.

In the September number of *Scribner* aboard the Lancastria I found an account of the Puritan discipline that was still possible in a Boston family only about half a century ago.[3] Such notions may still lurk among the "Wee Frees" in Scotland, perhaps in England among a few belated Sects or family groups. E. Gosse on the Plymouth Brethren (*Father & Son*) is, I suppose, known to you.

Yours ever,
F. P.

LONDON, January 29, 1931 [1]

My dear Holmes:

I have entered on my duties as Treasurer of Lincoln's Inn [2] — they are not crushing though some of the routine is a little tedious. One duty is to make a little edifying address to the young men who are called to the Bar in each of the four

[3] Arthur Train, "The Puritan Shadow," 88 *Scribner's Magazine* 314 (September 1930).

[1] Letters from Pollock, dated October 19 and October 30, 1930, are omitted.

[2] The Treasurer is principal officer of the Inn, and holds office for one year.

terms, which I have done once: as it is a different set of men every time not much variety is called for.

You ask whether I attach any weight to Bernard Shaw's opinions.[3] On things in general, none, but he does know a fair lot about art and letters and a great deal about writing plays, and on those matters is worth listening to when he is not wilfully playing the mountebank. The best thing (outside stage plays) he ever wrote, to my mind, was an essay on "The Sanity of Art" provoked by the thesis of an impostor called Max Nordau that all men of genius are mad or at least morbid. I have a mind to send it to you as a small birthday offering if it is still in print: it is good reading.

Doubtless you are hardening your head by appropriate exercises for the shower of *bunches* (is that still the young folks' slang for posies?) that will descend upon it in March. Meanwhile there are several pages about you in Owen Wister's book on Roosevelt, rather flowery in style, but with the substance and effect I respectfully concur. . . .

Yours ever,
F. P.

LONDON, February 5, 1931

My dear Holmes:

. . . As to what you note in the letter my wife got this morning concerning *The Newcomes*,[1] I conceive Thackeray's women are mostly dolls except in *Esmond*. Both he and Dickens seem to have been unlucky in knowing few women whom they could respect.

I am glad to hear that Miss Waddell's edition of medieval Latin lyrics has come in your way and pleases you, and I am sure it will please her to be informed that you enjoy her work. We have corresponded and occasionally met ever since she published *The Wandering Scholars*. . . . There are a few slips in her translations and a few omissions to notice obvious corrup-

[3] The letter in which Holmes asked this question is missing.

[1] The letter to Lady Pollock is missing.

tion of the text disclosed by grammar or metre having gone wrong, but in the main it is good scholarly work, and she has humour and imagination.

If you want to know about modern astronomy I recommend both of Sir James Jeans's books — the larger *The Universe Around Us* and the smaller—but tougher—*This Mysterious Universe*. Most of the notions of our youth, beyond the solar system, are now scrapped.

Who said, somewhere in your correspondence with Owen Wister, Horace was a light poet?[2] Certainly he wrote light verse, but also he wrote the great Ode on the defeat of Cleopatra "*Nunc est bibendum*," and the council of the Gods against rebuilding Troy: "*gratum elocuta conciliantibus Iunone divis*" and the *Carmen Saeculare* and so forth. He was no mere precursor of Matthew Prior, and anyhow Marvell did not think him a light poet when he called his ode on Cromwell's return from Ireland Horatian. Touch the patriot in Horace, and a true Roman speaks in his higher mood. I am waiting for time to improve my knowledge of his greater friend Virgil, now much to the front, in Mackail's edition of the *Aeneid*. Mackail is one of our best and most human scholars — in the first place a Latinist.

Yours ever,
F. P.

February 8, 1931

My dear Holmes:

Lord! by quoting Horace from memory I have saddled him (I think) with a *vox nihili* and a false quantity — all this by

[2] Owen Wister in his *Roosevelt; The Story of a Friendship* (1930), at p. 132, said: "How did he [Holmes] account, I asked him in later years, for the continual translations of a light poet like Horace? 'Because Horace,' he answered, 'sums up with unsurpassed felicity the philosophy of the man about town. Each great wave of thought, or science, or art, is left behind by successors. But the club man, the sceptical worldling, with his decencies and indecencies, had much the same standards in Rome as he has in New York. His point of view is constant. Therefore, whether he is dining out in sandals and a purple tunic, or in patent leathers and a boiled shirt, Horace is up to date with him.'"

mistake in one letter. So I repeat it right, adding the first lines of Juno's speech, which are magnificent Latin:

Gratum elocuta consiliantibus
Iunone divis: Ilion, Ilion
fatalis incestusque iudex
et mulier peregrina vertit
in pulverem, ex quo destituit deos
mercede pacta Laomedon, mihi
castaeque damnatum Minervae
cum populo et duce fraudulento.

(*N. B. Castae* is not an idle epithet but emphatic. The austere Goddess's anger is aggravated by her loathing for the *incestus iudex*, the effeminate Paris.)

The ode is best known by its no less magnificent opening lines "*Iustum et tenacem propositi virum* . . ." It must have been semi-official, written on a hint from high quarters. One can suppose Horace reading it to a select party invited by Maecenas to meet Augustus, who is waiving ceremony with just a touch of affection:

"My dear Horace, I don't know about drinking nectar with the Gods (between you and me, I have no pontifical knowledge that it is better than good Falernian) but you have made the glowing countenance true enough: indeed you put me to the blush. One must pose for Gauls and Greeks and such like, not to speak of barbarous Africans and Asiatics in the East and barbarous Britons in the far West — here among friends I am a Roman citizen on whom Senate and People (for reasons it would be ungracious to dispute) have heaped honours that I may the better serve them. The rest of your ode is first-rate; you need affect no fear of letting your Muse go. I speak of the poetry: for the matter, if ever I have to speak my mind on that it must be in my place in the Senate."

And when Augustus has gone Maecenas joyfully embracing Horace: "Excellent well, most excellent, you have surpassed yourself — neither matter nor form could be better." "Dear patron, indeed I took some pains about the thing: amply repaid by your approval and Caesar's, need I say?" "Well,

Horace, I don't think we shall hear any more of that hare-brained scheme for rebuilding Troy." . . .

Yours ever,
F. P.

WASHINGTON, February 22, 1931 [1]

My dear Pollock:

You always have me on the tongues, and specifically I can recite very poorly on Horace. I never read the *Odes* until within the last ten years, and then rather rapidly. Still I don't think I can have spoken of him as a light poet, unless for some particular antithesis. I don't remember. Certainly I don't defend the phrase. He said eternal things. But this adjournment has not brought the hoped-for leisure. They rarely do. Of the 3 weeks the first was work. The next smashed by sitting every day for a bust (I think for the Columbia Law School),[2] the last just ended. Now work, a case to write and 36 or so *certiorari* — all done but 5 or 6. So literature has had to wait. I wish your remembrances were on the table before me.[3] I should not be writing to you. You must have a lot to tell. I couldn't do that sort of thing — I remember only in a hazy way. I sometimes think of the chap I met when carrying an Order in 1864. I was face to face with him and meant to kill him, but I don't believe that I should recognize him if I met him. Even if I were told who he was. However, the chances are that he is only a skull by this time — and one doesn't remember skulls.

What a wonderful advantage Europe has in having its past before its eyes, so that you all learn without effort by seeing what we have to get from books and pictures. Even the background of novels generally is European. I remember the effect

[1] A letter from Pollock, dated February 19, 1931, is omitted.

[2] Presumably the reference is to the bust by Sergei Konenkov which was to be placed in a number of American law schools. A photograph of the bust was reproduced in 31 *Columbia L. Rev.* 349 (1931).

[3] Lady Pollock had recently written to Holmes telling him of her husband's intention to write a book of reminiscences. It was published in 1933 under the title *For My Grandson: Remembrances of An Ancient Victorian.*

of a detective story that opened with a death in our best known theatre in Washington. The theatre had been darkened for Macbeth's witches — when the light is turned on a man's head is drooping forward. He is taken out — he has had a fit — "No, he has been murdered." Elegant for a commencer?

I seem to be all right now. I stoop but I haven't lumbago. The doctor said little processes like icicles had grown from my spine and there was nothing to do but grin and bear it. Don't you wish that you had icicles growing from your vertebrae? My love to Lady Pollock. I suppose you two will be sports when I am eating dandelions by the roots.

Yours ever,
O. W. H.

LONDON, February 26, 1931

My dear Holmes:

. . . I have begun to look at Henry Adams's *Letters* (ought to have been in two handy volumes and not one big clumsy one with too much print on the page), opened at random in the South Seas, honestly don't think that part so very much better than other travellers' letters, but the sketch of R. L. Stevenson, wholly clear from any halo of hero-worship, is amusing. I expect to find the home part more interesting.

It's a cranky world. The last crank in music is one Mossolov, a young Russian who has made a piece of so-called Music of Machines, inspired by the noises of a big factory. We heard it last night. Either M. has not done justice to the factory he studied or the manager should be sacked for not seeing that the machinery is better oiled. And an Oxford law lecturer now retired who is quite a good lawyer has gravely proposed to the Selden Society to reprint the whole of Selden's works with English translation (including those on Mosaic Law and such like, for he would rather like to edit the *Uxor Ebraica* himself).

Now the only work that really wanted to be edited was the *Dissertatio ad Fletam*, and that is already very well done by a young Oxford historian.[1]

[1] *Ioannis Seldeni ad Fletam Dissertatio*, edited by David Ogg (1925). The volume was reviewed by Pollock in 42 *L. Q. Rev.* 107 (1926).

Finally a woman has published a *fundamentalist* commentary on Blake's prophetic books,[2] as I see by a review.

Yours ever,
F. P.

Do they maintain even in Tennessee that the winged creatures Ezekiel saw were real animals?

LONDON, March 5, 1931

My dear Holmes:

Salve Magister de Banco Hospitii Lincoln:[1]

Our rules require the election of an honorary Bencher to be unanimous. The unanimity was cordial.

Semi-officially I may add that the Bench would be much pleased if you would send us your photograph to be put in our album, and still more if you could add a rather larger one to be framed, for which purpose a good reproduction of the portrait in the Law School of Harvard might perhaps be better than a photograph from the life. . . .

It is the first time we have gone outside the four seas or I think even our own Inn.

Our English practice of reading the Latin poets at large at an early age dates, I suppose, from the Renaissance and the grammar schools of the 16th century. At Eton I must have gone through the whole of Horace (except the *Epodes*) more than once. As for the hard places we fudged them by some sort of traditional constructs. I don't remember how much Virgil we read. Ovid, as being more elementary, was not continued beyond the lower forms. Not that any Augustan Latin is really easy.

Never heard of vertebral icicles before — hope they don't worry you much. . . .

Yours ever,
F. P.

[2] Emily S. Hamblen, *On the Minor Prophecies of William Blake* (1930).

[1] On March 4, 1931, Pollock cabled to Holmes: "You are elected Honorary Bencher Lincolns Inn.

Pollock Treasurer"

WASHINGTON, March 15, 1931

My dear Pollock:

Herewith is a formal acknowledgment of the honor done me by the Benchers of Lincoln's Inn. . . . I sent a small photograph from the painting for the album to Cyprian Williams yesterday, at his suggestion. I will see what I can do for a bigger one, according to your letter of this morning, but I hardly know which way to turn for the moment, I am so overwhelmed by things requiring immediate attention. "Don't shoot the organist, he is doing his best."

My love to Lady Pollock.

Yours ever,
O. W. H.

LONDON, March 19, 1931

My dear Holmes:

I am waiting to hear that you are none the worse for the shower of birthday congratulations and tributes in writing and print which must have fallen upon you. . . .

The work of the Treasurer is interesting and pretty mixed. It includes Presiding at the Council (full meeting of the Bench) with dinner to follow, about once a month. Attending chapel services (in fall term only, not necessarily all of them) with lunch party of Benchers and guests to follow. Frequent committee meetings to deal with the several branches of the Inn's business from finance to sampling wine, appointing a new cook, or reporting on the merits of pictures offered for sale (the last professed to be a portrait of Richard Cromwell who was a student of the inn — identity of subject not clear — painting so much and so clumsily renovated as to destroy any merit it ever had — *ideo inde nihil*). The minor Committees may be quite informal.

So that a Treasurer who attends to the business, as not all do, may say *mutatis mutandis* as a Dartmoor parish clerk said to the Rural Dean: "Iss, when I've a-cleaned up the lisle (aisle) and the t'other lisle, and a-dusted the Commandments and a-brushed the Belief, 'tis a tidy little chower (chore)."

Spring has just broken out all of a sudden. . . .

Yours ever,
F. P.

WASHINGTON, March 21, 1931

My dear Pollock:

In the dense pressure of the last two weeks I fear that I have said nothing of what you wrote for the *Columbia Law Review*,[1] received only in these last days. Friendship for a moment became articulate and uttered tender and moving things. Of course we have known the friendship long. It is part of my life. But to hear the note of affection along with praises that are so precious when they come from you, is a surprise in spite of all that I know without being told. It would put heart into a brass andiron and I shall die the happier for it.

My love to Lady Pollock.

Yours ever,
O. W. HOLMES

WASHINGTON, April 12, 1931

My dear Pollock:

Tomorrow we sit again and all the birthday row sinks into the past. . . .

I have been listening to *The Maritime History of Massachusetts* by Morison which I found fascinating — the names and places familiar to me from childhood. I get on more slowly with Cohen's *Reason & Nature* which I have to read to myself. An able man — my inclinations generally with him. I regretted at the proper place not to see him refer to the composite photograph: there you have a generalization effected mechanically by physical means and the only need for consciousness

[1] "Ad Multos Annos," 31 *Columbia L. Rev.* 349 (March 1931).

is to recognize it when achieved. No bother about particulars and universals.

The apple trees around the Potomac basin are in full flower today and the place is packed with automobiles. It is a sight to come hundreds of miles to see.

Also the magnolias are coming out and generally I wish the sitting of our Court was at the devil. I want to idle and take in the Spring, but it may not be.

Yours ever,
O. W. H.

LONDON, April 23, 1931

My dear Holmes:

We envy you the apple blossom. Europe (for it is the same report all over the continent) is still wondering whether the obstinate rearguard fight of Winter against spring (and specially summer time in the Western parts) is really over. On Sunday, our first summer time day, we had bleak wind and cold rain.

Tuesday was our Grand Day at Lincoln's Inn and went off well. I rather think the Treasurer's convivial duties take up more time than the business matters — anyhow if you count dining with the other Inns.

Cohen's work is not known to me. Does not the generalization of a composite photograph, likewise its value, depend on the compositor's intelligence? A dozen dogs of various breeds would not give you a typical dog, nor a dozen men of divers races from Mongol to Patagonian a typical *homo sapiens*. Three or four Europeans of sorts, a Brahman, a Rajput and a Parsí might give an instructive typical Indo-European portrait: if you threw in a Bhíl or any other wild aboriginal Indian the result would signify nothing.

I am reporting, with some reluctance, a case on the damnable pretended doctrine of *res gestae*,[1] and wishing some high authority would prick that bubble of verbiage: the unmeaning

[1] Probably Homes v. Newman, [1931] 2 Ch. 112.

term merely fudges the truth that there is no universal formula for all the kinds of relevancy. Now to a Committee.

Yours ever,
F. P.

LONDON, May 4, 1931

My dear Holmes:

I was on the point of asking you for the original of the quotation with which you wind up your speech of thanks (not the least of your minor works and I hope not the last), when I found in Miss Waddell's reprint that *Mors aurem vellens, Vivite, ait, venio,* is the end line of the pseudo-Virgilian *Copa.* The author understood life in a pretty different fashion from yours, but all is fair in quotation and especially of tags. Your approximate dating leaves room for conjecture to place that curious poem anywhere in the whole range of ancient Latin verse.[1] To my mind the rather affected use of out of the way words can hardly be earlier than the silver age, and some of the lines are too good to be much later. But one good living scholar thinks the Virgilian tradition may be plausible just because it is so improbable that no sane man would have invented it: *credo quia impossibile.* In that case it would have to be reckoned a very early skit of Virgil's. But surely the pretended tradition is bad for remoteness, like the William Tell fable, whereas a tradition that can be shown to have been current within living memory of the events is interesting in any case, and entitled to some credit if not grossly absurd or contrary to better evidence.

The Treasurer of an Inn is *animal epulans*: I have dined with the Middle Temple and Gray's Inn and am going to dine with the Inner Temple. A really good book on the Inns of Court has yet to be written: the materials for it are collected in volume

[1] On March 9, 1931, Holmes had responded, over the radio, to birthday congratulations of Chief Justice Hughes and the American Bar. His closing words were quoted from Helen Waddell's *Medieval Latin Lyrics*: "Death plucks my ear and says, Live — I am coming." See Shriver, p. 142. Holmes ascribed the lines to "a Latin poet who uttered the message more than fifteen hundred years ago."

2 of Holdsworth's *History of English Law* (an extraordinarily accurate work and quite good reading).

Looking at the preface to Bernard Shaw's *The Sanity of Art* I find it was first published in America as a letter to *Liberty*, edited by one Benj. Tucker — largely distributed to the press, since become a curiosity for collectors — but this original form can't well have escaped the Library of Congress. G. B. S. has a lot of common sense under the Shavian swagger, and good critical faculty: his large wildernesses of ignorance are due to want of any regular education. . . .

Yours ever,
F. P.

WASHINGTON, May 15, 1931

My dear Pollock:

A delightful letter from you, that flabbergasted me as usual with your critical knowledge. I am afraid that it wouldn't have occurred to me to think the lines of the *Copa* attributive to one time rather than another. I thought it permissible to use the last line with a more serious significance than it had in its context. It seems to me a privilege of quotation. How easy it is to quote. I think one could get an available line from a column of advertisements if one were put to it. I am proud to think that you represent me among others when you dine at the various Temples and Inns. What is it that the Benchers of Lincoln's Inn can do when drinking the health of the King? remain seated or keep on their hats? There was a man here somewhere who was said to have a right to go to the King's palace and demand a meal, etc. I suppose there may really be some queer relics of the past in that way.

We draw near to the end. In 15 minutes I go to the last conference until the one just before final adjournment on June 1, and for June 3 I have bespoken berths and tickets to take the whole crowd to Boston. The women go on at once to Beverly Farms Thursday morning and I expect to drive down on Saturday. I am divided between two fears — that it will be cold and cheerless at Beverly and soul destroyingly hot if we remain here for another week. But the peculiar heat of Washington, as it sometimes comes about this time, I fear more than anything else.

I have just finished reading Morris Cohen's book *Reason & Nature*, a very thorough exposition, quickly disposing of the humbugs of which we most hear, and I think admirable for learning and logic. The title suggests a sort of challenge to John Dewey's *Experience & Nature* to which it is much superior as a piece of writing and in the domain [?] of the finite. But although Dewey's book is incredibly ill written, it seemed to me after several rereadings to have a feeling of intimacy with the inside of the cosmos that I found unequaled. So methought God would have spoken had He been inarticulate but keenly desirous to tell you how it was.

I may have mentioned a very interesting book on the Medici by G. F. Young — a cheap reprint in the Modern Library of a handsome one said to contain striking portraits and published some time ago — the preface dated 1910.

This finished, my secretary reading it to me, I intend to listen to Mark Twain's *Connecticut Yankee at the Court of King Arthur*, and by then I hope it will be time to go.

My love to Lady Pollock.

Yours ever,
O. W. H.

HOTEL SAN REGIS,
PARIS, May 29, 1931

My dear Holmes:

Your letter written a fortnight ago has come on to me here, and I find that by posting today I can catch a mail going by the *Mauretania*.

Concerning the King's health: The Templars (Inner and Middle) stand. Lincoln's Inn and Gray's Inn do not. Our legend is that when King Charles II dined with us (a historical fact attested by the signatures of the King, Prince Rupert *et mult: al:* in a well preserved book) he perceived at the end of dinner that some of his retinue were not capable of standing, and desired that they might be excused. Gray's Inn has no reason to give. In the Navy they don't stand because in the old men-of-war there was not always head-room for standing. . . .

I excused myself from representing the English Bar at a French Bars Association at Versailles (you know the old provincial divisions survive in several courts of appeal each with its own Bar): it has really been too hot for going about in a crowd.

We have been driving a good deal in the Bois de Boulogne, especially its less frequented rustic parts, and have had a general outside view of the Colonial Exhibition at Vincennes, which is admirably planned and laid out, and there is a complete lifesize reproduction of the great temple of Ang-Kor (Cambodia). See if you can the photographs and drawings thereof in the special number of *L'Illustration* — the best illustrated paper in the world, I believe. They call it Indo-Chinese art but the main lines are South Indian.

This morning to the Luxembourg — found almost a clean sweep of everything painted before 1900, likewise of sculpture. I don't see any genius coming on among the young painters, but they know their trade on the whole better than ours, and the sculptors are still our masters, unless certain British carvers of oddities are the sculptors of the future. I must look up Morris Cohen, I don't seem to know about him.

Yours ever,
F. P.

LONDON, June 22, 1931

My dear Holmes:

Here is a dream — not prophetic I hope. Walking down a staircase I met two ruffians who, as I perceived, had come to waylay me, whereupon I slew them both with no other weapon than an umbrella, giving each of them the point exactly in the eye left them there and reported the fact to some friends with a perfectly clear conscience but without elation.

I trust you are well recovered from the fatigues of the term by this time. . . .

The learned Victor Bérard has collected a lot of Homeric study in two small volumes *sub tit. La résurrection d'Homère*, not without aid of recent Cretan diggings. I am not so sure as he is that there was only one Homer, tho' I think the *Odyssey may* be the work of the poet of the *Iliad* in advanced years, minded to leave behind him something designed as a whole and all his own. You have heard of Samuel Butler's paradox (a man of genius but a crank) that the *Odyssey* was written by a woman who lived in Sicily — the latter branch even more absurd than the former.

Yours ever,
F. P.

BEVERLY FARMS, July 16, 1931

My dear Pollock:

What with *certiorari* and people calling, etc. I have waited too long to felicitate you on your destruction of the two ruffians by giving them the point of your umbrella in the eye. John Gray when taking lessons in Single Stick was told in like circumstances to give a straight thrust, guiding with his left hand, at the pit of the stomach (?). "And he will turn green and die," said his teacher. Bernard Shaw's *Sanity of Art* came this week and I read it with amusement and pleasure. . . . Yesterday I sent back my second batch of *certioraris* and am free till the next one comes. Meantime I am reading Plato's *Laws*. My memory weakens, but didn't you have a whack at them recently? Much that is unreal to us but enough remaining to impress. I was delighted with his quotation of Hesiod that the half was greater than the whole. I once said much the same as to the law. A man can give his goods to a carrier but he can't exonerate (by the [?] contract) the carrier from liability for negligent injury to them *in transitu*. It so happened that on the day when I came on the quotation my secretary had been arguing to me that my remark was logically fallacious — as of course in strictness it was — and I showed him the passage in triumph.

He is just finishing reading to me *Our Mutual Friend.* Mawkish sentiment, unreal and impossible discourse, a thousand artistic errors, but what a splendid thing it is in spite of everything. Still I doubt if I ever take up another Dickens. But last night Richard Hale left here a book that looks amusing, *Mock Turtle*, Barnaby Brook,[1] which I suppose is fiction but which promises to revive old sensations and recollections. I mean to try it for odd moments. I never heard of Butler's paradox about the *Odyssey* before and don't know his arguments but I approach it with prejudice. I am not as well up in the *Iliad* and *Odyssey* as I ought to be, though I read the *Odyssey* a few years ago. It is good to renew contact with the very great, but when time is limited, new truth is entitled to a larger share of it than old greatness (I think). I should like to read *La Résurrection d'Homère* but doubt if I shall live to do it. . . .

Yours ever,
O. W. H.

LONDON, July 16, 1931

My dear Holmes:

. . . Last week we gave a dinner to our granddaughter and some of her young friends before an Etonian dance they went to after the first day of the Harrow match (cricket — were you ever in London at that time? Eton is well up now — won by an innings with 5 wickets to spare this time — 70 years ago it was the other way). It was a festive party. . . .

There is a brilliant *tour de force* in the way of a historical novel about Dante's exile, with the odd and blind title *A Ship without Sails*, by a Miss or Mrs. Barclay Carter, who is soaked in not only Dante but all the relevant medieval literature: but unless you are already considerably interested in Dante I don't much think it would interest you.

Is there among your printers a new-fangled trick of dropping out the useful (to my mind necessary) comma before a dependent clause in a sentence — of the kind that begin with *as, for*

[1] Collin Brooks (Barnaby Brook, pseud.), *Mock Turtle: Being the Memoirs of a Victorian Gentleman* (1931).

and the like? It started here about half a year ago, I think, on what pretence I don't know. It seems to me likely to worry and even mislead readers, but I can't get the printers of the *Law Reports* to stick to the sound old way, which is right whether you consider punctuation rhetorically as marking a pause for the voice or grammatically as a caution that a new construction is beginning.

On August 8 my wife and I sail for a Baltic cruise and shall have no address for three weeks. . . .

Your President will surely deserve a monument (or a Nobel prize?) if he succeeds in rescuing the world from a general financial crash,[1] a danger we should have been spared if the chief framers of the Peace Treaties had either known something of economics and European politics — though Clemenceau may have known a little, not much anyhow — or been pleased to consult some one who did know.

Yours ever,
F. P.

Beverly Farms, July 27, 1931

My dear Pollock:

This ought to reach you before you are *englouted* in the Baltic. No, as usual, I jumped at the wrong date — but I shan't risk any fancy address but shall stand by the ancient ways. Your letter speaks of two or three things to be answered. (1) I know nothing of the Eton Harrow Cricket Match — or indeed of cricket. (2) I am afraid that Miss (Mrs.) Barclay on Dante must wait, although reading him was one of the great sensations of life. (3) I think the dropping of commas has been a fashion here for years. It has affected me so far that in cases of doubt I often leave them out, but I am apt to put them in, *as* they help the reader. This last sentence raises a question on which Fowler in his delightful *Dictionary of Modern English Usage* expatiates. The only passage in which I don't agree with him so far as I have noticed. He says the causal *as* placed late (not at the beginning of the sentence) is "intolerable to anyone with a

[1] On June 20, 1931, President Hoover published his proposal that there should be a moratorium of one year on payments of intergovernmental obligations.

literary ear." It seems to be mainly a question of actual usage. I know of no eternal *a priori* juridical objection to using *as* instead of *because* or *since*. Fowler has frightened me out of this use so far as I have remembered him, but under protests. In this same way I have been more or less bullied into beginning a letter with "*My* dear" instead of "Dear." But to me "Dear" sounds more familiar and I don't see the objection to it. I don't know exactly how I came on Fowler's pronouncements. I rarely look at a dictionary, which after all is merely somebody's estimate of polite usage, a matter on which one can form one's own opinion.

I have had another portrait painted by Hopkinson who did the one in the Harvard Law School full length, sitting this time, ordered by my former secretaries and intended for the new Law Building for us. I shouldn't think they would admit a full length of a side judge, but that is not my funeral.[1] Also I have read Plato's *Laws* — unreal atmosphere with some real flashes of lightning. They had clear notions of what a gentleman should be. Also a book on the *Mesta*,[2] Spanish association of owners of herds of merino sheep migrating annually from high to low lands and back — the history goes from 1273 to 1836. My eyes were turned to Spain also by Mauclair, *L'âpre et splendide Espagne* with bully talk about Goya, Velasquez and El Greco — and also about the country.

My secretary has read to me *Lavengro* and *The Romany Rye*. My enthusiasm dimmed somewhat on recurrence — . . . and now *Vanity Fair*, which impresses me more than ever. I think I was tired and blue when the vacation began but now I am in very good shape and sufficiently interested in the details of daily life. But I don't keep what the newspapers call abreast of the times, and have no views on the insolvency of Germany, etc., etc. I cultivate my garden and don't try to meddle with the workings of time.

My love to Lady Pollock.

Yours ever,
O. W. H.

[1] The portrait now hangs in one of the two lounging rooms for members of the bar in the Supreme Court Building in Washington.

[2] Julius Klein, *The Mesta; A Study in Spanish Economic History, 1273–1836* (1920).

LONDON, August 5, 1931

My dear Holmes:

This is the last you will hear of us for some weeks: on Saturday we go for a cruise round the Baltic in a 20,000 ton liner. . . .

In my Cambridge days we read Plato's *Republic* but were not encouraged to read the *Laws*, said to be comparatively dull as being Plato's compromise with what he thought the world capable of in practice, and less instructive than Aristotle's *Politics*. But I suppose it is really more interesting than it was to our preceptors at a time when political science was little studied — less at Cambridge than at Oxford I think.

Delisle Burns, a publicist who has written divers books, has brought out a new one called *Modern Civilization on its Trial* — contents hardly up to the title, judging by a cursory inspection: he seems to me a well-meaning industrious man who has read enormously and bitten off a little more of everything than he can chew. But this may be a hasty impression.

I have just put in writing, by request, an offhand address given a fortnight ago to a party of Canadians who dined with the Bench; they said they were very ignorant about the history of the Inns of Court and would like to be told something, so I fired off what I could after dinner. To be privately printed I believe, but I will see that you have a copy.[1] No new facts in it, but perhaps a summary statement free from fabulous matter was rather wanted.

La Résurrection d'Homère is rather too scrappy to be good reading, and the French habit of never quoting the text in the original rather annoying.

Dickens: where do you put *Great Expectations*? I read it when it was new and I was an Eton boy: reading it again about a year ago I thought very highly of it.

Yours ever,

F. P.

[1] *The Origins of the Inns of Court; An Address Given to Canadian Guests at Lincoln's Inn, July 21, 1931* (Oxford, 1931).

BEVERLY FARMS, August 16, 1931

My dear Pollock:

Will this letter hit you as you sink to shore from the billows of the Baltic, or how otherwise? I know not. It is hard to deal with such sports as you two. But I owe a line to both of you. I have read nothing of Dickens except *Our Mutual Friend* for many years. I have given *Vanity Fair* my first adequate reading. It seems to me to be a great novel — very great. The greatest drawback to me in this and *The Newcomes* is that mundane motives and interests seem to be Thackeray's own ultimates, *non obstant* pious ejaculations when he talks of Amelia. Of course I am not talking religion but of the scale of intellectual preoccupations. I admit that the bias is more natural in London than elsewhere. The prizes are greater — and there was splendor in Thackeray's time — and even in mine.

I don't think Plato's *Laws* is dull, except as all antiquity is, and I don't see why it should be thought to have been a compromise. Perhaps what seems queerest to us in his infinitesimal state is that the citizens never have to think about making a living. That is left to the slaves and foreigners. I think one likes the old fellow as he drools on (I speak as a modern). I await your address about the Inns of Court with interest. The last few days my secretary has been away and I have taken the opportunity to read some detective stories for which I have an ignoble liking. I have read four running. My wife used to remark that many could begin a novel well but few could end one well. That struck me with all these — the conclusion generally impotent and one that one didn't like.

I also have read Strachey, *Portraits in Miniature*. For the most part (one or two exceptions) they did not seem to me up to his earlier work. Also I didn't care much for his *Elizabeth & Essex*. The only moment that I remember when Essex interested me was when he spoke ill of the figure of his Mistress. A minor work by Willa Cather [1] (American). She seemed to me really great in *My Antonia*. Except for the interjection of slumber I really should have had some of those longed for

[1] *Shadows on the Rock* (1931).

hours when I wondered what to do, but such hours are very rare. Apart from all else more people come than I want, though each individual is welcome. Perhaps I make a mistake in not trying to walk but it is an effort and I doubt if it is wise to try even an eighth of a mile. Time is slowly taking down the house. I suppose next month the American Bar Association intends to give me a medal and I am expected to say a few words by radio — details not yet settled — at any rate, not a very exciting occasion.[2]

In view of uncertainties I will write no more. My love to my dear Lady Pollock . . . .

Yours ever,
O. W. H.

I have been accompanying Rémy de Gourmont in some of his *Promenades philosophiques*. He is so clever that he ought to have been a little bigger.

London, August 29, 1931

My dear Holmes:

Your letter has found us back from our cruise, spending one day at home. We have seen Stockholm, and a still more beautiful city, Helsingfors, where Finnish friends, acquired when I was one of a committee working in support of Finnish liberties in the days before the war, gave us a delightful welcome. Quite right about Thackeray: his world is much smaller than Dickens's. I rather think posterity will consider Dickens, the Brontë sisters, and Thomas Hardy the greatest English novelists of our fathers' generation, with Thackeray, George Eliot and Meredith, perhaps also Trollope, in the second bracket of the first class. None of the lot quite up to the level of the 19th century giants, Balzac (greatest of all), Turgenev, Tolstoy. I am carrying about a very solid and rather long-winded study of Spinoza's philosophy, with much confutation of recent critics,

[2] The American Bar Association, at its thirty-fourth annual meeting, in September 1931, conferred on Holmes a medal "for conspicuous service in the cause of American jurisprudence." Prevented by ill health from responding by radio, Holmes sent a letter of thanks to the Association which is published in 56 *Am. Bar Asso. Report* 136–137 (1931).

called *Aeternitas,* by one Hallett. I agree with him in thinking meanly of Greenwich time, which I am sure has nothing to say to eternal life.

We had very fine weather in the Baltic tho' rather cold while Western Europe was being rained and stormed upon. Now it looks like a fine September.

I hope our ignorant and reckless Labour men may now be powerless for mischief, at least for a season.[1]

Yours ever,
F. P.

[1] On August 24 the Labour Ministry resigned and the Coalition Government was formed immediately thereafter.

LONDON, October 29, 1931 [1]

My dear Holmes:

Our General Election is over.[2] The common sense of our people has decided with more emphasis than any one expected (about 2 to 1 in votes cast, more than 8 to 1 in the new House of Commons: this large amplifying in Parliament of the actual majority in numbers is nothing new in kind) that:

(1) the supremacy of Parliament is an inviolable landmark of our political tradition: the Trades Union leaders tried first to overawe it by the abortive general strike, and have been trying to nobble it by wire pulling ever since. Some years ago President Lowell showed how an attempt to transfer political control from the House of Commons to outside party machines had failed in both the great parties: I don't think the importance of this has been generally recognized.

(2) Officers who quit the ship in a storm deserve no confidence. Only two or three of the seceding Labour Ministers are returned. Among people who try to think I suppose there was a pretty strong conviction that the Trade Union Congress policy

[1] A letter from Pollock, dated September 28, 1931, is omitted.

[2] On August 25, 1931, following the resignation of the Labour Ministry, a Coalition Government under the premiership of MacDonald was formed. On October 7 Parliament was dissolved and MacDonald began the campaign for the return of the Coalition Government at the General Elections. By those elections on October 28 the Government was returned by a large majority.

of reckless spending would have brought us to national bankruptcy if not pulled up: but what proportion of the electors have any rudiments of public economy is more than I know, certainly some of the leaders have none.

The exaltation of Ramsay Macdonald as a kind of national hero and the total eclipse of Lloyd George are two of the most curious political incidents within my memory. R. M. has purged himself from the reproach of his discreditable shuffling in the matter of the Zinoviev letter, which put an end to his first term of office,[3] and has somehow grown a backbone, put into him it would seem by the King or Snowden[4] or both. Lloyd George's case is less surprising. He is wholly lacking in judgment and very ill informed, and has an inveterate habit of taking advice anywhere except in the right quarters — plenty of energy and resource when once aligned on a right direction, but that is not enough to make a statesman. He, his son and daughter, and one other Welshman, are all that remains of the so called Independent Liberal party.

Of course the National majority is too large to be stable. When the financial crisis is past the split is like to be on economic policy, dogmatic Protectionists on one side and moderates who support a tariff only for present expediency on the other. There are no more dogmatic Free Traders, or not enough to count; on the other hand the Protectionist dream of some pan-Britannic customs union (Empire Free Trade they call it) is chimerical while the Dominions insist on taxing British manufactures for protective reasons. I don't see what else there is to split about, but one never knows. The Bolsheviks must be pretty sore. I should not wonder if they lost their temper and did something compelling us to break off relations, which would be a good riddance. . . .

I shall be pretty well content when my year of office as Treasurer comes to an end (Jan. 11, beginning of Hilary Term) both as to work done and that it is over. You would hardly believe

[3] The publication of the Zinoviev letter in October 1924, during the general election campaign, and the somewhat uncertain position of Premier MacDonald as to the authenticity of the letter had done much to bring about the Conservative victory and the fall of the first Labour Ministry.

[4] Philip Snowden, 1st Viscount (1864–1937), was Chancellor of the Exchequer under MacDonald.

how large a proportion of our really troublesome questions are raised by the conduct of our members (mostly Indian or African) in (or from) jurisdictions beyond seas. . . .

Yours ever,
F. P.

LONDON, November 23, 1931

My dear Holmes:

. . . Yesterday Dean Inge gave his first Warburton Lecture at Lincoln's Inn.[1] (Did I ever tell you about that curious foundation of the eccentric and Controversial bishop?)[2] We had more than 100 Benchers and guests to lunch (not part of the foundation but a fairly recent addition. I don't think lunch was a professionally recognized meal much before 1850) and a considerable congregation besides. He talked as if the permanence of the material universe had become an established belief and been rudely shocked by the latest astronomico-physical theories: I believe it is really a new-fangled thing: all the ancient cosmogonies point to destruction of some sort leading either to a new cycle or to a different kind of world. It is the difference between being knocked on the head and dying of old age.

I am entirely at one with you on the whole bag of tricks and delusions vulgarly called spiritualism. Apart from the *a priori* improbability of intelligible communications from the dead to the living (not less but more gross if one believes that eternal life has nothing to do with our 3-dimensional space, or now strictly speaking 4-dimensional space-time, which seems also to knock out Greenwich Time), I have never seen any such alleged communication that was beyond the invention — or in a charitable view the waking dream — of a half-educated medium. As for the things the medium is supposed to have had no means of knowing, the natural ways of accounting for them

[1] The lectures, expanded in length, were later published under the title *God and the Astronomers* (1933).

[2] William Warburton, Bishop of Gloucester (1698–1799); author of *Divine Legation of Moses Demonstrated* (1737, 1741); founded lectures to be given at Lincoln's Inn upon the proof of Christianity from the prophecies.

are by no means exhausted. Thought transference (or coincidence), if proved—as to which I have an open mind—is obviously a natural fact occurring under conditions at present obscure (as plenty of quite familiar facts still are).

Dissociated personality is I think established by unimpeachable witness, and that is quite odd enough; however, be it more or less explained, it provides a pigeonhole to put demoniacs in. If one did accept the attribution of the so-called communications to extra-terrestrial agency, there would be much to say for the good old explanation of the Church that the agency is diabolical — nothing heretical in supposing a dull loutish kind of devil whom Satan can't trust with a bigger job. Do I understand that this last impostor had the impudence to personate Bill James?[3] who could be paradoxical but was never flat or dull. . . . I must go to a committee, getting on for the last of my official duties. After the new year I may have some time for reading and writing.

Yours ever,
F. P.

LONDON, December 10, 1931

My dear Holmes:

Here I am *aet.* 86 today, not feeling decrepit and encouraged by your example to hope that at 90, if I so long live, I may still have my wits about me. . . .

It rather shocks me to learn from a symposium on *U. S.* v. *Macintosh* in the *Illinois Law Review* how great are the ravages, even in your Court, of the post-war State jingoism mania (*diss. totis viribus*, Holmes & Brandeis, JJ.),[1] but you will ultimately

[3] It seems likely that Holmes, in a recent letter had mentioned Jane Revere Burke, *Let Us In; A Record of Communications Believed to have come from William James*, with a foreword by E. S. Martin (1931).

[1] 283 U. S. 605 (1931). A majority of the Court, in an opinion by Sutherland, J., held that an alien's conditional refusal to bear arms in defense of the United States unless he believed the war to be morally justified barred him from naturalization under Federal statutes. Chief Justice Hughes wrote a dissenting opinion in which Holmes, Brandeis, and Stone, JJ., concurred. See "United States v. Macintosh — a Symposium," 26 *Illinois L. Rev.* 375 (1931), reprinted in 2 *Select Essays on Constitutional Law* 1265 (1938).

be justified. Apart from the particular merits it seems to me all wrong to make naturalization a judicial or quasi-judicial matter: it is better dealt with by administrative discretion. Not that I believe it ever occurred to the Home Secretary here to ask an applicant whether he (let alone she) had scruples of conscience about bearing arms for the defence of the realm — a common law duty in case of war within the realm, never abrogated though in practice long ago superseded by statute.

At last I have got Morris Cohen's *Reason & Nature* from the London Library. So far as I have yet looked up and down it, he seems to me very independent, very sensible, and on sound lines, only the constant discussion of other people's opinions in detail is rather distracting except for minute students. I don't want to know whether Avenarius and Mach, of whom I never read a word, do or do not agree with Cohen; but this fault — a literary defect which in experts' eyes may be a substantial merit — is common to most recent philosophical books. Now and then I doubt whether the condemned opinions were really quite so absurd as they look in his statement — once or twice think him captious. It is quite rational *e.g.*, to call science organized common sense if it is an important function of common sense to pick out and attend to the facts relevant for one's purpose. . . .

Yours ever,
F. P.

LONDON, December 17, 1931

My dear Holmes:

Now I think I have read as much of Morris Cohen as I can with the time I have to give to things in general; moreover much of it is, so far as concerns me, preaching to the converted. Sometimes I have wondered whether the opinions he denies are or were quite so devoid of plausible reasons as he makes them look. I seem to perceive as through a glass dimly — I hope not quite darkly — that in many places Cohen's dialectic position is notably strengthened by his skill in the mathematics.

The dispatch of the copies of my address to our Canadian

visitors is waiting for their envelopes, which I understand were specially ordered, but I hope they will be sent off by the beginning of next week. You may think me credulous about the 13th–14th century Earl of Lincoln having been our ancestors' patron, in face of the later known tracing of our local name to the later Thomas Lincoln, a King's sergeant.[1] But the casual coincidence of the two names appears to me less improbable than an invention so impudent as the fiction of the Earl's patronage and assumption of his arms, not a thing easily done without censure in those days, would have been. Elizabethan and Jacobean antiquaries were audacious in guesses no doubt, but I think not quite so far as that. . . .

This evening I preside for the last time as Treasurer and am glad to have done with the routine part of the work. Has any one written on the art of managing committee meetings? There are certain *arcana imperii* there.

Yours ever,
F. P.

Radiogram: Pollock to Holmes

January 13, 1932[1]

ANNIS NON ANIMO SENI IAM RUDE DONATO SALUTEM PLURIMAM AMICUS SENEX

POLLOCK

[1] In his address *The Origins of the Inns of Court*, at p. 10–11, Pollock said: "Henry de Lacy, Earl of Lincoln, was an eminent and trusted minister of King Edward I. By tradition of which we have no written warrant we regard him as in some sort an eponymous patron of our early predecessors. His lion is borne on a canton in our coat of arms as finally approved by the Heralds' College in 1700. . . . On the other hand it now appears that our predecessors did occupy a site in Holborn which in the fourteenth century belonged to one Thomas de Lincoln, King's Sergeant, and was described as '*hospitium vocatum Lyncolns Ynne*.' That is a definite historical connection. Must we therefore renounce Henry de Lacy and regard our appropriation of his lion as at best a trespass excusable by lapse of time? I suggest with diffidence that both tales may be true."

[1] On January 12 Holmes had resigned from the Supreme Court of the United States.

WASHINGTON, January 24, 1932 [1]

My dear Pollock:

It is such a pleasure to get your letters that I am anxious lest the meagreness of my replies discourage you from keeping on. I know not why but I find it very hard to do my part. The physical act of writing has become difficult. However, I still live and take interest in matters within my scope.[2] My secretary is reading to me now Lea's *History of the Inquisition in Spain*, which I long have had in mind. I don't doubt the learning but the literary performance seems to me poor. Perhaps the fault is with me, but the facts seem to me muddled. Other lighter books alleviate the rather weary task, but nothing much. Some essays by H. Belloc [3] & others by S. M. Ellis about Wilkie Collins *et al.*. One doesn't quite see why the author felt called on to print, but the product is well enough for a leisure half hour. I am rather glad to have a notion of the author of *Verdant Green* — and at the time of the Civil War *Guy Livingstone* etc.[4] moved all of us. But I am idling a good deal because I feel tired most of the time.

My love to Lady Pollock.

Yours ever,
O. W. HOLMES

LONDON, February 8, 1932

My dear Holmes:

I am glad to hear from you however shortly, and hasten to assure you that I have had occasion to consult Lea's book now and then but have never felt tempted to read on: so I have little doubt that your poor opinion of his style is justified. Cer-

[1] A letter from Pollock, dated January 7, 1932, is omitted.

[2] In Pollock's omitted letter of January 7, 1932, he had written to Holmes: "I am sorry to hear you are feeling tired. So far as my own experience goes *Anno Domini* may not blunt one's faculties — if one keeps them in exercise — but does command one to go slower, and that command may not be neglected."

[3] *A Conversation with a Cat and Others* (1931).

[4] Ellis's volume, *Wilkie Collins, Le Fanu and others* (1931), contained an essay on Edward Bradley (1827–1889), author of *Adventures of Mr. Verdant Green, an Oxford Freshman* (1853), and an essay on George Alfred Lawrence (1827–1876), author of *Guy Livingstone* (1857) and *Sword and Gown* (1859).

tainly not a few learned and judicious historians are dull. Such is Gardiner, our best authority for the early Stuart and Civil War period. In 1893 a learned Frenchman, Tanon, published *Histoire des Tribunaux de l'Inquisition en France* and called attention to the influence of the procedure of the Holy Office on the criminal procedure of secular courts.

Concerning histories that are not dull, James Truslow Adams's *Epic of America* is excellent: a friend of the author with whom he is staying in London lent it to me — a history of a new kind, on the social characters of the people of the U. S. and the sections thereof, with only so much outline of political history as is needful to show what the conditions were from time to time. It has taught me a lot of things, for one, that the Civil War might have come twenty years earlier, possibly with the North as the seceding party, but for the rush for westward extension in the 1840's diverting attention from internal controversies. Apparently I have plenty of company in finding it good reading: Mr. Adams tells me more than 100,000 copies have been sold. . . .

I wonder what you make of Hilaire Belloc: he is clever and more or less a scholar, but flashy, impudent and not too scrupulous about facts. During the first autumn and winter of the war he prophesied once a week — with plans and elaborate reasons — that the Germans must be thoroughly beaten within two months or so. It made a little fortune for the paper he wrote in and seemingly did him no harm.

A volume of Laski's[1] just come to the *L. Q. R.* with a chapter on your political philosophy, not mentioning where first printed. However, the book has an index, so he will not be damned ten miles beyond Hell where the devil can't get for the stinging nettles.

What are your plans as to abode? I can conceive you still at Washington as a spectator of public life in the winter, climate being I presume better than on the North Shore.

Yours ever,
F. P.

[1] *Studies in Law and Politics* (1931).

WASHINGTON, February 17, 1932

My dear Pollock:

Such a pleasant letter from you — incidentally comforting me for my difficulties with Lea. He, Lea, also insisted on the influences of the procedure of the inquisition on the criminal procedure of the civil tribunals, but I didn't pay much attention to it because I supposed the whole business was older than inquisition, and went back to the first royal inquiries in search of revenue — but my memory is 50 years old.

Belloc struck me much as he does you, cheeky and hoping to make you sit up. Not first rate but with enough spark to keep you awake and enable you to finish his book (but without regret). I am going through the Sherlock Holmes stories with a good deal of pleasure. He is better than his imitators. I am about to turn to graver matters. A little book by Wm. McDougall, *World Chaos* . . . to be followed by a big dull one not yet seen and title forgotten. Said to be good at beginning and end. It is time that I turn to other interests than murder. But I tell you, so far I do enjoy idleness and irresponsibility hugely. My love to Lady Pollock.

Yours ever,
O. W. H.

LONDON, March 7, 1932

My dear Holmes:

I am glad to have a good report of you, having been a little anxious: and the celebration got up by your Federal Bar Association confirms it. The secretary of our Bar Council asked me for a message: from his answer I perceive that it has been edited into official form:[1] I have just sent an untouched one signed in the plural, signifying thereby not only our two selves but our son and daughter-in-law. . . . Did I tell you of Bertram Thomas's *Arabia Felix*, a real good travel book, and

[1] On March 8, the Federal Bar Association at its annual banquet in Washington celebrated Holmes's 91st birthday. Messages of tribute from Pollock and others were broadcast by radio. Pollock's message of congratulations, as read at the dinner, is printed in 1 *Fed. Bar Asso. J.* 35 (1932).

John Buchan's *Sir Walter Scott* — not yet seen — is very well spoken of. Another book about him with a fancy name seems to me by the reviews to be altogether too *precious* — tho' written by an old friend.[2]

I have no use for jeremiads about the world being in chaos — unless the writers know of a remedy. Anyhow it was much worse in these parts a thousand years ago, and pretty dirty weather when my grandfather took his degree (1804). But I have been reading again, after a long interval, your father's "Hunt for the Captain." He was a right good optimist. Incidentally it is now a historical document for various local details. . . .

Yours ever,
F. P.

WASHINGTON, March 17, 1932

My dear Pollock:

Have many letters gone unanswered? I hope not, but I believe that I have told you that writing comes hard in these days. . . . But I have nothing to complain of. I wonder if I am witnessing the approach of the end, but the doctors talk as if I had a good prospect ahead. I don't care much, but I still enjoy life and am very willing for it to keep on, especially since I have finished C. D. Broad's *The Mind & Its Place in Nature*. That is, it was read in my presence — I taking an occasional snooze — not thinking much of the work & finding it very dull as well as not believing it. I have sweetened it by rereading all Sherlock Holmes & *The Moonstone* which I think the best there is in that line. Other books, not mentioned. I hope I answered the message of your Bar Council. I meant to, but have lost the run [?] of letters and telegrams. My love to Lady Pollock.

Yours ever,
O. W. HOLMES

[2] Dame Una Pope-Hennessy, *The Laird of Abbotsford* (1932).

LONDON, March 23, 1932

My dear Holmes:

Tomorrow my wife and I are off for a cruise in the Mediterranean, a sea we are now no strangers to, but we are to touch at some ports we have not visited before such as Tripoli. Back on April 14. . . .

I have just passed for the *Law Reports* the proof of a House of Lords decision which I think is wrong in law, reversing by a majority an unanimous decision of the Court of Appeal affirming one of Wright's [1] (who is now promoted to be a Lord of Appeal himself), and I am sure is mischievous in fact as encouraging shifty people to say they forgot the things it was their business to remember: the name is *Lever Bros.* v. *Bell.*[2] I assume you are not quite of Blackburn's [3] mind, who when he retired said "Damn the law," and read nothing but French novels. Another little editorial find is that once Cockburn, C. J.[4] quoted Story (W. W.) on *Contracts* with great respect, taking it for Story the father's work. Not that it was bad work, but *Roba di Roma* is better.

Yours ever,
F. P.

WASHINGTON, April 5, 1932

My dear Pollock:

You will have returned from the Mediterranean when you receive this and are welcome back. . . . I think I have cut

[1] Sir Robert Alderson Wright, Baron Wright, appointed Lord of Appeal in Ordinary, April 11, 1932.

[2] [1932] A. C. 161. In this case the defendant and the plaintiff had entered into a contract by which defendant was to be employed by the plaintiff for a certain period of time. During the term of the employment the defendant was guilty of such misconduct as would have entitled the plaintiff to discharge him, but the plaintiff, remaining ignorant of the defendant's breach of contract, entered into a new agreement with the defendant by which the contract of employment was rescinded and the defendant was paid a substantial sum as compensation. Thereafter plaintiff learned of the defendant's earlier misconduct. A majority of the House of Lords held that the mutual mistake of the parties did not entitle the plaintiff to repudiate the contract of rescission and to claim a refund of the money paid to the defendant.

[3] Colin Blackburn, Baron Blackburn (1813–1896); Judge of the Court of Queen's Bench, 1859–1876; Lord of Appeal in Ordinary, 1876–1886.

[4] Sir Alexander James Edmund Cockburn, Lord Cockburn, Lord Chief Justice of England, 1859–1880.

most of the filaments that connected me with the Court, and see a [illegible] good and able man in my place — Cardozo. My idleness is pretty busy and I enjoy it greatly and should like it better if it was a little idler. . . . I have a thought of the possibility of writing a little book embodying my views on the ultimates of the law, but I have expressed them *passim* and I desire only repose. I am persuading myself that one has no duties at 91.

Yours ever,
O. W. H.

WASHINGTON, April 21, 1932

My dear Pollock:

Probably you will have returned from your I hope successful trip to and on the Mediterranean. I envy you, but I am being happily idle and persuading myself that 91 has outlived duty. I can imagine a book on the law, getting rid of all talk of duties and rights — beginning with the definition of law in the lawyer's sense as a statement of the circumstances in which the public force will be brought to bear upon a man through the Courts, and expounding rights as the hypostasis of a prophecy — in short, systematizing some of my old chestnuts. But I don't mean to do it or to bother about anything. We are reading Spengler, *The Decline of the West*, a learned, original book, written with incredible German arrogance, and not in all believed by me, but wonderfully suggestive — an odious animal who must be read. A lot of other stuff is being waded through and I am lightly skipping through the little book on Marcel Proust.[1] The cherry trees around the Potomac basin have been as beautiful as ever but probably are near their end. My love to Lady Pollock.

Yours ever,
O. W. H.

[1] Leon Pierre-Quint, *Marcel Proust* (1925, translated, 1927).

London, [Undated]

My dear Holmes:

Returning from our cruise (Thursday last), I am pleased to find satisfactory advices from you. By the way, your script has become minute while your pen—quill, I rather think—remains broad, and the width of the nib sometimes swallows up the form of one or more letters.

Our weather was, for the Mediterranean, rather cool and unsettled, but we had a fair amount of sunshine and anyhow it was much better than the rain and cold winds that have prevailed here all the time. I went for only one whole day excursion on shore — Naples to Amalfi by way of Pompei and the hills, and back by the coast road passing through Sorrento, mighty fine cliff scenery. Since I saw Pompei a quarter of a century ago there have been more diggings: pretty much the whole city is now laid open. The decoration and (so far as found) movable ornaments of an ordinary Pompeian house put us moderns to shame when one remembers that it was only a second-rate provincial town, say like a minor summer resort on Long Island. No doubt the element of Greek taste counted for something in Southern Italy. Likewise we saw Tripoli, where Italian improvements are proceeding at a great rate — meaning, I suppose, to cut out Tunis. The ship was very much up to date, too much in some ways: the craze for making believe that a ship is just like a smart hotel on shore is being worked to death, and the perpetual fuss of sports and entertainments is a bore when one can't take part in it. But the swimming bath (a good sized tank) on deck is a pretty sight, and it must be very good — both the water and the sun — for the young folks. It is pleasing to see that the young women swim quite as well as the men. The number of the whole crowd of passengers (over 400) in a big liner cruising — of course the ship has to be full to make it profitable — makes it very difficult to discover the conversible ones among them, and on the whole I don't feel like wanting another cruise very soon.

Certainly Wilkie Collins with *The Moonstone*, perhaps still more *The Woman in White*, was the father of our whole tribe of detective tales. I think the influence of the French school, Gaboriau, etc., has been slight.

I am reading (in anticipation of a Spinoza celebration at the Hague in Sept.) a short book on Spinoza by a Polish(?) count, Dunin-Borkowski,[1] who is also a Jesuit, also one of the most acute and fair-minded philosophical critics I know: I seem just to sniff a faint exotic atmosphere in his German, but am not sure: whereas with Nietzsche, whose name is obviously Slavonic (only four letters in the Cyrillic alphabet) there is no mistaking it.

Yours ever,
F. P.

WASHINGTON, May 15, 1932

My dear Pollock:

It is less than a month before I go to Beverly Farms, if nothing turns out wrong. It is wonderful and incredible to have no duties. I can't tell you how much I like it. I ought to be getting cultivated, for my secretary calculates that, roughly, we have read 4,500,000 words since we got here, but I am afraid that a good deal buzzes through my head without much profit to me. I forget if I have mentioned the accursed Spengler, *Decline of the West*, whom I now have read in translation (vol. 1 years ago in German with a dictionary). He has as swelled a head as man can have and live, but the beast has ideas, many of which I don't know enough to criticise. I wish he was dead. On the other side is that dear delightful Wodehouse, whom I read and even reread with guffaws. I accept with humility your criticism of my writing. I don't know why it has become so small & I suppose it is old age makes me get my letters wrong at times. We began today a book by Sir A. Salter, *Recovery*, which I like very much, though the criticisms on *Laissez Faire*, mentioned by him and now generally prevalent, leave me not fully convinced. There has been a lot of rain and the Potomac is high, but falling. I must take my lad up to Great Falls — which I have not seen this year. . . . Is this enough of my gossip?

Yours ever,
O. W. H.

My love to Lady Pollock.

[1] Probably Stanislaus Dunin-Borkowski, *Spinoza nach dreihundert Jahren* (1932).

TABLE OF CASES

TABLE OF CASES

INDEX

INDEX

X 2

For EU product safety concerns, contact us at Calle de José Abascal, 56–1°, 28003 Madrid, Spain or eugpsr@cambridge.org.

www.ingramcontent.com/pod-product-compliance
Lightning Source LLC
LaVergne TN
LVHW090305210926
848480LV00001B/141
* 9 7 8 1 1 0 7 5 1 2 0 9 2 *